DETACHMENT AND CONCERN

DETACHMENT AND CONCERN
Conversations in the philosophy of teaching and teacher education

Margret Buchmann and Robert E. Floden

with
Deborah Loewenberg Ball
Maxine Greene
Michael Huberman
D. C. Phillips
John R. Schwille
Lee S. Shulman
Steven Weiland

CASSELL

Published in Great Britain in 1993 by Cassell, Villiers House, 41/47 Strand, London WC2N 5JE

Published in the United States of America by Teachers College Press, 1234 Amsterdam Avenue, New York, NY 10027

British Library Cataloguing-in-Publication Data

A catalogue record for this book is available from the British Library.

ISBN 0-304-32739-5

Printed and bound in the United States of America

Contents

Foreword

This is an unusual book that invites and carries on serious, thoughtful and open-ended conversations about education, research, teaching, learning, and teacher education. In it, Buchmann and Floden explore a number of topics by often rejecting "common sense," and they bring a number of people into their colloquy about uncertainty, moral obligation, professional socialization, theory-practice, mature reflection, learning, and knowledge utilization.

Sometimes they engage in extended vicarious conversations with such seminal thinkers as Dewey, Vygotsky, James, and Geertz. More often, they draw selectively on the ideas of many other major and minor figures in philosophy, psychology, education, anthropology, sociology, history, linguistics, and even literature and poetry to carry their dialogues forward. In fact, literary references play a large role in keeping the conversation going; as Buchmann and Floden call on the likes of Woolf, Eliot, Coleridge, and Wordsworth to join in.

As one reads, there is an ever-present feeling that in this book ideas and arguments won't just be presented and developed as is most often done in this kind of academic writing, but rather, themes and ideas will be constantly turned over in the minds, metaphors, images, and words of others along the way, thus inviting reflection, reexamination, and reconsideration of what teacher education should be about. An example of this is a late chapter that is built around a fictitious symposium on coherence and consistency that uses the actual words of Scheffler, Lindbloom, Kolakowski, Frye, Wollheim, Rodriguez, Hampshire, Canetti, Lakoff, and Johnson to bring a variety of penetrating lights to bear on this issue.

Also, at the end of each set of essays, formal respondents set the scene for Buchmann and Floden to engage directly in real conversations by way of rejoinders to their respondent-critics, D. C. Phillips, Michael Huberman, Deborah Loewenberg Ball, and Steven Weiland. And, fittingly, Maxine Greene begins this volume with an insightful introduction that imagines Margret Buchmann as Mrs. Ramsay, the presiding hostess to conversations at the dinner party in Virginia Woolf's *To The Lighthouse*. Greene provides her summary version of the conversations in this book and adds her own unique contribution to them. Finally, in his concluding chapter, Lee Shulman joins in to reflect wisely as only he can on the previous conversations, and urges their continuation.

This is a book for teacher educators who want to think about possibilities and transformations, about the moral obligations and virtues of teaching, about the utilization of knowledge in a kind of practice that will always be variable and uncertain, about research, theory and practice, and about teaching as a kind of life-long learning project. It is an invitation to join in on a new conversation that will bring fundamental changes to teacher education in the twenty-first century.

As a key spokesman for a post-modern view of philosophy, Richard Rorty has urged philosophers to think of philosophy not as argument and the logical establishment of certain ideas, but as edifying conversation. To advance contemporary educational thought about teaching and teacher education, Buchmann and Floden and all their communicants in this book have shown us how such an edifying conversation can be carried on to the enrichment of us all.

Jonas F. Soltis
Series Editor

Acknowledgments

Composing a book always involves friends, family, places, and a great deal of labor. We are particularly grateful to Deborah Ball, Maxine Greene, Michael Huberman, D. C. Phillips, Lee Shulman, Jonas Soltis, and Steve Weiland, who have befriended our efforts and engaged in this textual adventure. Together with our families, Philip Jackson, Anthony Kenny, Robert Merton, and Israel Scheffler are among the less visible protagonists in efforts that go back years.

The Institute for Research on Teaching, College of Education, Michigan State University (funded in part by OERI—the U.S. Department of Education, Office of Educational Research and Improvement) has been the place where many of our essays' puzzles took shape and could be worked on with others; here we would like to mention, in particular, Sharon Feiman-Nemser, Susan Florio-Ruane, and Michael Sedlak, as well as Jere Brophy, Andy Porter, and Judy Lanier. We worked closely with Jack Schwille and Chris Clark on issues of learning from experience and teachers' uncertainties.

Over many years, Gail Nutter has had the patience and ingenuity to provide conditions of support that allowed Margret to ceaselessly rewrite her drafts. Among the people who carried out this work are Mary Mowry, Cathy Siebert, Jennifer Kubanek, and Christine Olsen. Bob drew on the resources of the National Center for Research on Teacher Education (also funded in part by OERI) and relied on John Zeuli and Kate Baird for assistance. Harold Morgan's stringent standards meant that every word and date in this text was twice and thrice examined; Marguerite Halversen carried on with this task. Our developmental editor at Teachers College Press, Cathy McClure, was cheerful, firm, and encouraging in seeing the book through; we thank her, too.

We gratefully acknowledge *Teachers College Record* for permission to adapt the following material originally published therein: "Breaking with Everyday Experience," by M. Buchmann, R. E. Floden, and J. Schwille (1987), Volume 88, pp. 485–506; "Improving Education by Talking: Argument or Conversation," by M. Buchmann (1985), Volume 86, pp. 441–453; Role over Person: Morality and Authenticity in Teaching," by M. Buchmann (1986), Volume 87, pp. 529–543; "Preparing Teachers for Uncertainty," by R. E. Floden and C. M. Clark (1988), Volume 89, pp. 505–534. We also thank Blackwell Publishers for permission to adapt "What is Irrational about Knowledge Utilizaton," by M. Buchmann (1985); appearing in *Curriculum Inquiry,* Volume 15, pp. 153–168.

With all the time this writing required and all the support and companionship we were fortunate to have, our efforts only go so far. We trust others will point out flaws that we cannot see and horizons of understanding beyond our sights.

There are three conditions which often look alike
Yet differ completely, flourish in the same hedgerow:
Attachment to self and to things and to persons, detachment
From self and from things and from persons; and, growing
   between them, indifference
Which resembles the others as death resembles life,
Being between two lives—unflowering, between
The live and the dead nettle. This is the use of memory:
For liberation—not less of love but expanding
Of love beyond desire, and so liberation
From the future as well as the past.
                   —T. S. Eliot, 1943/1971, "Little Gidding"

. . . she was at the moment pursuing a connection between the nature of quattrocento pigmentation, and lichenology as a method of dating the antiquity of landscape: a gratifyingly pointless and therefore pure pursuit which enabled her mind to wander in the direction of Italy and to hover about the abstraction of a particular shade of green-blue which she had noted in many a painted Italian scene as well as in the lichens of ancient English woodland. A pale, delicate, hard, metallic, heavenly, shocking, suggestive green-blue. It tinted dry artistic Italian cypress trees and the undersides of vine leaves, it lived on the damp bark of English oaks and thorns. It expressed both distance and presence: it was both of the background and of the sharpest proximity. An enigmatic colour, speaking of metaphysical correspondences. Signifying nothing but the search for itself. But an essential shade.
                   —Margaret Drabble, 1987, *The Radiant Way*

Introduction

Maxine Greene

"'He must have reached it,' said Lily Briscoe aloud, feeling suddenly completely tired out. For the Lighthouse had become almost invisible, had melted away in a blue haze, and the effort of looking at it and the effort of thinking of him landing there, which both seemed to be one and the same effort, had stretched her body and mind to the utmost. Ah, but she was relieved. Whatever she had wanted to give him, when he left her that morning, she had given him at last. 'He has landed,' she said aloud. "It is finished."'

. . . .Quickly, as if she were recalled by something over there, she turned to her canvas. There it was—her picture. Yes, with all its greens and blues, its lines running up and across, its attempt at something. It would be hung in attics, she thought; it would be destroyed. But what did that matter? she asked herself, taking up the brush again. She looked at the steps; they were empty; she looked at her canvas; it was blurred. With a sudden intensity, as if she saw it clear for a second, she drew a line there, in the centre. It was done; it was finished. Yes, she thought, laying down her brush in extreme fatigue. I have had my vision."

—Virginia Woolf, *To the Lighthouse* pp. 241–242

An invitation to write an introduction to a linked series of essays like the ones that follow here is like an invitation to enter into a muted and peculiarly civil conversation. In this case, it is a conversation marked by a

1

diversity of perspective, by an acknowledgment of inconclusiveness, and by an awareness that there is something that lies beyond—a significance, a coherence still to be attained. Conscious of the complexities and ambiguities involved, I think of Mrs. Ramsay's dinner party at the core of Virginia Woolf's (1927/1955) *To the Lighthouse.* Margret Buchmann works with colleagues; but the reader is tempted to respond to her as the one who sets the tone. She is the Mrs. Ramsay who strives to create a space of calm consideration in the noisy, banal domains of teaching and teacher education: a space where the probing questions can be posed; where the tensions can be lived out between what is and what ought to be. Near the end of the dinner, Mrs. Ramsay feels a moment of joy, as if she has reached an unexpected security. She recalls that "she had already felt about something different once before that afternoon; there is a coherence in things, a stability; something, she meant, is immune from change, and shines out (she glanced at the window with its ripple of reflected lights) in the face of the flowing, the fleeting, the spectral, like a ruby. . . . Of such moments, she thought, the thing is made that endures" (p. 158).

Indeed, the authors here seek transcendence and sustaining conceptual orders. They would, by means of teaching, move persons beyond the concrete, the relevant, the merely experiential. Like Mrs. Ramsay, they are altogether conscious of impending disintegration. They know that, outside the room where there "seemed to be order and dry land" there is a strangely rippling room, in which "things wavered and vanished, waterily" (p. 147). It is partially in response that they try to go beyond the "finitude" of firsthand experience and (through engagement with the disciplines and the arts) to expanded domains of knowing and awareness, to realms of what they call "possibility."

Buchmann and John Schwille begin by together sounding one of the major themes of this text: A reliance on firsthand experience and what they call an "analogical fusion of education and experience" derived from a "commonsense" view of knowledge or what used to be called "classical realism." They develop a critique, therefore, of the notion that reliable learning can begin through sense experience. If such a notion is taken seriously, the consequences will be extreme objectivism or subjectivism. There will be, the authors say, too easy an acceptance of things that happen to be vividly remembered or subjectively available. Gullibility and bias will take over from careful judgments based upon evidence; there will be inherent limitations in both growth and learning. What is required, these authors say persuasively and eloquently, is access to a range of theoretical systems, to novels and other works of art, to the "objective contents of thought."

Robert Floden joins Buchmann and Schwille in pursuing the theme of the importance of "breaking with everyday experience." Objecting now to the common concern for relevance and utility, they focus on curricula founded in a conception of continuity with daily life. For them, such curricula as the familiar social studies curricula that work outward from study of the family to the community to the world of work reinforce the "given" and thereby encourage the maintenance of what phenomenologists call the "natural attitude," with its incorporation of the taken-for-granted, of beliefs viewed as unquestionable. Calling for the kinds of "adventures" that create distances from the "natural" and the "everyday," the writers call for broad and encompassing views that move learners away from narrowly subjective ways of seeing. They refer to John Dewey, to anthropologists, to psychologists to strengthen their call for breaks with the everyday and the limiting. The opposite, as many point out today, may be an unjustified reliance on a false spontaneity, on a confining single-dimensional vision.

Buchmann alone goes on to examine further the dangers of submission to the "given." She is aware of a problem now drawing the attention of many educators, including post-modern scholars and feminists. It is the problem of reconciling the importance of going beyond the ordinary—toward the emancipatory, the transformative—and the equal importance of teaching what is pragmatically useful and relevant for the improvement of practice. Common sense and direct experience are not enough, Buchmann insists, especially when it comes to teaching teaching. She admits the importance of teacher folkways and lore but believes in "the instructive interruptions of many teacher habits and beliefs." It is extremely difficult, after all, for people to understand differences among people, as it is difficult for them to grasp the meaning of ideals like freedom and justice, if they are *not* provoked to abandon habits and routines.

D. C. Phillips (as if sitting at that dining room table) responds to these three chapters. He is concerned about a too-sweeping obliteration of firsthand experience, as he is about the neglect of the manner in which the young are to be liberated or moved from one domain to another. He also reminds us of the particular knowledge a teacher develops on the ground of common sense, the kind of knowledge that enables her to "psychologize" subject matter and make material accessible to the young. But, like Buchmann, Phillips makes the point that a teacher has to be "liberated" from common sense if such ends are to be achieved.

We move at this point to the second part, where Margret Buchmann herself deals with the use of knowledge from three points of view: the rationality of knowledge utilization; the importance of argument and conversation; the problems in research communication. In the first chapter here, Buchmann explores the conceptual problem of connecting knowledge and utility. Warning against reliance on research knowledge *per se*, she makes the interesting point that, in practice, as many problems arise due to tensions or deficiencies in moral frameworks as to deficiencies in knowledge. She not only calls for the definition of community norms governing acts of teaching; she asks for attentiveness to "public forms of reasonableness" as well.

The question then arises with regard to knowledge as instrumental, knowledge as a tool. The impacts of metaphor are investigated, as are the implications of Wittgensteinian linguistics. The idea of principled action driven by conviction needs to be held in mind, particularly when the fallibility of knowledge and the overestimation of "scientific" authorities are concerned. Buchmann concludes this chapter with suggestions that there are often wide gulfs between those gifted in theory-making and those engaged in practice. As she often does, she turns to literary artists for support. In this instance, Anthony Powell and T. S. Eliot, mocking (for example) brilliant scientists conceiving "grotesque judgments" with regard to poetry.

The author then takes up what has become an issue of widespread consideration: the uses of an ongoing conversation in sense-making and informed communication. She would like to see conversation characterized by "sweetness and light" and arguments "nested in" conversation against a background of friendship. One reason for this is to prevent a preoccupation with winning from taking over from a quest for understanding. Even as others have spoken of "love and logic" as a pair in the world of discourse, so does Margret Buchmann speak of "romance and reason." The sense of incompleteness and possibility remains; and it provides a context for what follows—an account of the problematic of what Buchmann calls "research communication."

The persisting problem of the connection between research knowledge and practice, like the related problem of persuasion, is examined. Here the way in which language is used to communicate compulsion as well as information extends further the discussion of the importance of tentativeness and the willingness to accept uncertainty. Buchmann is asking of researchers an ability to wonder, to question assumptions, to attend to contexts while living up to what they define as the expectations of their publics and their colleagues.

Michael Huberman, responding to these three chapters, takes issue with an incipient dualism or Manichaeism in Margret Buchmann's discussions of rationality in research and what happens in classrooms. Not only does Huberman argue for the multiple uses of research; he summons up the literature of critical theory to remind the writer that there are indeed traditions of challenge to excessive utilitarianism and to reification in research. But he also suggests the possibility of linking a rational commitment to passionate engagement in *praxis*. Among the various issues raised by the research-practice polarity is the issue of disseminating policy research, which is generally known to accomplish little in the way of practical guidance. There have to be interactions among people who construct their realities differently; there have to be the kind of reoriented inquiries that lead in time to real collaboration between and among institutions like research institutes or universities and schools. Huberman has seen this happen; and his stories provide Buchmann's inquiries with an enriched context, perhaps more in touch with the lived experiences of those beginning to work together, staying (as Huberman writes) "in touch."

Moving on from the epistemological dimensions of teaching and teacher education to teachers' thinking, attending, and remembering, Margret Buchmann spells out an interesting distinction between "role" and "person." It is not uncommon today, in the many converging attacks on bureaucracy, to discover something inauthentic in role-playing and to call for a recovery of the person in her candor and spontaneity. Buchmann, challenging this, says that it is out of membership in a norm-governed community that teachers seek good reasons for their choices. The most crucial teaching actions, she reminds us, are responsible acts with public significance. To choose to take on a teaching role is to choose a fabric of obligations that apply despite individual preference or personal choice, and that relate to what is being taught and learned.

She is emphasizing the fact that to take on the role of teacher is to be obliged to teach students worthwhile things and to take an interest in what they learn. In teacher education, therefore, there has to be a recognition that the teaching role demands that there be a "shift of concern from self to others." The writer is taking up themes announced earlier in this book: the need to move beyond the subjective reasons that so frequently offer a false sense of finality and the importance of accepting the constraints of facts and norms taken to be forms of public knowledge. As before, she is beckoning her readers to a domain wider than that of the personal, a world in which teachers locate themselves in larger and larger pictures, within communities that move them to strive to what they believe they *ought* to be. Even as she is pointing to the larger meanings of professionalism, she is also talking about aspirations and moral commitments that may inform teaching within community as it moves teachers to transcend relativism and self-concern.

She moves past this to an account of the ways in which contemplation—or "the moral disciplines of quietly receptive attention"—can become a source of guidance for thinking oriented to choice and action.

Drawing from the work of Hannah Arendt and others, Buchmann offers an account of the many dimensions of thinking, the many "thought-trains" that arise, the thinking of craftspersons and of artists, the moral destructiveness of "thoughtlessness." She adds new facets here to her conception of the acts of teaching as a normative practice embodying recognizable goods and excellences. Contemplation becomes another mode of setting aside self-involved willing and feeling, even another mode of rejecting the given. She sees truth and goodness converging in contemplative experiences linked to fidelity; and this leads, for her, into a conception of receptive attention to subject matter, learners, and "professional ideals." Margret Buchmann chooses to see teaching as "a virtuous activity that is a bearer of human goods" and that involves "enlightening and perfecting others." Again, tapping spokespersons from the arts, the social sciences, and psychiatry, she expands her readers' sense of possibility while remaining within the tradition of the liberal arts.

When Buchmann turns in the next chapter to the contesting mythologies she associates with differing views of teachers and teacher thinking, she develops an approach to memories (viewed here as a "luminous thread of life and personal meaning") that expands and deepens what appears to be a liberal arts approach to the education of teachers. This is not meant to suggest that she would substitute a traditional liberal arts curriculum for what is now taught in teachers' colleges, although (quite evidently) she would make literature, the arts, philosophy, and ethnography central to any curriculum she finds worth building. It is meant to draw attention to her interest in total visions of the human situation and in commitments to fostering freedom, life, and happiness. More than once she connects all this to a view of teaching rooted in a concern for improvement. Drawing from Virginia Woolf, she links memory to caprice and elusiveness, to uniqueness and release. Drawing from Thomas Mann, she speaks of memories as structure and quest, the meanings of which have to be achieved over time.

In part, this is meant to be a challenge to researchers who persist in treating teacher memories as part of their conditioning. Rather than being a source of understanding and illumination, memories are looked at as outside forces, congealing habit and old custom. She finds in the opening of texts a paradigm for the way memory feeds into what Northrop Frye called a "directed quest." Perspectives open as recalled experiences are interpreted; meanings are continuously and unexpectedly made as the past moves into the present and the present's vantage points transform the past. If researchers were to acknowledge and develop a concern for memories in this sense, if they were to come to terms with what lies beyond the horizons of empirical science, their evaluations would be sounder. In their own quests for meanings (themselves linked to mythologies), they might seek out a new kind of clarity that might increase the likelihood of finding truth.

At this juncture, there is a response from the world of practice by an elementary school teacher and scholar living through the tensions of teaching: the tensions between commitment to knowledge and respect for students; the power of personal experience in the absence of shared norms; and the struggle for a balance between external authority and teacher autonomy. The writer, Deborah Loewenberg Ball, effectively and sympathetically puts Buchmann's analyses to the test in a "real life" context. Offering a mathematics lesson as an example, she draws attention to the effects of cultural difference on the process of learning and on the presumed obligation to move students toward participation in impersonal knowledge. There has, she says, to be an overcoming of detachment in caring for students and caring for what they are taught. Young people's knowledge can be extended, as Dewey believed, by making into a continuous and vital process the connection between vital experiences and the subject matters they study.

Agreeing with Buchmann that the fundamental task of teaching is both moral and intellectual, Ball emphasizes the elusiveness of any conception of "ultimate good" as a compass for teacher action. But she pays more heed to the power of personal experience and to the need to make personal interpretations of practice, even when there are standards to be taken into account. She is far less sanguine than Buchmann about the likelihood of moral communities made up of teachers; and she is troubled by images of compliance in cases where existing requirements determine what is taught and how. Agents of change, concludes Ball, must often allow their personal judgments to overcome obligation. She goes on, in summing up, to agree that it is the striving for a justifiable balance that makes teaching the virtuous activity Buchmann describes.

Seeking once more a productive balance, Robert Floden and Margret Buchmann look at ways of educating teachers to confront uncertainty. Most teachers will probably agree that they can never be sure about what their students are learning, or even about what they know. People construct meanings differently; their misunderstandings may be as invisible as their understandings. In any case, tests can never be relied upon to provide absolute certainty with regard to what has been learned (or guessed at or picked up somehow by accident). The authors remind us of the ways in which discussions or clinical interviews can expose the limits of any assessment system, thus adding to the uneasiness particularly of beginning teachers who want to be sure of what they have taught.

Teachers also would like to be sure that the learning that does take place is linked somehow to prior teaching; and it is difficult for many to come to terms with such variables as the influence of social context or parental support or the acceptance of peers. Even the most fruitful research investigations into the merits of diverse approaches to teaching cannot suggest activities that will ensure classroom success. No research or inquiry can lead to predictions about the success or failure of individual children. Uncertainty is often increased, the authors tell us, by teachers' inadequate understanding of the subject matter or by difficulties in deciding what to emphasize and what to include.

Seeking (once more) a productive balance, Floden and Buchmann propose the understanding of uncertainty. This does not mean a preaching of the sort of "anarchy" involved when teachers become cynical and relativistic. Floden and Buchmann would remind them of the grounds available for assessing choices. At once, even as they would raise questions about uncertainty, they would still beckon toward "evolving disciplinary knowledge and ideals of autonomy and responsibility." They see the uses of habits and routines when it comes to structuring what occurs in classrooms; and it is evident to them that an appropriate reliance on routine may free people's attention for confrontation with the unexpected and the new. But they also stress the harm that can be done by an unreflective reliance upon the repetitive and routine. They suggest conversations with other teachers, the development of a "brisk assurance," and the capacity for "second thoughts" when teachers find themselves struggling to deal with the unpredictable and the unmanageable. At the very least, this might prevent a settling into a taken-for-granted kind of certainty, an illusion of order and control.

Following this, Margret Buchmann works with Robert Floden in contrasting consistency in teacher education to coherence, which they call "the rebel angel." They know they are confronting a stubborn desire for certainty, order, and control, along with a resistance to the unexpected and to the revisions and reweavings that keep thinking alive. They call to their aid an assortment of critics and philosophers meeting in a fictional symposium that is intended to clarify the values of disintegration, the inevitability of incongruities in the realm of disciplines, the unlikelihood of systematizing knowledge. The point is to find a way of constructing coherence, to achieve—not a hierarchy—but a web, a network of connections. They point to the indeterminacies that characterize works of art and to the kinds of incompleteness and inconsistencies in education that leave room for the shaping of multiple perspectives. They recognize the need for shape and for structure; but they want to see an interplay between "form and flexibility." As in many of the preceding chapters, there is an effort here to stitch together even as distinctions are made, and the obstacles of fixity and completeness are exposed. Implicit in all this is a critique of the frozen and the fixed.

Steven Weiland takes up the argument with regard to uncertainty and joins it to Richard Rorty's stress on the importance of contingency. He also recalls Rorty's writing about the significance of a "redescription of liberalism" and a replacement of Enlightenment linearity with a poeticizing of contemporary culture. It may be, as Weiland sees it, that Buchmann and Floden, tapping the literature of the humanities as they do, are attempting something very similar. Then he goes on to suggest that an intellectual life that allows for uncertainty and disruption, in the sense Buchmann and Floden speak of them, demands a kind of lifelong learning on the part of teachers. There is an implication that adult development must be attended to when intellectual life is described as it is in the foregoing chapters, a life that is reflective, norm-governed, detached, and open to change. Interested as they are in "pedagogical content knowledge" rather than curricular projects and programs, Buchmann and Floden have to deal with a dialectic in the space they create between intellectual development and the work (often managerial work) the teacher's role requires. They are asking for something serious and difficult when they propose bringing intellectual dilemmas, conflicts, and uncertainties into classrooms where there are so many demands for management and control. What Scheffler speaks of as the "double consciousness" is required of such teachers: a way of relating action to reflection, practice to critical thinking, in order to overcome the either/or.

With a sense of having moved around a table under shifting lights, I turn once again to Woolf's (1927/1955) *To the Lighthouse,* which ends with a vision of completeness when Lily Briscoe finishes painting a picture that resisted wholeness and coherence throughout the years of the novel's life. "I have had my vision" (p. 310), Lily thinks; and readers are aware that such completion can only be aesthetic. The dialectic remains between window and lighthouse, between palpitant changing life and the "x," the logico-linear definition of things. At the same moment, when Mr. Ramsay and two of his children reach the lighthouse, no one is quite sure what the aging man is thinking. It might be that "We perished, each alone, or he might be thinking, I have reached it. I have found it; but he said nothing" (p. 308). The text remains open, as this book remains open. Having opened what they chose to say for commentary and for dialogue, Buchmann, Floden, and Schwille are provoking their readers to go in search of their own meanings, to conceive of teaching and learning with a renewed passion, to wonder about and redefine their roles.

As someone who has spent many years "doing" philosophy in the contexts of teacher education, this particular writer finds herself stirred by what she has read and, at once, moved to reflect on her own journey against the backdrop provided by Margret Buchmann and her friends. There are many things we share; there is an intertextuality we all recognize. The language links us: incompleteness, unexpectedness, tension, dialectic, dialogue. We recognize the perspectives provided by ethnography, sociology, and the range of philosophies in the Western world. In my case, it must be said, I would be more conscious of the arguments raised against a taking for granted of the "canon" in our several fields. Yes, I would refer to Aeschylus, Dante, Shakespeare, Blake, Wordsworth, Keats, the Brontës, Eliot, and Joyce; but I would realize and declare the limitation of a worldview that excludes so many of the world's cultures and ways of seeing. It is not only that there are depths of experience in the works of the great Russian novelists that are untapped here. There are the perspectives of the long oppressed, of those who have resisted oppression, of those who have transcended: Frederick Douglass, Sojourner Truth, Harriet Tubman, W. E. B. DuBois, Zora Neale Hurston, the Reverend Martin Luther King, Jr. There are the Hispanic voices, only newly discovered by those of us in the north: Borges, Fuentes, Neruda, Octavio Paz, Isabel Allende. When I read Margret Buchmann on the meanings of memory, I cannot but recall Gabriel Marquez's *One Hundred Years of Solitude*. When I am moved to recall cultural myths, yes, and memories, I have to summon up Maxine Hong Kingston's *The Woman Warrior* and Ralph Ellison's *Invisible Man* and Toni Morrison's *Beloved*.

When I search my own accumulated understandings for visions of reason at work, visions of knowing, visions of visions, I think (as Margret Buchmann has also done) of Primo Levi (1975/1984), in *The Periodic Table*, naming each of his chapters after an element. Exploring what it means to "figure" the past, Buchmann quotes Levi on "inert" and "noble" gases; she relates what he wrote to a conception of memory's "inert" pictures, serving as ground or background for teachers' thinking, not the source of productive responses. There are other evocations: one to be found in the Czech novelist Skvorecky's (1984) *The Engineer of Human Souls*. He speaks of freedom being mainly a matter of youth and dictatorships. He thinks that "it exists nowhere else, perhaps because we are not aware of it. Just as we are unaware of air until, in the gas chamber of life, it is replaced by those crystals, tasteless, colourless, odourless" (p. 439). He is talking, in part, about what inertness, what taken-for-grantedness can mean. And, like Buchmann and Floden, he is calling for attention, for awareness.

Levi (1975/1984), in his text, was writing about being a chemist in a concentration camp and about overcoming the crisis of becoming part of the *Lager* system: ". . . and I must have developed a strange callousness if

I then managed not only to survive but also to think, to register the world around me, and even to perform rather delicate work, in an environment infected by the daily presence of death. . . . I was a chemist in a chemical plant, in a chemical laboratory . . . and I stole in order to eat" (pp. 139–140). Trying to remember it later, he explained that he and his companions were not normal because they were hungry, suffering a hunger that was "a need, a lack, a yearning . . . that had struck deep, permanent roots in us, lived in our cells, and conditioned our behavior" (p. 140). But then, in the last chapter, entitled "Carbon," he wrote about the role of that element in human life:

> "This cell belongs to a brain, and it is my brain, the brain of the *me* who is writing; and the cell in question, and within it the atom in question, is in charge of my writing, in a gigantic minuscule game which nobody has yet described. It is that which at this instant, issuing out of a labyrinthine tangle of yeses and nos, makes my hands run along a certain path on the paper, mark it with these volutes that are signs: a double snap, up and down, between two levels of energy, guides this hand of mine to impress on the paper this dot, here, this one" (pp. 232–233).

Primo Levi has provided a way of seeing that permits us to view the relations between swarming carbon atoms, the lives of cells, the chains and the breaking of chains—and the induplicable, personal moment of putting down a letter, leaving a thumb print, "here, this one." His background in an empirical science allowed him to write that; indeed, his being a chemist was what enabled him to survive. But then the clear and soluble questions and descriptions led him to the unanswerable. How *explain* life in the Lager as a reasonable man? To what will "this one" lead? Buchmann's centering on uncertainty and the need to live with uncertainty is altogether important. But I want to break through the atmosphere of detachment here and there. I want the presence of the silences to be felt, what Albert Camus called "the muteness of the spheres."

It may be that I want to remind these authors of the experience of the absurd, which Camus (1955) told us emerges when we feel within us a longing "for happiness and reason" and find ourselves face to face with the irrational. As Camus notes, the absurd arises from a confrontation between human need and the world's silence, which is unreasonable. And, later, there are words that might well be Buchmann's words, up to a point: "Thinking is not unifying or making the appearance familiar under the guise of a great principle. Thinking is learning all over again how to see, directing one's consciousness, making of every image a privileged place" (p. 43). Camus went on to relate this to phenomenology, to an approach that declines to explain the world but merely attempts to describe actual experience.

The writers' replies to their respondents make me somewhat less inclined to charge them with a narrow, incomplete view of experience, and I realize that they may not be identifying it with what phenomenologists call the "natural attitude." (In fact, the "natural attitude," for all its assumption of the existence of an independent, "given" world, goes beyond merely experiential claims. For Husserl (1931), the world—from the natural standpoint—"is the totality of objects that can be known through experience (*Erfahrung*), known in terms of orderly theoretical thought on the basis of direct present (*aktueller*) experience" (p. 52). The natural sciences, in fact, are all given by the natural standpoint; since all assume the givenness of the world as a totality of objects of possible experience interrelated by universal causal laws.)

There are, as Buchmann and Floden themselves recognize, other ways of looking at experience. Surely, it is not enough to view it mainly in terms of the "everyday," the restricted, the unaware. Dewey, refusing a one-dimensional view of experience, went further than these writers, even in their rejoinder to Phillips, when they agree that reasonable thought and practice cannot be accounted for in terms of "formal reason and consistency alone." In a remarkable chapter called "Existence," in *Experience and Nature*, Dewey (1925/1958) sounded some of the themes sounded so frequently in the present book—but in connection with the interactions of experience. The important problems in life and philosophy, he said, have to do with "the rate and mode of the conjunction of the precarious and the assured, the incomplete and the finished, the repetitious and the varying, the safe and sane and the hazardous" (p. 75). And then

> If we trust to the evidence of experienced things, these traits, and the modes and tempos of their interaction with each other, are fundamental features of natural existence. The experience of their various consequences, according as they are relatively isolated, unhappily or happily combined, is evidence that wisdom, and hence that love of wisdom which is philosophy, is concerned with choice and administration of their proportioned union. Structure and process, substance and accident, matter and energy, permanence and flux, one and many, continuity and discreteness, order and progress, law and liberty, uniformity and growth, tradition and innovation, rational will and impelling desires, proof and discovery, the actual and the possible, are names given to various phases of their conjunction, and the issue of living depends upon the art with which these things are adjusted to each other. (pp. 75–76)

As Dewey saw it, a true wisdom, devoted to "an opening and enlarging of the ways of nature" discovers ways of administering the "unfinished processes of existence so that frail goods shall be substantiated, secure goods be extended, and the precarious promises of good that haunt experienced things be more liberally fulfilled" (pp. 76–77).

Thinking experientially, he had in mind an organic movement of expansion within the contextual situations in which cognition began. It was an expansion, an ordering reaching toward the horizons. In many respects, his description evokes what Maurice Merleau-Ponty (1964) described as a "route, an experience which gradually clarifies itself, which gradually rectifies itself and proceeds by dialogue with itself and with others" (p. 21). Like Vygotsky, as quoted in this book, Merleau-Ponty understood the importance of awareness of our thinking. For him, of course, thinking began in a perceived landscape; and "the experience of perception is our presences at the moment when things, truths, values are constituted for us; . . . perception is a nascent *logos*; . . . it teaches us, outside all dogmatism, the true conditions of objectivity itself; . . . it summons us to the tasks of knowledge and action" (p. 25). He was concerned about the birth of knowledge, the growth of consciousness of rationality against the background of nature, of the world as sensed.

There is nothing here nor in the Deweyan view to prevent a movement forward and outward into a conceptual order—beyond the everyday, the routing, or what is described as "finitude." Indeed, I find it hard to believe that the movement outward, the taking of the "route," would be likely without the tension and the sense of the problematic that can only arise within lived situations where there is a felt need to "adjust," as Dewey said, the "traits, and tempos" of the transactions among experienced things. In some dimension, this book attends to the multiplex character of experience and its contingencies; and I feel great sympathy with the writers' invigorating concern with the quest for structure, for coherence, for a vision. There is something haunting and important for me in the view that the text is always open, that there can be no final moment, no completion to be found.

Still, I want to argue for a greater attention to situation, to location, to point of view. There is relatively little in these chapters that suggests the range of languages, images, and meaning structures that young people bring to school. To suggest that what they bring is necessarily to be equated with innocence, unreflectiveness, and narrowness is to ignore the possibilities that may be applied if multiple perspectives are taken into account. There are, today, plentiful examples of this in the journals kept in "whole language" classes and in such articulations as Deborah

Loewenberg Ball describes. Whether it is mathematics or history or paint-ing or writing, learners come with different ways of mediating what is presented to them. This is not to deny what even William Blake noted long ago: the tension between innocence and experience. Nor is it to deny the need to make accessible the perspectives implicit in the disciplines or the importance of informing the perceived with the conceived. The power in the present book is to be found in the possibilities of knowing and understanding that it discloses. The young people who are to be brought to take initiatives in the face of such possibilities, like the teachers who are being prepared to teach them, must be viewed in their situatedness, provoked to move from where they know they are into a more expansive, more challenging, defamiliarized world. It is in that world and in the communities they may find there that they may be empowered to pose the questions, perhaps even to love the questions. It is in that world, reaching out to one another, that they may find some images of coherence and clarity and hope, even as they discover diverse ways of structuring and looking at what is conceived as "real."

The authors' rejoinders to their respondents do indicate somewhat more attentiveness to the contextual than I originally saw. Still, however, there is a frequent air of groundlessness in the book; it is hard to locate ourselves in particular spaces and moments of time as we read. I think of the pulsations and colors of cities, and the walls of cities. I think of tumultuous streets and empty homes (lacking books, lacking study cor-ners). I think of alienation and hatred, of noise and garbled dreams. And then I ponder what they signify for teaching and learning in these times, for all the "sweetness" of the friendships sought, for all the concern for "form and flexibility." I think of the influences of popular culture, the play of images, what semioticians call our "mythologies" (Blonsky, 1992) and certain artists, our "imagology" (Kundera, 1991, p. 114). There is the erosion of community (including the normative community); there is the persistent cacophony. Somehow or other, the moral and intellectual com-mitments that glow in this book must be related to the vacancies and longings within the culture. Of course, there are no clear solutions; nor are there any certainties the deficiencies can be repaired. The dialectic here can be given more content, however, should be given more content. It does not simply involve the tensions between window and lighthouse, between the theoretical and the practical, the generative and the routine, the unpredictable and the systematized. There are the living, uncertain human beings of all ages: Some are newcomers; some are too embedded in the ordinary to perceive alternatives; some feel such a sense of entitle-ment they no longer care; others feel abandoned, without homes or with-out trust. We need somehow to picture their faces and their eyes, to make them visible in books like this one. We need, as Cynthia Ozick (1989) writes, to "imagine the familiar hearts of strangers" (p. 283) as we work to recreate our moral communities. There are many strange voices, many contesting voices still to be heeded. There are excluded groups still yearning for acknowledgment; there are women still reaching out for recognition as *who*, not what they are. A shallowness and a carelessness mark too many of our atmospheres; there are distances that alienate and continue to chill. It is not detachment that causes it; it is not even a sometimes necessary distancing. It is deadly cold indifference; it is a thoughtlessness that withers if it does not kill.

No book, even one as authentic, scholarly, and lustrous as this, can encompass all the unmet needs or deal with all the open questions. But it can (and this book may have that power) persuade; it can address the sense of restiveness readers feel; it can awaken responsibility. If the conversation rendered in these chapters engages more and more persons in search of meaning, in search of coherence, we know at least that there will be openings. Margret Buchmann and her colleagues provoke us to move through those openings, sometimes beyond the actual. They ask us to think about our own thinking, to reflect upon our changing practice, to become what it is possible for us to be.

Part 1

EXPERIENCE AND EXPERTISE IN TEACHING AND LEARNING

CHAPTER 1

Education, Experience, and the Paradox of Finitude

Margret Buchmann and John R. Schwille

"Experience is the best teacher." In U.S. education there is a common belief in the educative value of firsthand experience, of "being there" and "doing it" and "seeing for oneself." Teachers claim they have learned from classroom experience most of what they know about teaching. In deference to this belief, preservice education gives more and more time to classroom experience, while inservice programs stress teachers' sharing their experiences with one another. Teachers in turn are advised to build on the firsthand experiences of children. There is a fear that without such foundations learners will have neither interest nor understanding.

Firsthand experience is trusted implicitly as both the means and content of education. It is supposed to be down-to-earth, personal, and practical. Ideas encountered in books are pale in contrast. Compared with life as a school of hard knocks, the school of hard books seems irrelevant and ineffective. Immersion in the "real world" teaches people "what is what." Those who want students to learn about the world of work firsthand often do not challenge limits set by present occupations and social structures.

In a four-part argument, we question presumptions that favor firsthand experience. First, we look at the language of education as a language of experience with presuppositions, entailments, and functions that stem from this view. Next, we analyze limits and fallacies of learning from firsthand experience. Third, we consider how firsthand experience can close avenues to conceptual and social change. As specific examples, we discuss learning to teach and career education. Finally, we argue that, in general, books and art can give better access to the real world and to the realm of the possible than can firsthand experience.

EDUCATION AS THE VOICE OF EXPERIENCE

Historians of education have argued both that the American language of education is a language of experience and that the belief in the educative value of experience has not been subjected to critical analysis (see Clifford, 1975). As Eisele (1980) points out, we "say things like . . . 'you have to learn from experience,' 'that was a real learning experience'" (p. 32). People feel that they "learn by doing" and that "practice makes perfect." "Experience is the best teacher," so "live and learn" and "let experience be your guide." Colloquial reason thus casts experience as teacher, school, and learning context and as the means by which education and its perfection are accomplished. The connection between the concepts of education and experience appears to be an analogical fusion—the essence of metaphor (Lakoff & Johnson, 1980; Perelman & Olbrechts-Tyteca, 1958/1969).

Firsthand Experience: From Metaphor to Theory and Action

We think, talk, act, and live under the guidance of metaphors. Understanding things in terms of each other, we fuse them in action. Metaphors prescribe and commend; they "sanction actions, justify inferences, and help us set goals" (Lakoff & Johnson, 1980, p. 142). Thus, the analogical fusion of education and experience implies and imposes a theory of learning, of the relationship of mind to reality, and of people to the social world.

What is taken for granted in language becomes, quite literally, second nature. The integration of metaphorical expressions into ways of speaking and acting masks the fact that these expressions make a case whose merits need to be examined. To understand the fusion of education and firsthand experience and its effects on what is taught and learned in schools, it is necessary to consider the commonsense theory of knowledge and mind on which this analogical fusion depends and on which empirical and prescriptive claims about the educative value of firsthand experience rely.

The Bucket Theory of Mind

The commonsense theory of knowledge is deceptively straightforward. "If you or I wish to know something . . . ,we have to open our eyes and look round. And we have to raise our ears and listen to noises, and especially to those made by other people" (Popper, 1972, p. 60). Sense experience is central to the commonsense theory of knowledge, in which the mind figures as an empty container. Popper calls this the *bucket theory of mind.*

In this view, what comes to the mind through the senses can be relied on as objectively true; it appears directly apprehended and in no way interfered with. Immediate experience therefore cannot be false; to question it makes no sense. Error can be remedied by taking another hard look at the facts, the externally "given." The mind is seen as an impassive and efficient instrument that registers, adds up, and digests incoming sensory data.

The commonsense theory of knowledge turns on the notion of a simple sensory function dismissed by scientists and philosophers of science. Scholars of various disciplinary stripes and orientations agree that there is little of which people can be certain; they call for systematic criticism and openness to new data and ideas. However, many beliefs and practices in education presuppose the commonsense theory of knowledge and mind. Such presuppositions also inspire problematic interpretations of the work of Dewey and Piaget. Educational applications of these theories tend to emphasize the practical and concrete, in the expectation that conceptual frameworks will be acquired "naturally" through an immersion in practical problems.

The commonsense theory of knowledge assumes that subjective (i.e., individual, possibly idiosyncratic) experience is a sufficient foundation for knowledge. Pushed to its logical conclusion, this theory leads to relativism. If individual experience is the basis for knowledge, it is impossible to adjudicate between conflicting claims. In the absence of interpersonal, objective criteria for judging the validity of knowledge claims, it is possible to say only that something is "true for you" or "true for me."

The dogma of subjective certainty is closely associated with epistemological nihilism, the counterintuitive notion that we cannot know anything. Epistemological objectivism likewise takes firsthand experience as a starting point; it focuses, however, on the sensory and descriptive rather than the personal element in sense experience. As indicated earlier, the assumption of the self-sufficiency of immediate experience—on which both epistemological subjectivism and objectivism depend—is faulty. Common sense, which pretends to realism, leaves one stranded in extreme objectivist or subjectivist positions. Critically examined, it refutes itself.

The central educational thesis of the commonsense theory of knowledge is that we learn most, if not all, of what we learn in a reliable fashion through sense experience. The analogical fusion of education and experience, supported by the commonsense theory of knowledge and mind, has entailments regarding the goals of education, the methods of effective instruction, and the social adaptation of young people, especially those with working-class origins. In what follows we discuss traps inherent to learning from firsthand experience, traps that lead people to untenable conclusions and narrow the range of investigation, choice, and imagination.

IF SEEING IS BELIEVING, GULLIBILITY IS THE RESULT

Sense experience can be misleading. Consider the following examples: "The sun seems to move around a stationary earth. Except when the wind is blowing, air seems to be empty nothingness—a vacuum. When standing still, we feel voluntarily motionless on stationary ground—there is no sense that we are spinning at 1,000 miles per hour and held in place by a balance of powerful physical forces" (Brophy, 1982, p. 28). Hard facts and firsthand experience often go their separate ways. Sensory evidence may feel compelling; one's persuasions, however, don't prove anything. Apt explanations can fail to persuade, while persuasive explanations may be riddled by logical and evidential shortcomings. In the words of John Stuart Mill (1843/1900), "Evidence is not that which the mind does or must yield to, but that which it *ought* [italics added] to yield to, namely, that, by yielding to which, its belief is kept conformable to fact" (p. 370).

Research in the psychology of judgment shows that learning from firsthand experience is not the same as sticking to the facts. Ordinary judgment strategies reduce complex tasks of inference to simpler operations. Many of these commonly used heuristics are not trustworthy.

Firsthand Experience and Misguided Inference

For example, the relative availability of objects or events in memory tends to influence people's judgments about their relative frequency, plausibility, and causal efficacy (Tversky & Kahneman, 1973). Much of what is readily remembered has been experienced firsthand. But the firsthand experiences of individuals necessarily are restricted in number by the length of any given life and are systematically influenced in kind by the location of people in social systems. The selection of a person's firsthand experiences is unlikely to be a controlled probability process in the sense of scientific sampling. Firsthand experience is not a suitable means of sampling from an environment that is variable; it is an unreliable basis for making inferences about the real world.

Nisbett and Ross (1980) exemplify the inferential shortcomings associated with the *availability heuristic* by the hypothetical case of a pollster who asks people to estimate the current rate of unemployment. Unemployed respondents will tend to overestimate the rate of unemployment, while people who are currently employed are likely to underestimate it. The bias in subjective availability can be traced to sampling bias.

> The unemployed individual is likely to share the neighborhood, socioeconomic background, and occupation of other jobless individuals. He also is likely to encounter other unemployed people in such everyday endeavors as job-hunting, visiting employment agencies, [and] collecting unemployment benefits. . . . Thus, to the extent that the unemployed person relies upon the sample generated by his personal experience, he will be misled about the commonness of unemployment. In the same manner, employed people, who are apt to live, work, and shop near one another, are apt to err in the opposite direction. (p. 20)

For the availability heuristic to be valid, the availability of acts and events in memory must be determined by a mechanism that keeps track of their frequency and causal efficacy. But salience in memory often has little to do with the evidential or probative value of information. Take, for example, the *vividness criterion*, that is, the influence of the sensory, cognitive, and affective salience of data on the weighing of evidence. The probative value of evidence is not necessarily related to the emotional interest it may have for a person. Similarly, the degree to which evidence is concrete and vivid is no predictor of sound conclusions.

Most of the factors that contribute to the vividness of information are factors that characterize firsthand experience. Firsthand experience is close to us, concrete, and interesting simply because what happened did happen to us or to people we know. It prompts sensory images, hopes, and desires. But what makes an experience vivid may be irrelevant for the purposes of inference and judgment, and feelings have no intrinsic connection to defensible thought. The availability heuristic and the vividness criterion will not invariably determine what is learned from firsthand experience. Nevertheless, these common strategies of judgment do suggest that firsthand experience will often prejudice attempts at education based on better evidence or reasoning.

Cognitive and Behavioral Traps

In the hypothetical case discussed above, survey information in the form of employment statistics could be used to estimate the rate of unemployment. Contextual factors and other possible sources of unreliability could have been considered to adjust any initial subjective guesses. However, experimental evidence shows that people are generally swayed by availability and not much disposed to adjust for the biases of firsthand experience. As Nisbett and Ross (1980) point out, common parlance attests to the importance of firsthand experience in evidential weighting: "People often say 'I was there,' or 'I saw it myself,' in order to enhance the credibility of their assertions. Doubters are urged to go see for themselves" (p. 50).

The experiences of teachers provide further illustrations. When teachers say, "I tried individualized instruction and it does not work," or "I have read that book to fifth-grade children and they are not interested," they rely on the availability heuristic. Classroom experiences can be quite vivid. For instance, an excitable child may calm down greatly after being struck with a ruler. Organizational ramifications, the teacher's feelings, and the child's reactions can make this event salient. Little can be learned from it, however, about the effectiveness or appropriateness of corporal punishment in general, or for hyperactive children in particular.

Imagine what can be learned from firsthand experience in student teaching: Punishment works; punishment doesn't work; silence is an indication of busy minds and student engagement; silence is an indication of irrelevant and ineffective teaching; cultural difference is deprivation; cultural difference is desirable; whole-group instruction is less effective than individualized instruction; and so on.

In principle, no one need rely on the vividness and biased availability of data based on firsthand experience. Research information in the form of anthropological descriptions or experimental evidence from psychology could inform and correct beliefs founded on firsthand experience. But another effect of the vividness criterion—unjustified skepticism of secondhand information coded in texts or summarized by figures in tables—makes such adjustments less likely. As methods of first choice, judgment heuristics associated with firsthand experience can thus become cognitive traps.

Platt (1973) has analyzed traps of firsthand experience from the perspective of reinforcement theory. People tend to get trapped in behaviors that are rewarding in the short term, even when these behaviors have negative consequences in the long run. Behavioral traps also occur when something initially rewarding becomes less so over time and is punishing in the end. In itself, firsthand experience does not provide a long-term view of likely consequences: Such a view depends on information and imagination.

The impact of firsthand experiences over the course of the teaching career illustrates how cognitive traps can interact with behavioral traps. After student teaching, many novices act as if maintaining an orderly and busy classroom amounts to good teaching. Their work conception gets shaped by their initial successes. What typically helps teachers survive in their beginning years (i.e., the activation of models of teaching acquired in the lengthy course of their own schooling) may arrest their professional development. It is here that ideas about what is possible and desirable could help. But the rewards of survival are self-evident and reinforce associated behaviors, derived from firsthand experience to begin with. The relative isolation of teachers throughout their careers makes cognitive and behavioral traps associated with firsthand experience particularly effective.

In view of the experimental and anecdotal evidence on the problematic role of firsthand experience in judgment, Nisbett and Ross (1980) are surprised that there are so few cautionary sayings about concrete, sensory data. They even invent a few caveats for this purpose: "'Just because it's punchy doesn't mean it's important,' 'Yes, it's interesting, but what does it prove?'" (p. 61). In contrast, there are many sayings to protect us against secondhand data: "Don't believe everything you read"; "You can prove anything with statistics." Both phenomena—scarcity of caveats about the inferential pitfalls of firsthand experience and the diversity of cautionary statements regarding secondhand information—signal an implicit endorsement of the commonsense theory of knowledge.

In everyday judgment and behavior, strategies of judgment and evidential weighing are neither devised nor employed deliberately. Here, one might think, is a mission for educators: Challenge the implicit trust in firsthand experience and clarify misleading assumptions of the commonsense theory of knowledge. But the very language of education, as a voice of (firsthand) experience, gets in the way. Indeed, educators themselves are long on homilies about the value of firsthand experience, short on inferential and evidential homilies, and prey to the mystique of firsthand experience. This mystique has not only cognitive but also political and social consequences.

FIRSTHAND EXPERIENCE, ENEMY OF FREEDOM?

Getting firsthand experience is often a process in which one comes to terms with the "real world." In viewing learning as adaptation, the role of imagination is limited and that of imitation paramount; learning from experience, then, means learning to adhere to given practices and standards. Thus, the experience of schoolteaching, as Waller (1932/1961) wrote, "disciplines the creative impulse out of many" (p. 391). When young people are told, "It will be a good experience for you," the expectation usually is that they will come out of it chastened.

Aspiration presupposes thinking that the limits of firsthand experience are not the limits of what is possible. Actuality and imagination stand in a relation that Bourdieu (1967/1971) calls the *paradox of finitude:* "The individual who attains an immediate, concrete understanding of the familiar world, of the native atmosphere in which and for which he has been brought up, is thereby deprived of the possibility of appropriating immediately and fully the world that lies outside" (p. 205). Firsthand experience limits not only personal understandings but views of the social and political worlds. Everything actual is by its nature finite and necessarily excludes what Whitehead (1933) calls "the unbounded welter of contrary possibilities" (p. 356); this doctrine, he adds, should be "a commonplace of political philosophy" (p. 356).

To transcend the paradox of finitude, people need to overcome their purely experiential frames of reference. Understanding one's own experiences does require access to the behavior, thoughts, and knowledge of many individuals whom one cannot know personally. If such knowledge cannot be mustered, people trying to learn from their experiences may become subject to the manipulation of others. Other people need not be evil, but taking their disinterestedness, benevolence, or wisdom on faith is unwarranted. As Lipsky (1980) points out, "Citizens in general and poor people in particular will resign themselves to inferior levels of service if they have nothing with which to compare their experiences and have no basis for thinking that they deserve any better. Their frame of reference, if any, is experiential" (p. 53). Clients of public bureaucracies usually do not receive information that allows them to judge the way they are treated or to compare their own treatment with that of clients in other years or at comparable agencies.

Karl Marx hoped that increasing hardships would act to break the barriers of isolation among the poor and enlarge their scope of vision. He believed that objective circumstances, if only harsh enough, would lead to an understanding of oppression and to revolutionary commitment. But, after analyzing the events that led to the coup d'état of Louis Bonaparte, Marx (1852/1963) judged that poverty and isolation among the small-holding peasants in France made them, in fact, a conservative force. The peasants were restricted by their mode of life. The small holding, in the words of Marx, "admits of no division of labour in its cultivation, no application of science and, therefore, no diversity of development, no variety of talent, no wealth of social relationships" (p. 123). Revising tenets at the heart of his own theories, Marx came to conclude that commitment to change is no outcome of material hardships alone, but requires a change of consciousness.

The Schooling of Followers

As Willis (1977) has shown, British working-class boys still tend to accept—almost embrace—what they take to be their place in the world. Disaffected, the "lads" enact their skeptical stance toward the social order as a rejection of school and intellectual activity in general. They celebrate manual labor as a test of manhood. It gives evidence of their superiority over women: To be a man is to accept the physical demands of industrial work as inevitable. As presented in careers teaching, the British equivalent of career education, the organization of work in industry appears as timeless as the class distinction between manual and mental labor.

The absolutism of this perception rests on a conflation of things as they are with things as they will and must be. It is the absolutism of common sense, which claims the world as its authority. "For 'the lads' this hegemony of commonsense surrounds them all the time.... It supplies naturalized social divisions and an omnipresent sexual chauvinism. Perhaps most important, ... it supplies an overpowering feeling that the way of the world is the way of work. Work of a certain direct and concrete kind" (Willis, 1977, p. 162). The naturalist's view of the social world and of people's destinies within it implies that "there is no one to blame, no action to be taken" (Willis, 1977, p. 163). The "hand-mindedness" of the lads and their stoic pride are touching—and saddening, too—because they are self-defeating.

In the late nineteenth and early twentieth centuries, advocates of manual training or vocational education in the United States saw first-hand experience as a means of insulating the "rank and file" (Snedden, 1924, p. 554) from undue aspirations. The trend toward social predestination was so strong that in 1908 Harvard president Charles W. Eliot (1908/1974) reversed his earlier position and argued, "Teachers of the elementary schools ought to sort the pupils ... by their evident or probable destinies" (p. 137). He later added that "it is the very best thing that a teacher can do for a child, to tell him or her in what line he or she can have the most successful and the happiest life" (p. 137). One of the most influential documents in the history of vocational education in the United States, the report of the Commission on National Aid to Vocational Education (1914/1974), put it this way:

> Vocational training will indirectly but positively affect the aims and methods of *general education* [italics added]: (1) By developing a better teaching process through which the children who do not respond to book instruction alone may be reached and educated through learning by doing; (2) by intro-

ducing into our educational system the aim of utility, to take its place in dignity by the side of culture and to connect education with life by making it purposeful and useful. Industrial and social unrest is due in large measure to a lack of a system of practical education fitting workers for their callings. (p. 117)

Two of the most important advocates of a purposefully limited education were David Snedden and Charles Allen Prosser. A key person in the passage of the landmark Smith-Hughes Act of 1917, Prosser (Prosser & Allen, 1925, chap. VII) contended that vocational education should be based on the actual experiences of people working in an occupation. Subjects such as mathematics or science should be organized in short units that apply directly to the "specific needs of workers in the performance of specific tasks or operations" (Prosser & Allen, 1925, p. 207).

In 1916, Snedden argued that industrial education in the schools should mean real work on real machines, turning out marketable products. Attempts to mix job-specific education and general education would turn the whole into a useless "hash." He predicted the replacement of the short, "soft" school day with a workday equal in length and conditions to a day of industrial labor (Rodgers, 1978). Today, Snedden's (1924) tone is likely to offend; for example, when he writes that the multitude "can follow well—if trained thereto—in voting or in war, [or] in working" (p. 554). The training for "following well" was to be supplied by vocational education.

The entailments of the analogical fusion of education and (firsthand) experience are played out here in the social and political arenas. Educators saw learning by doing, for the world of work, as both the content and means of an education openly class-based and oriented toward political quietism. Vocational education has been reformed as "career education," which stresses developing career awareness in advance of some specific training. Social predestination is not assumed. The progression from vocational schooling to career education thus permits a wider opening to the social world than simple firsthand experience. Nevertheless, critics of career education (e.g., Grubb & Lazerson, 1975; Wagner, 1980) maintain that it results in a lowering of aspirations and educational quality as well as an unquestioning commitment of young people to the social order.

Education that merges the immediate goals of the world of work with those of education limits people's awareness and their choices. Confounding things as they are with things as they must be closes avenues to conceptual and social change. Immediacy is also ahistorical. "The ideal of immediate experience denies the desire for reflection, tradition, and cumulative knowledge" (Shiff, 1978/1979, p. 105). This desire is affirmed in encounters with texts and other human creations to which imagination responds by drawing "upon an immense accumulation of interacting memories and associations, layer upon layer combining and recombining" (Hampshire, 1989, p. 126).

COMING OF AGE THROUGH DISCIPLINED IMAGINATION

"Perhaps the immobility of the things that surround us is forced upon them by our conviction that they are themselves, and not anything else, and by the immobility of our conceptions of them," reflects Proust (1913/1956, p. 7). Book learning and the languages of art advance the mobility of conceptions—their capacity to move and to be moved—and expand one's scope of thoughts and sensibilities:

> The vast capacity and scope of the art of Shakespeare or of Titian create a space into which a great variety of fused memories can enter: suggestions of happiness, of loss, of transience, of love, of innocence, and of old age. Into these inchoate and unparticularised suggestions, as into a vast, unfurnished cave, each person insinuates some highly specific version of these indefinite themes, which he finds sharply realised in the specific forms of the works before him. (Hampshire, 1989, p. 127)

Yet the person who drifts into a museum without guidance or picks up a book here and there and reads without deepening attention and critical awareness is subject to many of the pitfalls of accidental firsthand experience.

Are Texts to Be Preferred to Reflective Experiences?

Text has its own authority, not always well deserved. Reading can be disconnected and—though massive—shallow, while experience can be a basis for considering received opinions. The traps of firsthand experience may partially be overcome by a knowledgeable person with the means to plan experiences carefully, anticipate what they may have to offer, and select them with a view toward some systematic variation. Even so, books and other objects of thought retain advantages. In any circumstances, firsthand experience is difficult to control. It involves natural and social facts and other people—amenable to thought, often intractable in life. The person who wants to choose experiences is more constrained by time, expense, inevitable evanescence, and other obstacles to access than someone who selects a book.

The reader is free to be daring. Experiments in reading are less risky than firsthand experience in even a mildly adventurous vein. Besides, opportunities in life are limited and fleeting. How does it feel to be a medieval knight, a Flemish lace maker, or a Mexican immigrant in Texas? Firsthand, these experiences cannot be checked out from a friendly librarian. But libraries have historical records and works of fiction and social theory that describe and analyze feudalism, lace making, and U.S. immigration from many points of view. Holding them steady for examination, books incorporate the experiences, thoughts, and feelings of people remote in time and place.

People who live by action alone may never ask what is happening; their critical faculties are in abeyance. However, when one is not the person peering through a visor, bending over lace bobbins, or looking for a job in San Antonio, necessity is in abeyance. Necessity and chance are often joined in ways not calculated to advance goals of learning. What texts and the arts make possible through ever-increasing attention is less vulnerable to potent subjective and objective constraints than is firsthand experience.

Nor are learning conditions dependent upon the logic of action; "learning can occur when neither of the primary conditions for learning through contingent experience—self-initiated action or direct knowledge of its results—is fulfilled" (Bruner & Olson, 1977–78, p. 3). Psychologists have shown that knowledge can be acquired by observing and imitating others and, more directly relevant to our argument, by extracting knowledge from vicarious experience coded in text.

Pallid Numerical Information Raises Questions

Unlike firsthand experience, secondhand information (particularly in the form of pallid numerical data) lends itself to a consideration of what is typical, what is generalizable, and what can be found that is different from what is already known. It enlarges the number of cases that can be considered and can include rare occurrences of high value for learning, while representing more adequately than firsthand experience the distribution of events in the real world.

Secondhand information works against conceptual, temporal, and spatial parochialism and can protect people against the fallacy of misplaced certainty. Take, for instance, the lads and their naturalistic conception of the social world, accepted with stoic pride. In 1844, Marx (1963) quoted the following figures on the composition of the English labor force: "In the English cotton spinning mills only 158,818 men are employed as against 196,818 women. For every 100 male workers in the Lancashire cotton mills there are 103 women workers. . . . In the English flax factories in Leeds there were 147 women for every 100 male workers" (p. 80).

These data should shake one's assumption of male superiority for factory work; yet for the lads, these figures might shake a self-definition that seems to entrap them. If anything, working conditions at the height of early industrial capitalism were harder than today. However, these data do not settle the question, for we do not know that women's work equaled men's in terms of physical requirements, how mortality rates compared, what contribution to female mortality rates was made by childbearing, and so on. In short, the data help raise further questions. Nisbett and Ross (1980) warn laypersons as well as scientists against the fallacy of misplaced certainty.

> An important step in reducing people's overconfidence would be taken by leading them to recognize that their interpretations of events, rather than being simple read-outs of data, are inferences that make heavy use of theory. Once one recognizes that the same data would look quite different, and could easily support different beliefs, if those data were viewed from the vantage point of alternative theories, the groundwork for a humbler epistemic stance has been laid. (p. 293)

Epistemic humility makes room for surprise (Scheffler, 1977a). Facts as we know them can appear in a new light. Persuasions erode as new connections are made. Ways of knowing and being do change. Resulting shifts and uncertainties are unsettling. But they are less confining than a life in which everything is what it is and nothing else. Still, change means losing as well as gaining things. In an educational memoir that is poetic and poised, Richard Rodriguez (1982) sums up his coming of age: "It is education that has altered my life. Carried me far. . . . To admit the change in my life I must speak of years as a student, of losses, of gains. . . . I remember what was so grievously lost to define what was necessarily gained" (pp. 5–6).

Freedom and Generosity

Art and fiction do not derive the possible from the real; in objects of shared insight and pleasure, they affirm wonder. Appreciated in a spirit that accepts artistic conventions—neither taken for reality nor dismissed for lack of fit with the facts—fiction allows us, in Frye's (1976) words, to "send out imaginative roots into that mysterious world between the 'is' and the 'is not' which is where . . . ultimate freedom lies" (p. 166).

Literature provides an opening to the life of the mind, with its countless, but not arbitrary, renderings of experience. There is no end to the imagination from which the written word springs and no limit to the thoughts and feelings with which the reader can answer. Intended or not, meanings overflow. As a work of art, a book is a path of transcendence.

> If the painter presents us with a field or a vase of flowers, his paintings are windows that open onto the whole world. We follow the red path which is buried among the wheat much farther than Van Gogh has painted it, among other wheat fields, under other clouds, to the river which empties into the sea, . . . to the other end of the world. (Sartre, 1948/1988, p. 63)

In attending and responding to art, one allows oneself to be moved by the free creation of another self.

Freedom on either side is not unruliness, however. "In creating his forms the artist is operating inside a continuing activity or enterprise, and this enterprise has its own repertoire, imposes its own stringencies, offers its own opportunities, and *thereby* [italics added] provides occasions, inconceivable outside it, for invention and audacity" (Wollheim, 1968, p. 108). Moreover, both the decision to write and one's actual writing presuppose that an author "withdraws somewhat from his feelings, in short, that he has transformed his emotions into free emotions *as I do mine while reading him* [italics added], that is, that he is in an attitude of generosity" (Sartre, 1948/1988, p. 61).

The generosity of writer and reader is a complex liberality of spirit— responsiveness joined to detachment. Involving some renunciation, this generosity is an ascesis in the service of generation, for it liberates capacities for growth and understanding. Energies that may drive artist and audience away from reality are harnessed in finding a path back; this recovery is also a path of transcendence (see Wollheim, 1968). Anton Chekhov put a sense of personal freedom above an author's talents, spontaneity, or an abundance of materials; as he wrote to a friend in 1889:

> Try and write a story about a young man—the son of a serf, a former grocer, choirboy, schoolboy and university student, raised on respect for rank, kissing the priests' hands, worshiping the ideas of others, and giving thanks for every piece of bread, receiving frequent whippings, making the rounds as a tutor without galoshes, brawling, torturing animals, . . . needlessly hypocritical before God and man merely to acknowledge his own insignificance— write about how this young man squeezes the slave out of himself drop by drop and how, on waking up one fine morning, he finds that the blood coursing through his veins is no longer the blood of a slave, but that of a real human being. (Karlinsky, 1973, p. 85)

This is Chekhov's own story. The detachment and compassion of his writings lend support to Sartre's belief that literature evokes and displays freedom and generosity; and it lends life to Hegel's (1821/1952) statement of the ends of education: "The end of reason . . . is to banish natural simplicity, whether the passivity which is the absence of the self, or the crude type of knowing and willing, i.e. immediacy and singularity, in which mind is absorbed. . . . The final purpose of education, therefore, is liberation" (p. 125).

Reality: Neither Empirical nor Subjective

Objective knowledge, art, and literature are contained together in what philosophers of science as well as literary critics have termed the *third world*. This realm of objects of thought is equally removed from the physical world and the world of subjective experiences. It comprises theories, questions, the contents of books, libraries, and computer memories. Like creations of art, they are human products of objective standing. Ideas are autonomous and impersonal because they are distinct from the people who hold or debate them. And theories are, in the words of Polanyi (1958/1962), "a kind of map extended over space and time" (p. 4), in much the same way that "even a geographical map fully embodies in itself a set of strict rules for finding one's way through a region of otherwise uncharted experience" (p. 4).

Objective does not mean absolute. Scientific theories and artistic creations invite debate and criticism (Leavis, 1962; Popper, 1972). They draw on analytic, descriptive, and appraising uses of language. Language has evolved as a social creation that contains all manner of assumptions about the world. Since these assumptions are easily mistaken for in-the-grain-of-nature realities, crucial questions are, "To what extent is this socially constructed world the only world available to us? To what extent are we locked into it and to what extent are we free to go beyond it or contrary to it? To what degree does formal education make us more of a prisoner of that social world or on the other hand provide us with the means to achieve some measure of freedom to transcend it?" (Soltis, 1981, p. 100).

The measure of education is the degree to which it allows all people access to the objective contents and revelations of thought, to artistic creations, theoretical systems, and ideas with intimations of the unknown. By the biological and structural limitations of firsthand experience, everyone is deprived of knowledge and understandings commonplace to other groups and other times. Education that affirms the absolutism of common sense and of subjective, untutored perceptions is a contradiction in terms. The analogical fusion of education and experience and its enactment in schools enshrine this contradiction. By definition, firsthand experience cannot overcome the paradox of finitude.

CHAPTER 2

Breaking with Everyday Experience For Guided Adventures in Learning

Robert E. Floden and Margret Buchmann

During this century, U.S. schools have increasingly come to be seen in a continuum of experience that spans family, community, and the world of work (see, e.g., Powell, Farrar, & Cohen, 1985). Secondary school teachers are urged to make courses relevant to their students' lives and expected careers. Elementary school teachers are advised to stress the utility of mathematics and spelling. Many educators assume that without such links students will not be motivated and will have difficulty learning.

Emphasizing continuity with everyday life, however, can confuse regard for students and their interests with accepting all personal beliefs and overly stressing the practical relevance of school learning. Emphasizing this continuity also conflicts with two central goals of schools: promoting equality of opportunity and disciplinary learning. For unless students can *break* with their everyday experience in thought, they cannot see the extraordinary range of options for living and thinking; and unless students can give up many commonsense beliefs, they may find it impossible to learn disciplinary concepts that describe the world in diverse, surprising ways.

Everyone lives in a particular, restricted time and place, "but school and university are places apart where a declared learner is emancipated from the limitations of his local circumstances and from the wants he may happen to have acquired, and is moved by intimations of what he has never yet dreamed" (Oakeshott, 1975/1989, p. 24). By emphasizing continuity with everyday life, educators destroy some of the strengths of schooling. If family, job, church, or other social institutions were to take responsibility for developing children's power to break with everyday experience in an environment sheltered for purposes of learning, the school's role would be less important. Currently, though, no other institution takes that responsibility, and schools seem to lose sight of that role. Hence, many students do not learn to see the limits and idiosyncrasies of the given.

We aim to recover the meaning of school as a place set apart, where truth and the social order do not coincide. To this purpose, we examine breaks with experience as adventures in learning, show why they are required for equality and disciplinary knowledge, and discuss how educators can foster such breaks. We consider objections to our argument that can be derived from the call for meaningfulness in instruction, research on cognition, and aspects of Dewey's philosophy of education. Central to our argument is the contention that, in the words of John Dewey (1916/1966), it is "the office of the school environment . . . to see to it that each individual gets an opportunity to escape from the limitations of the social group in which he was born, and to come into living contact with a broader environment" (p. 20).

WHY BREAKS WITH EVERYDAY EXPERIENCE ARE NECESSARY FOR EVERYONE

Everyday life is not set up for learning that transcends its own boundaries and suspends its immediate purposes. It is rich in experiences that are vivid and compelling, while appearing self-evident in their meaning. All of these attributes are two-edged swords. While giving contextual learning power, they also restrict people's scope of vision, exaggerate the reliability and importance of close-to-home experience, and make it difficult to grasp concepts from the disciplines of knowledge.

When someone is in what phenomenologists describe as the natural attitude, the world feels centered in time and space around oneself, and objects are important mostly for achieving personal ends. The structure and reality of this egocentric world are taken for granted and ordinarily not made the object of reflection. Immersion in the natural attitude supports the false belief that the actual and the possible are identical and that local perspectives are unassailable. Just as it seems that one's individual perspective gets at the nature of things, so it appears that one's social or ethnic group has the proper views. These sociocentric and ethnocentric natural attitudes are even more powerful.

Sociocentrism can affect scientists just as it affects garment workers; ethnocentrism can affect whites as much as Hispanics. No individual or group is immune to the deceptions of the natural attitude. People go about their lives assuming that *their* group's patterns of acting and thinking are not open to question; these patterns are so familiar that they become invisible. When such patterns are not seen, alternatives are not envisioned either. Even if alternatives could be considered, the natural attitude gives undue weight to the familiar, which is both vivid and readily available in memory (see Nisbett & Ross, 1980)

Limitations and distortions make it important to break with the natural attitude and to achieve greater distance from egocentric and sociocentric patterns of acting and thinking. Educational philosophers characterize this change of perspective as a move toward objectivity (see Green, 1971; Peters, 1966). Greater objectivity means moving away from the point of view of a particular self or social group, living in some definite time and place. The crux is that objectivity means seeing the world not from within but, as it were, from without. Oneself or one's group is not seen as the center of things, but as part of a larger, variegated picture.

Objectivity also allows seeing circumstances and phenomena from more than one perspective, varying in distance to the contingent self. Another part of objectivity's appeal stems from the sense that breaking with the natural attitude implies responding to the ideal of truth: "We flee the subjective under the pressure of an assumption that everything must be something not to any point of view, but in itself. To grasp this by detaching more and more from our own point of view is the unreachable ideal at which the pursuit of objectivity aims" (Nagel, 1979, p. 208). Moving toward objectivity requires being able both to recognize other perspectives and to select those perspectives that are most appropriate for a matter at hand.

The detachment presupposed by objectivity is not indifference, but rather the sense that many modes of thinking and acting familiar to oneself seem strange to other people and that some of one's ideas and actions may have to be changed for good reasons. However, we usually are not ready to abandon the natural attitude "without having experienced a specific *shock* which compels us to break through the limits of this 'finite' province of meaning and to shift the accent of reality to another one" (Schutz, 1945/1962, p. 231). This shift may happen in dreaming, watching a theater production, switching from one language to another, or having an adventure.

The image of an adventure provides a metaphor for educative breaks with experience. An adventure interrupts the integrated consistency and predictable flow of life and thought. An adventure may be educative if it also centrally connects with a person's sense of self, capacities, and developing understandings. As Georg Simmel (1911/1959) puts it,

> An adventure . . . occurs outside the usual continuity of this life. Nevertheless, it is distinct from all that is accidental and alien, merely touching life's

outer shell. While it falls outside the context of life, it falls, with this same movement, as it were, back into that context again … ; it is a foreign body in our existence which is yet somehow connected with the center. (p. 243).

Such adventures, like educative breaks with everyday experience, are linked to the springs of human learning.

Breaks with everyday experience are more likely to be educative if they occur in a setting created to make the most of deviations from the usual or seemingly fated course. Ordinary life, however, does not screen breaks for worthwhile directions and effects, warding off those that are untimely or damaging. In a sense, every self-chosen action means that "a human being lets go a mooring and puts out to sea on a … largely unforeseen course" (Oakeshott, 1975/1989, p. 23). Schools can turn some vicissitudes of existence and ordeals of consciousness into guided adventures in learning. The separateness of school can shelter youngsters from the enveloping nature of the taken-for-granted and the press of immediacy, so that they can confront the world they inhabit through conscious knowing and valuing.

Everyday Experience Reinforces Inequality

More often than not, life teaches people that they have to fit themselves into the scheme of things. As part of their socialization, children learn what to expect from life. They learn how they are expected to act and how other people will act toward them. They adopt notions of what is true and right, often without much capacity for judgment and reflection. Such expectations stretch into the future of jobs, families, and community roles—and they are not the same for all children.

Some youngsters see themselves progressing through high school, university, and professional school, imagining vacations in the Caribbean and a condominium in the mountains; others plan to escape from school at the earliest opportunity, to help out at home or save their overtime pay for a new car. Some envision campaign contributions to politicians who will protect their interests; others expect to give their votes to whichever party will keep their streets in good repair; and some see no point in voting.

To have more equal opportunities, children must imagine themselves in futures not determined by their immediate environments and local beliefs. No matter how much a school is able to raise a student's achievement test scores, the increase does little to equalize opportunities unless students can see and act on the possibilities created. Understanding what happens to oneself and envisioning what could require more objective perspectives and lively imagination.

Everyday Concepts Frustrate Disciplinary Learning

The academic disciplines provide perspectives that draw on accumulated, systematically tested, and creatively imagined human experiences. They are also guides in judgment, preventing people from falling into the relativistic trap of thinking that all perspectives have equal merit. Arguments for disciplinary understandings as a central educational goal resemble our general case for breaks with everyday experience. As with equal opportunity, acquiring such distancing and liberating understandings is frustrated by relying on everyday experience.

Students enter school with concepts and methods for understanding and acting on the world around them. They have ideas about physical principles and about people. But many of these naive conceptions conflict with disciplinary understandings. Moreover, some disciplinary concepts do not refer to everyday experience at all. When children encounter science in school, this subject conveys fascinatingly new and *different* information about the world: It is the sun, and not the earth, that stands still; hammers dissolve into electrons and protons; water is actually a combination of gases; and so on. There are also concepts with no counterparts in the everyday world, such as latent heat.

Because of the human tendency to try to incorporate new experience into old frameworks (see Mayer, 1979), students often assimilate school learning into their naive conceptions, even when those conceptions are not appropriate (Clement, 1982; Nussbaum & Novak, 1976). Thus, many students may continue to believe that the earth is flat or that continual force is needed to maintain constant velocity. This tendency is so strong that everyday conceptions persist, even in the face of instruction that contradicts them (Eaton, Anderson, & Smith, 1984). In part, their robustness may be due to the fact that everyday conceptions have served students well outside school (Viennot, 1979).

To learn the disciplines, students need instruction that helps them to see the limits and distortions in their everyday conceptions, not instruction that encourages them to think that disciplinary concepts are mere variants of their everyday beliefs (Anderson & Roth, 1989). People are beginning to understand the conditions under which students will give up everyday beliefs and replace them with disciplinary concepts. One prominent model of conceptual change learning suggests that a sense of conflict and dissatisfaction with old conceptions is an important prerequisite (Posner, Strike, Hewson, & Gertzog, 1982).

EFFECTING BREAKS WITH EVERYDAY EXPERIENCE

If schools are to develop students' capacities to break with everyday experience for purposes of learning, changes in the content and methods of instruction are needed. The work of Vygotsky (1934/1962, 1930–1966/1978) lends support to instructional approaches that strive for greater separation from—not more continuity with—students' everyday experiences. Vygotsky concludes from his studies of school learning that children do not acquire systematic understanding of academic subjects by drawing on the concepts they bring with them. Children are not consciously aware of these concepts and thus cannot work with them abstractly. For example, concepts of family relationships (e.g., brother, sister, mother) can be applied to concrete situations, but not to answering abstract questions of kinship (e.g., the identity of a brother's father's sister). Children eventually become conscious of these logical relations, but may be confused because everyday concepts are "saturated with experience" (Vygotsky, 1934/1962, p. 108). By contrast, abstract concepts (e.g., the concept of exploitation) are learned consciously; their lack of concrete reference allows children to keep conceptual relations straight.

Teachers should be wary of introducing students to new ideas by pointing out their relations to everyday concepts and ways of thinking. Instead, teaching should often begin with material divorced from everyday life. Links to experience can eventually be made, but within the abstract conceptual system. Vygotsky (1934/1962) contends that this instructional approach—favoring awareness of one's own thinking—also favors reflection.

> School instruction induces the generalizing kind of perception and thus plays a decisive role in making the child conscious of his own mental processes. Scientific concepts, with their hierarchical system of interrelationships, seem to be the medium within which awareness and mastery first develop, to be transferred later to other concepts and other areas of thought. Reflective consciousness comes to the child through the portals of scientific concepts. (p. 92)

Acquiring the ability for systematic reflection is a process of several steps; in it an adult takes responsibility for directing the student's learning. First the child is led through the steps of some task, without being able to do the task alone or, presumably, understanding why the individual steps are being taken. As the child learns to repeat these steps habitually, she learns to do the task independently. In a study of mothers teaching their preschool children, Wertsch (1979) examines how children make the transition from adult-directed performance to independent appropriate action. Wertsch suggests that, because children are motivated to make sense of what they do, being guided to perform a strange task creates the incentive for moving toward new capacities and understandings. School instruction could likewise lure students into unfamiliar subject matter.

Adventures in learning can occur with guidance from a teacher, but without initial clarity about their purpose and promise. This argument applies to learning in the liberal arts as well as to learning scientific or moral concepts. Universities may attract students on the supposition of career benefits, but actually deliver human goods—including the capacity to stand back from the particulars of everyday experience—that students will appreciate only after they have made them their own (Peters, 1966, chap. V). Learning what good literature is and what it can give (e.g., in offering multiple and deepening readings of life and people) may depend on a leap into reading good literature. Similarly, students must acquire habits of moral thought and action before they can become autonomous moral agents.

To conclude, in many areas of school instruction, students can transcend given ways of thinking and acting by first acquiring habits whose components they can imitate and practice but whose purposes they initially do not understand. Such transcendence requires schooling that breaks with the natural attitude and everyday understandings. While this separation may forfeit immediate relevance, there are distinctive educational gains. However, the popularity of continuity with everyday experience as a principle of curriculum and instruction derives, in part, from cultural and commonsense beliefs that identify the value of education with its practical usefulness. This view of what makes education valuable in part underlies the call for "meaningfulness" in school instruction.

SHOULD NOT SCHOOLING BE MEANINGFUL?

A seemingly straightforward objection to having schools provide breaks with everyday experience is that such breaks will make schooling less meaningful. Instructional content that is not meaningful, people argue, will be difficult for students to understand and remember; they will also not be motivated to learn it. This objection to our case for educative breaks for purposes of learning rests on the ambiguity of the term *meaningful*, which has at least three senses. To call something meaningful can signify that it is related to prior knowledge, practically relevant, or closely tied to everyday life.

In its first sense, meaningfulness is important for learning; but this sense does not support an objection to breaks with everyday experience, for educative breaks do not require discontinuity with *all* knowledge. Breaks with everyday experience do lead to loss of meaningfulness in the second and third senses, but the educational value of practical relevance and continuity with everyday life is, as we argue throughout this chapter, debatable. Moreover, getting access to new concepts and meanings is not inconsistent with opening up new systems of practical relevancies, as well as creating *new* patterns of thought and action that grow to be "close to home" (i.e., habits of reflection). The force of the meaningfulness objection seems based on the fallacy of equivocation: using the first sense to argue that meaningfulness is crucial, then drawing on the commonsense appeal of the other senses to suggest that breaks with *everyday* knowledge are not defensible.

Relationships to Prior Knowledge

Meaningful instruction in the first sense—as instruction relating to prior knowledge—is endorsed by common sense and psychology (see, e.g., Ausubel, 1968; Bruner, 1972; Resnick, 1987). Smith (1975), for example, writes in a cognitive psychology textbook for teachers that a central requirement for learning is that "there must be a point of contact between what the student is expected to know and what he knows already" (p. 9). It is trivially true that things to be learned must in *some* way be related to *some* prior knowledge. Research supporting this sense of meaningfulness relies on interpretations of "related to" that encompass a wide variety of relationships, from simple associations to conceptual links. Thus people's capacity to memorize a list of objects may be increased by imagining a familiar walk and associating each item on the list with a place passed during this mental journey.

The argument for guided adventures in learning would be damaged if educative breaks with experience were meaningless in this first sense. But the breaks we advocate are with *everyday* knowledge, not with all knowledge. As psychological studies of meaningfulness show, one can meet the general requirement for relationships to prior knowledge by interpreting "relationships" and "prior knowledge" in diverse ways. Having lessons relate to disciplinary knowledge or conceptual systems acquired in earlier instruction fits this sense of meaningfulness.

The criterion of relation to prior knowledge is not an all-or-nothing affair. Although psychologists occasionally write as if meaningfulness (in this sense) were dichotomous, "there are differing degrees of meaningfulness, depending on the extent to which the material to be learned can be related to what the learner knows already" (Smith, 1975, p. 160). In working with methods and content different from everyday experience, students may begin with only a faint idea of what it all means, but that beckoning glimmer of understanding could suffice to make the instruction meaningful. A gradual deepening and spreading of significant relationships is consistent with the picture of educative breaks described earlier.

Practical Relevance

In its sense of practical relevance, meaningfulness is commonly considered a prime source of motivation for learning. This sense merges making instruction meaningful into demonstrating to students that instructional content can be put to use outside of school, either now or in the future. Meaningfulness in this second sense depends on an instrumental view of school knowledge and an understanding of value in terms of utility. Since practical relevance implies integrated relations with everyday activities, this interpretation of meaningfulness is inconsistent with the educative breaks we advocate. If practical relevance were decisive for valuable and successful instruction, it would support a serious objection to making schools break with everyday experience. Developing motivation to learn, however, does not depend on showing the practical relevance of schoolwork and may, in fact, be hindered by such an emphasis.

In his analysis of the literature on instructional motivation, Brophy (1983a) emphasizes the difference between two types of motivation. With exogenous motivation, students complete tasks for reasons not linked to what they learn from engaging in the task; with endogenous motivation, students are motivated by the tasks themselves and seek to learn what they can from engaging in those tasks. Linking school tasks to activities outside school tends to develop exogenous motivation at the expense of endogenous motivation. Telling students about the inherent value of the tasks tends to develop motivation to learn. Hence the fact that breaks with everyday experience fail to provide meaningfulness in the second sense supports, rather than undercuts, the argument for breaks with everyday experience for purposes of learning.

In its third sense of close ties to everyday life, meaningfulness is a characteristic of instruction that builds on familiar patterns of thought and action. Actually, this is a specialized version of the first sense of meaningfulness. Breaks with everyday experience, by definition, run counter to this requirement. Yet such meaningfulness has considerable commonsense appeal and seems to be supported by cross-cultural cognitive studies and research on everyday cognition.

TEXTS VERSUS LOCAL KNOWLEDGE

Research on everyday cognition in Western and other cultures describes and appraises everyday modes of thought in ways that contest the value of breaking with them (see, e.g., Rogoff & Lave, 1984). Scribner and Cole (1973), as an important example, argue for "bridg[ing] the gulf between school and practical life" (p. 558) in both the methods and content of instruction. What is needed, they write, is "to move everyday life into the school so that its subject matter and activities deal with some of the same aspects of social and physical reality that the pupils confront outside of school. . . . Education must be stripped from the schoolroom and made instrumental in traditional settings" (p. 558).

Other cognitive anthropologists study everyday thinking in situations like grocery shopping (Lave, Murtaugh, & de la Rocha, 1984), navigating (Gladwin, 1970), or selling fish (Hallpike, 1979). Their work draws attention to the many unschooled abilities people have and to their general capacity for making sense of things. Like the third sense of meaningfulness, this research tradition emphasizes the importance of building on everyday modes of knowing in school learning. Like supporters of the second sense of meaningfulness, these scholars suggest that practical relevance is necessary to make learning worthwhile and motivating. Surprisingly, this research grows out of a line of work that tends to support our argument for breaks with everyday experience.

Cross-cultural studies of thinking often focus on whether learning a written language is a central feature in learning to think abstractly (see, e.g., Goody & Watt, 1963/1968; Scribner & Cole, 1981). This research tradition spells out the advantages of breaks with everyday experience. Instruction based on text can put people into contact with the unfamiliar, with what is different and distant in time, place, and culture; the oral mode tends to preserve continuity with local experience, with what can be seen, touched, or heard. Bruner and Olson (1977–78) link this distinction between oral and text-based instruction to differences between everyday learning and the text-based mode of learning that characterizes schooling. They argue that skills for working with written material have three interrelated advantages.

First, these skills enable students to see their current world as just one of a number of possibilities. Second, text-based instruction allows for more flexible and general application of what is learned. When learning is closely tied to the local context, it is more difficult to adapt to changing circumstances or to strike out in new directions. Third, the skills learned through text-based instruction increase students' tendency to be analytic. Oral lore requires memorization and is structured for this purpose; oral arguments are hard to pin down and often appeal to authority and the emotions. Through written argument, analysis, and critique, people can comprehend and judge reality and the claims of others.

However, writing can be closely tied to everyday life, and oral instruction can provide the basis for reflection or for thinking about an unknown audience. The important distinction may be whether learners assume the role of spectator or participant (see Britton, 1982), rather than whether the instructional mode is written or oral; in other words, it may be taking a more or less objective stance that makes the difference. Also, scholars interested in the "great divide" between oral and written literacy have recently concluded that it is not writing *per se* that benefits students, but some of the practices associated with *formal* schooling.

In their seminal study of the effects of written literacy, Scribner and Cole (1981) compared illiterate, literate-but-unschooled, and literate-and-schooled groups within the Vai people of Liberia to determine whether literacy accounted for, among other things, people's tendency to think analytically. They found that such thinking was barely more prevalent in the literate-but-unschooled group than in the illiterate group they studied. Those in the schooled group, however, were significantly more analytic than those in the other two groups. Scribner and Cole attribute these effects to school instruction that is based (at least in part) on requiring students to describe their mental processes and give reasons for what they say. Teachers ask questions such as, "What made you give that answer? How do you know? Go to the board and explain what you did" (Scribner & Cole, 1981, p. 255). These school practices are consistent with our emphasis on objectivity and educational content considered in its own right, rather than in terms of continuity or practical relevance.

For what reasons, then, are these researchers so intent on tying schooling to everyday life? Why does Olson (1977), for example, describe schools as "bookish, detached from reality, devoid of personal meaning, and useless practically" (p. 69) and conclude his comparison of oral and written modes of instruction with an impassioned plea to reduce schools' reliance on text? Or why do Scribner and Cole (1973, p. 558), after enumerating the benefits of instruction removed from local contexts, argue that schools should strengthen their ties to people's everyday experience?

These scholars may be ambivalent because of the costs entailed in breaking with everyday experience, even for purposes of learning. These costs have been recognized since Plato, who was torn between recognizing the analytic value of written argument and feeling nostalgic about the sense of continuity inherent in oral tradition (Goody & Watt, 1963/1968). Some intellectuals, such as Rousseau and his followers, continue to yearn for "the peasant's simple but cohesive view of life, the timelessness of his living in the present, the unanalytic spontaneity that comes with an attitude to the world that is one of absorbed and uncritical participation" (Goody & Watt, 1963/1968, p. 61).

If these primeval attitudes are goods, breaking with them brings losses that will be accelerated by literacy and education. The question is, however, to what extent an orientation toward the present and an absence of dispositions for analysis *are* goods and—if they are—to what extent these goods may conflict with other valuable dispositions, such as exercising prudent foresight and distancing reflection. Usually, people praising the simplicity of others—children, "natives," working-class people—are not themselves spontaneous and uncritical, nor members of such groups, sharing their typical experiences. People who luxuriate in the communal, richly passionate lives of others are themselves practitioners of the *reflective* life, aware of its value. The praise of the unlettered by the highly educated is, as Richard Rodriguez (1982) learned at college, a primary theme of elitist nostalgic literature.

Ambivalent scholars may also believe that breaks with everyday experience will contribute to existing social and educational inequalities. Where breaks are found, they are typically breaks for working-class and minority children that are implemented in ways that seem to exclude them from the benefits of instruction (Labov, 1982; Philips, 1983). John Dewey's complex position on continuity in education seems similarly shaped by worries about what schools will actually do to provide breaks.

DEWEY'S AMBIVALENCE ABOUT CONTINUITY

Like the cognitive researchers, Dewey recognized the value of breaks with everyday experience, yet sometimes seemed ambivalent. He, too, may have emphasized continuity with everyday experience in part because he feared that schools would divorce instruction from experience without using breaks as an opportunity to expand students' horizons. Dewey was incensed by the ways many schools blinded students to new ideas, destroyed their desire to learn, and killed their interest in books. He was also disturbed by the apparently deteriorating significance of community in the United States.

For the most part, our argument is consistent with Dewey's positions. Apparent differences arise in the strongly worded essays Dewey wrote in opposition to the school practices of his day. Based on these statements, Dewey is often considered a champion of tight ties between home and school. However, he took a complex position on breaks with everyday experience. To understand why Dewey is considered an enemy of breaks, consider, for instance, what he writes in his early, emphatic, widely re-printed pamphlet, "My Pedagogic Creed": "The school life should grow gradually out of the home life; . . . it should take up and continue the activities with which the child is already familiar in the home" (Dewey, 1897/1959, p. 23). Forty years later, in *Experience and Education*, Dewey (1938) avers that, for an educator, "connection with life-experiences" is a "fundamental principle" (p. 95) and "connectedness in growth must be his constant watchword" (p. 90). Spanning the period of most of Dewey's educational writings, these quotations suggest a fervent commitment to connections with everyday experience in education.

Yet Dewey's view of schooling also centrally features the advantages we have attributed to the power to make breaks. Educative schooling "opens a way to a kind of experience which would not be accessible to the young, if they were left to pick up their training in informal associa-tion with others, since books and the symbols of knowledge are mas-tered" (Dewey, 1916/1966, p. 8). Dewey (1902/1959) also links learning academic subjects to acquiring a sense of intellectual method and objec-tivity, or the

> ability to view facts impartially and objectively; that is, without reference to their place and meaning in one's own experience. It [i.e., a sense of intellec-tual method and objectivity] means capacity to analyze and to synthesize. It means highly matured intellectual habits. (p. 94)

Dewey also saw education as an adventure; experiences are not educative if they give students only "greater skill and ease in dealing with things with which they are already familiar" (Dewey, 1938, p. 90).

Moreover, Dewey believed that schooling ought not to be closely tied to definite future occupations, and he attacked plans for vocational edu-cation aimed to fit workers into existing jobs; rather, such education should make workers the "masters of their own industrial fate" (1915, p. 42). Dewey wanted to integrate occupational concerns into the education of *all* students, not to substitute occupational skills for disciplinary knowledge by occupational skills for some groups.

Both Dewey's emphasis on reflection and his conception of education as extending the limits of experience resonate with our call for breaks. We disagree, however, with Dewey's belief that education requires begin-ning with everyday experience. Although Dewey insists that instruction must use knowledge of the local world as "an intellectual starting point for moving out into the unknown, not [as] an end in itself" (1916/1966, p. 212), he also maintains that instruction must begin close to home and maintain continuity with everyday experience as other realms are explored. But, as Vygotsky argues, sticking to everyday experience can make it more difficult for students to learn new concepts or become reflective.

By pointing to the problems schools have created when they provided instruction divorced from everyday experiences, Dewey articulates a plea for continuity that has emotional power and wide appeal. Yet any educational reform may be carried out poorly or in self-defeating ways. This is a reason to urge care in making changes, not a reason to abandon the implications of one's analysis or worthwhile aims of learning distinctive to schooling.

EDUCATIVE BREAKS ARE NEEDED FOR ALL CHILDREN

In stressing the drawbacks of schooling tied to close-to-home experience, there is a danger that our argument could work to the disadvantage of working-class or minority students who currently achieve less, on the average, in U.S. schools. If providing breaks makes school more difficult for students already at a disadvantage, it might create yet another situation in which middle-class students reap the greatest benefits of schooling. One explanation of this situation is that typical schooling is closer to the everyday experiences of middle-class students than those of other children (see Heath, 1982). Some argue therefore that, to eliminate the advantages for middle-class children, school should be made equally familiar to all children. In other words, they advocate relying more on instructional content and methods that are tied to the home experiences of children from working-class or minority groups (see, e.g., Au & Jordan, 1981).

Our argument, however, questions the educational value of everyday experience for *all* students. It is not directed just toward those groups whose home experience is already largely discontinuous with what is expected in schools. Furthermore, while middle-class homes may provide children with concepts and ways of talking that help them succeed in school, that is by no means the same thing as possessing the ability to break with the natural attitude in mind-opening ways. We contend that all students should have adventures in learning, not that all students should come to share the everyday experiences of one segment of the population.

We have belabored the drawbacks of everyday experience, in part because its constraints and distortions are not sufficiently understood, especially among U.S. educators. Yet for detachment, as for most things, virtue lies in moderation and appropriateness; objective pictures of the world are only partial, appropriate for some, but not all, purposes. Transcending personal and group experiences leaves behind ways of knowing and being that have intrinsic worth. Schools should therefore help students to move toward objectivity, but without denying that everyday experiences have their place and meaning.

Withdrawal from connection with surrounding things has to be balanced with engagement and relatedness. Since everyday experience tends to support subjective and local perspectives, it is itself unlikely to provide a balance. Supporting students in the continuing effort to find that balance presupposes their ability to break with everyday experience. Yet this ability does not imply a permanent divorce from the everyday world, nor a loss of all personal or local meaning. As Richard Rodriguez (1982) says in his poised and lucid educational autobiography, although learning to separate from home experience is painful, it can also provide the distance needed to understand—and perhaps ultimately return to embrace—that experience: "If, because of my schooling, I had grown culturally separated from my parents, my education finally had given me ways of speaking and caring about that fact" (p. 72).

Weighing Gains and Losses

Every gain is a loss of some kind. Breaks with everyday experience are necessary for helping all children to think and act with a sense of methods and ideas that reach beyond the immediately given. The concept of adventure indicates that everyday life occasionally includes such breaks for people. Public schooling is, however, the primary North American institution in which attention can be paid to equality of opportunity in ensuring educative breaks with experience, in which the frequency and nature of these breaks can be controlled in the interests of learning, and in which students can be sheltered from the press of everyday life to bring that learning to fruition. Although discontinuity is not in itself an educational goal or guarantee of worthwhile learning, schools are unlikely to further equal opportunity and disciplinary understanding if their curricula remain within a continuum of experiences spanning home and work.

While the ability to make breaks with everyday experience is valuable for all, such breaks come at a cost. Equalizing opportunities often disconnects individuals from their backgrounds. Objectivity brings progressively greater distance from things intimately known and cherished. In general, education means losing the sense that life is seamless and whole and the comforting—but false—assumption that things, once learned, are safe from change and challenge. The attractions of close ties to everyday experience and local traditions must be weighed against the benefits of breaking away from such experience for purposes of equality of opportunity and learning. Our conclusions bring to mind the words of Israel Scheffler (1985):

> The capability to learn is the capability to alter what one is and has been; it places the present at risk. Made quite general, such capability is consonant with the vision of a democratic society, in which learning is not restricted but opened wide, in which the risks of learning are more than justified by the human quality of the community sustaining them. (p. 122)

CHAPTER 3

Making New or Making Do: An Inconclusive Argument About Teaching

Margret Buchmann

Rather than feeling themselves absurdly placed among things, people live, above all, in the realm of the given, where they think like others around them and take much of their world for granted. What is learned by participation and the chances of group membership—common sense, tradition, tacit knowledge—directs and shapes what people see, want, know, and remember. As a champion of change, John Dewey (1916/1966) confronted these facts with a sober appreciation that few educational reformers have equaled:

> Even in present-day societies, [direct participation] furnishes the basic nurture of even the most insistently schooled youth. In accord with the interests and occupations of the group, certain things become objects of high esteem; others of aversion. . . . The way our group or class does things tends to determine the proper objects of attention, and thus to prescribe the directions and limits of observation and memory. (p. 17)

If the given is well entrenched, it is also embattled ground. For what surrounds one often seems mean—tolerable at best, but lacking in elevation and dignity, generosity and justice.

This paper explores the meaning of these generalizations about ordinary thinking, socializing experiences, conservative powers, and discontents for teaching and teacher education by considering a plea for transformation in relation to a halfhearted case for what people learn about *teaching* through schooling and life. I argue that there is an inherent tension, perhaps a dilemma, in what to make of and how to deal with the relationships between transformative education and the education for

50

teaching incidental to life and practice. In working out this point, together with its implications for the teaching profession and its knowledge, I examine two arguments in support of the stance that, to alleviate abiding discontents, the education of teachers must involve breaks with ordinary ways of thinking and acting.

The first argument in support of breach-making approaches to teacher education might be called the dead-hand-of-the-past argument. People's apprenticeship of observation (Lortie, 1975, chap. 3) in schools and the socializing effects of practical experience are strong conservative forces in teaching; together, they seem to account for most of teachers' working knowledge. This is the reason why many university educators want to challenge teachers' entering beliefs and arm teachers with ideas that will stand up against the norms of schools. The second or "professionalization" argument involves a bid for power and comparisons of teaching with other lines of work. In becoming a doctor or lawyer, learners go through deeply felt upheavals. Claiming expertise for teachers as they strive for teacher empowerment, many reformers contend that their socialization should likewise result in teachers' alienation from common-sense beliefs.

DOES EXPERIENCE INDUCE THE SLEEP OF REASON?

Probably a boy or girl of 12 years will not be able to say this clearly, but typical, conservative classroom practices such as lectures and whole-class recitations have the virtue of allowing for some content coverage, some participation, and some classroom control by structuring who gets to say or do something, when, and, by and large, what. The folkways of teaching (Buchmann, 1987)—the common patterns of teaching, learned and practiced in the half-conscious way in which people go about their everyday lives—hence meet some functional needs of schooling. And in the catalog of means to ends in teaching, which people absorb through schooling and other experiences, we have the makings of a modest science—a science that is imperfect, partial in outlook and technical in orientation (see Schwab, 1959/1978b).

Why Folkways of Teaching Are Well Entrenched

Exposed to the folkways of teaching, youngsters learn many things, incidentally acquiring some teaching knowledge as well. Thus, fond of it or not, we are all amateurs of teaching knowledge. The power of experiential learnings derives from both what people learn and how they learn it. In schools, much of what people learn fits with the views of common sense that fix attention on what seems palpably obvious. To be sure, people need to learn, for instance, their number facts. But it seems one can teach them as one has been taught, that is, mostly by telling—if necessary, repeated telling—which is supposed to make facts sink into the mind.

"Teaching as usual" is reinforced twice by experience: by the experience of success in learning (even if it is a partial, intermittent, and unevenly distributed kind of success—which is just what common sense would lead one to expect) and by the experience of participation, or the act and condition of taking part in activities with people. Doing things in concert with others leads to automatic readings of situations—inducing habitual meanings and actions—and is itself a powerful test. At school, at home, or at the workplace, it shows what does and does not work, often given ends that are limited and plain, such as getting done or getting it right. These ends are seldom examined because of being obliquely affirmed in institutional structures and patterns of social life, supported largely by common sense.

For teachers, who have to act, it stands to reason that they have to find quickly what works in the range of situations they are most likely to encounter, and learn to do these things, together with children, reliably and well. Having a repertoire of concrete patterns and vivid images of teaching and learning is a great help in that, as is working in ways that fit with the expectations of others. The placid assurance of common sense gives teachers a confidence that they need and that will reassure pupils besides. Are all these learnings like a dead weight that people must shake off to prosper as teachers? The answer is not clear-cut.

The Equivocal Benefits of Direct Experiences for Learning to Teach

For one thing, it would be good to remember that people always undervalue what they have never been without. Teacher educators are no exception. Could an aspiring lawyer picture a day between chambers and courts or imagine the wiles of witnesses and judges? Doctors rarely come to their training familiar with a wide variety of bedside manners and ways of dealing with patients' questions. Teacher educators, by contrast, can rely on their students' knowing quite a bit about teaching through observation and participation—with the strengths and defects of these ways of knowing.

The two faces of common sense. For another thing, acting and thinking within the system of common sense is not the same as being dead to reason. Patterns of action can be simple without being foolish. In addition to mastered patterns of action for familiar circumstances, the types of action consistent with the folkways include flexible ways of acting for variable situations that require some artfulness in modifying steps or sequences in patterns. Schwab (1959/1978b) places these types of actions in levels one and two of "pragmatic intellectual space" (see pp. 175–176), where there is an active intelligence though no knowledge in the scientific sense.

Common sense makes a case that is different at different places and times. Its inherent feeling of self-evidence, however, chokes off questions. Given change, error, and limited knowledge, these are high costs. Furthermore, preferences for the mundane bias people and limit their vision. For the case of morality, William James (1891/1969) points out, "The moment you get beyond the coarser and more commonplace moral maxims, the Decalogues and Poor Richard's Almanacs, you fall into schemes and positions which to the eye of common-sense are fantastic and overstrained" (p. 171). To the extent that being a good teacher requires loyalty to causes and ideals entwined with loyalty to other people, these limits are troublesome. Josiah Royce (1908/1969), greatly admired by James, makes clear why that is so:

> Loyalty . . . is an idealizing of human life, a communion with invisible aspects of our social existence. Too great literalness in the interpretation of human relations is, therefore, a foe to the development of loyalty. If my neighbor is to me merely a creature of a day, who walks and eats and talks and buys and sells, I shall never learn to be loyal to his cause and to mine. (p. 958)

Obfuscations of natural understandings. What further qualifies my grudging case for what people learn about teaching through direct experiences is that some school practices and their assumptions do not live up to common sense. Most people realize that children are quite taken with the extraordinary, far removed from the banalities of basal readers or insipid facts about postal carriers and "my town" that often count as social studies. Some of the vapidity of school knowledge can be traced to research on word frequencies and a confusion of the frequency with the *importance* of words in composing texts and learning to read. That is, just because a word appears often in spoken or written language (e.g., "the" or "does"), the word does not necessarily mean much to learners—or for the development of their capacities. Hence, an obfuscation of natural understandings can sometimes be traced to research and its mistaken authority in education, that is, the false belief that finding out some things about the world can tell people what they ought to do.

The example of social studies highlights another source. As Brophy (1990) argues, the stability of the usual concentric pattern of teaching in social studies—family, neighborhood, hometown, state, and so on—may be explained by the capacity of that pattern to adapt to all kinds of educational fashions with which teachers have to cope. This shows how functional adaptivity may override ordinary good sense in the life of institutions. It also shows that—while dominant modes of teaching have the advantage of being functional and while that is better than being non-functional—functionality is certainly not everything. Here, then, is a place for transformative education. In my particular examples, however, university instructors would find themselves sorting out the detritus of academic misunderstandings (e.g., about how to choose worthwhile educational content for school readers) and challenging current fads (many of which originate in the academe), thus returning to natural understandings where schooling and schools of education have departed from common sense.

The Twofold Authority of the Given Confronted with Ideas

Regardless of their merits and the directions in which they might tend, transformative ideas have to match the authority of the lessons that teachers absorb through experience. Authority means, first, impressiveness. What is impressive produces deep, lasting effects on the mind or feelings. Resting on features of firsthand experience such as closeness to self, vividness, and concrete familiarity, such authority may be disconnected from validity and value. But the authority of direct experiences of teaching and learning derives also from their practicality, or the objective chances as success embedded in them. Not unreasonably, people will be impressed by what they can see works in teaching: allowing some content to be put across to some pupils some of the time, while maintaining order and tractability in the group.

The authority of the folkways is empirical—that is, based on first-hand experience, not on theoretical reasoning. It derives from people's actual participation in them and the likelihood of getting results. Having a catalog of means to given ends is nothing to be despised. The folkways are an integral part of personal biography and collective tradition. For ordinary people and situations, acting on them accomplishes what is needed, avoiding fuss and risks. The folkways thus have the practicality of common sense: prudence and astuteness in sizing up persons and situations and in adapting means to given ends without much cogitation. This practical orientation implies a likelihood of success that makes people feel secure and capable.

The heart's response to ideal claims. In addition to their vital familiarity, folk-ways have thus proven themselves to be practical within a given system of thought and action. Where ideals do not fit that system, educators have to make strange, pale abstractions speak to future teachers, so that they can recognize the intellectual and moral force of ideals and respond wholeheartedly to the claims on their powers of imagination and action. This point is related to a standard problem in moral education, namely, that people must want to do the right thing because it is right and not for an extrinsic reason (e.g., someone told them to, they were forced or expected to do it).

There is a tricky point about learning here, too. Because of what they are, ideals (and any notions remote from what seems real to people) can-not rely on the authority of the given, experienced firsthand. Their impres-siveness must come from other sources, notably from a quality of sympa-thetic imagination that—nascent in the learner—engages a disposition to believe, perhaps to act. William James (1891/1969) puts this memorably.

> The only force of appeal to *us*, which . . . an abstract ideal order can wield, is found in the "everlasting ruby vaults" of *our own human hearts* [italics added], as they happen to beat responsive and not irresponsive to the claim. . . . A claim thus livingly acknowledged is acknowledged with a solid-ity and fullness which no thought of an "ideal" backing can render more complete; while if, on the other hand, the heart's response is withheld, the stubborn phenomenon is there of an impotence in the [ideal] claims. (p. 178)

Happen in two of its senses is a key word in this clear-sighted obser-vation. Transformative education must evoke answering vibrations in stu-dents' imagination. At the same time, the actual response (i.e., that which does, in fact, happen) depends on what each learner happens to come with (i.e., that which has fallen to his or her lot or come into people's way in the course of experience). Being responsive, in this sense, does not simply consist in learners' following teachers' suggestions or answering their questions. It is more like offering a rejoinder to a reply dependent on a previous question that the teacher can see intimated in what *students* feel, say, or do. And in all of this, some vital sparks must be flying.

To many, James's insight into the limits of cognitive and behavioral control (power of directing, checking, and regulating) in teaching or, looked at positively, into the need to trust in and depend on learners (and their hearts) makes not only teacher education intolerably chancy and hence provokes a tensing of instructional muscles rather than their atten-tive relaxation. A similar inversion of customary hierarchies or, at least, muting of one-sided powers can be found in how Wordsworth (1850/ 1904) reverses the places of the "living mind" and general truths in learn-

ing. As he considers how nature and education may have made him fit
for his work, the poet writes:

> ... I neither seem
> To lack that first great gift, the vital soul,
> Nor general Truths, which are themselves
>   a sort
> of Elements and Agents, Under-powers,
> Subordinate helpers of the living mind. (p. 126)

Overhauling Conceptions of Learning and Knowledge

The view that learning is not introduced or caused externally but
brought forth, assisted by kindly attention and judicious prodding, by
learners themselves is, of course, ancient. Joined to historical and socio-
political understandings of knowledge, one of its current variants is constructivism.

Yet teaching as usual brings with it tightly meshed, well-worn answers to questions such as "Who knows?", "What is knowledge?", "How
can knowledge be acquired and learning be demonstrated?" The teacher
knows (and what she or he doesn't know isn't knowledge); knowledge is
in the textbook, film, and computer (not in students' actions, heads, and
affecting experiences to begin with); students demonstrate learning by
dovetailing right answers into given schemes (fixed results—and not the
arts of learning and knowing—are educational outcomes). On these
views of knowledge and learning, there are few qualitative transformations of knowledge, or of learners, including *teachers* as learners. Nor can
we be sure that quantitative additions of knowledge will stick, that is, get
into students' minds and stay there.

Jackson (1986) sums up compacted assumptions about teaching and
learning implicit in teaching as usual, which he terms the *mimetic tradition*. The taken-for-granted grounds of school knowledge—considered
justified by their correspondence to personal understandings or to con-
textually embedded, codified knowledge, typically not of a scholarly
kind—fit with operating criteria for success in teaching and learning.

> [Knowledge] can be judged right or wrong, accurate or inaccurate, correct
> or incorrect on the basis of a comparison with the teacher's own knowledge
> or with some other model as found in a textbook or other instructional mate-
> rials. Not only do judgments of this sort yield a measure of the success of
> teaching within this tradition, they also are the chief criterion by which
> learning is measured. (p. 118)

Workable, self-sealed, socially acceptable and reinforced, this conceptual
network is not very open to analysis. In teacher education, the task of

overhauling flawed but well-integrated conceptions of what it means to learn and to know is a tough variant of the "ideals" problem with its attendant perplexities.

Its peculiar difficulty stems from the fact that, to the extent to which knowledge is seen and used in schools in a theoretically more appropriate fashion (that is, as fashioned by people in accordance with reasonable conventions, thus evolving and debatable), straightforward bases for student evaluation are eroded. Rightly making room for uncertainties in knowing and learning hugely complicates the institutional and (societal) judgment functions of teachers, through raising questions of practicality and fairness. This example shows that the folkways of teaching are not easily replaced by something else that will meet most of the needs of schooling.

Workable replacements (e.g., of prevailing conceptions of knowledge and learning) must pick up important pieces of whatever else tumbles down (e.g., manageable and generally intelligible forms of student evaluation). If reforms do not go *some* way toward providing functional replacements, most people will adhere or revert to the folkways of teaching without being subject to blame. On the other hand, if some theories—deep and accurate though they may be—remain impractical, this is not fatal as long as there are some relatively crude theories with which people can "make do" (see Schrag, 1981).

Weighing the Case for Folkways Against the Plea for Breaks

Taking into account what I have argued so far, one cannot be surprised that most reforms in schools and teacher education do not take hold. At worst, some muddle what is sound in common sense and practice through fads and quasi-scientific dogma. My qualified defense of common sense, and halfhearted case for the folkways of teaching, throws doubt on the notion that learning to teach must include breaks with experience and that all such breaks will be salutary. Yet the characteristic kinds of learning (both in content and modes of acquisition) associated with schooling and living also provide good reasons for instructive interruptions of many teacher habits and beliefs. When we weigh the drawbacks of incidental teacher learning heavily, the question of how professional education can transform people becomes urgent.

IS PROFESSIONAL LEARNING LIKE SEEING THE WORLD IN REVERSE?

The beliefs of students in medical school are often upset. Contrary to lay assumptions, the reasons why someone gets sick or recovers often remain unclear to doctors—a muddle of physical, environmental, and social-emotional factors, eddying inward and outward; medical students present at the opening of a corpse find out that the cause of death often remains a mystery to their tutors (Fox, 1957). Law students get used to the fact of professional life that, in law, it is the better-prepared case and not the more defensible cause that wins. They learn to think like lawyers, in specialized modes of reasoning and case analysis remote from common sense (see Bodenheimer, 1962; White, 1985). Passing through the professional mirror, doctors and lawyers learn to see the world, as it were, from behind it.

Converting Teachers?

What many reformers want for teachers parallels the conversions of professionals in occupations with higher status. Shrinking from novices' eager affirmations of liking kids as a reason for going into teaching, they aim to substitute motivations having to do with worthwhile learning and social justice. Dissatisfied with teachers' plain views of teaching as doing and telling and their concomitant desire for procedures and techniques to follow, reformers aim to replace these views and desires by elevated understandings of teaching and learning as *thinking*, with a focus on why rather than on how. Some urge concerns, moreover, for the equal distribution of the human good of learning, productive of many other goods, moral and social. (See the Holmes Group and Carnegie Foundation reports, discussed—especially the first—from various angles in *Teachers College Record* [Soltis, 1987].)

Such teacher education goals imply a shift from habits, observables, and dominant patterns (with deep, entangled root systems) to remote ideas of knowledge and justice. Neither everyday experiences nor ordinary ways of making sense of things and other people are much help in preparing teachers for the pursuit of these ideals in school. From the point of view of common sense, people who are different may seem inferior, and this tendency can solidify into demeaning stereotypes. Many scholarly understandings that reveal *processes* of learning (including errors and reversals) never make it into undergraduate education, let alone the public schools. Even understandings included in the school curriculum often conflict with common sense and everyday experience.

The shifts that transformative educators envision for teachers are hence at least as dramatic as the separations, almost alienations, from the "real world" that other professionals undergo. One might conclude that—just because future teachers are already well versed in schooling (and routinely have many extramural experiences of teaching and learning besides)—their professional socialization must be even more of a turning point. Are ever-more complete conversions, more decided breaks with experience, required for the teaching profession? This seems an irrational conclusion. In all helping professions, a separation from ordinary beliefs and concerns can be carried too far and may become self-serving.

Counterpoints and Inherent Tensions

> Men sail a boundless and bottomless sea;
> there is neither harbour for shelter nor floor for anchorage,
> neither starting-place nor appointed destination.
> The enterprise is to keep afloat on an even keel;
> the sea is both friend and enemy;
> and the seamanship consists in using the
> resources of a traditional manner of behaviour in
> order to make a friend of every hostile occasion.
>   (Oakeshott, 1951/1989b, pp. 149–150)

To return to where we started: Teachers' minds are no tabula rasa, no blank slates, but scratched in deeply with plain characters. Can people replace the slates, wipe out what is upon them, or reverse interpretations, as breach-making approaches to teacher education suggest? Can we do this for all teaching subjects, all concepts, topics, and methods within them? What about interpretations of human differences? Conceptions of knowledge and learning? The weight of experience alone, downward bearing in quality and quantity, makes effective breaks on all these counts seem unlikely.

Yet this weight cannot solely be seen as the dead hand of the past. While the common experiences of future teachers are no reliable sample of the real or ideal worlds of school and society, they include much that— deserving a skeptical respect or, at least, an attempt at understanding— tends to be overlooked by the clever absorbed in their self-imposed missions of change. As long as classrooms and people remain by and large what they are, transformative perspectives can compete with the folkways of teaching only if they are supplemented by workable, effective, new patterns of action that give ordinary teachers, with ordinary preparation and resources, a chance to meet the demands of their work.

While being critical, academics do not always take a hard look at their projects and themselves. They may propose radically new perspectives in hopes of shocking teachers into abandoning their folkways, or perhaps only in hopes of shocking. As Donald Campbell (1975) warned his fellow psychologists, "With our conceptual framework still heavily

shared with popular culture, our narcissistic motivation for creative innovation overlaps into the motivation to advocate shocking new perspectives" (p. 1121). In the social sciences, as lines of inquiry where people
look at themselves, it is an open question whether scholarly frameworks
can ever be expected to depart radically and *validly* from what people (at
some level) already know, feel, and do. Uncomfortable or unthinkable to
most academics, this is a fundamental question in education (see Schrag,
1981, 1983; also Stephens, 1967).

Common Sense and Experience as Starting Points?

Schoolteachers may be intellectual leaders, but they are social managers as well, shepherding groups of youngsters along a meandering path
with some purpose and kindness. Do they plan classes? Reprimand and
praise where appropriate and fair? Do teachers work at getting pupils to
finish their assignments and themselves try to return them on time? More
subtly, are they tactful in quieting down attention-seekers while encouraging the timid? Of course, teachers try to do these and other things that
pupils can see or figure out in a fashion. Children can also make sense of
school because—though inmates behave somewhat strangely in places
such as hospitals, prisons, or schools—people are still people and all children grow into understandings of what *that* means.

Are everyday understandings of knowledge as facts and names utterly bizarre? Granted that science dissolves the objects of ordinary experience, we can still sit on chairs, and their everyday use tells us what they
are. The commonsense assumption—entrenched in schools—that facts
and names are essential for knowledge does connect with the empirical
and conceptual pursuits of science, though falling short of their characteristic elaborations, especially in terms of methods and criteria of knowing.
Still, unless museum visitors, for instance, are "equipped with [a] basic
stock of words and categories by which differences can be named and,
thereby, apprehended—proper names of famous painters . . . , concepts
designating a school, an age, a 'period' . . . and rendering possible comparisons . . . or contrasts—[they] are condemned to the monotonous diversity of meaningless sensations" (Bourdieu, 1967/1971, p. 195). This
suggests that common sense and experiences are, at least, among the
starting points of teacher education: sometimes to be abandoned on examination, more often to be refined or deepened, and sometimes to be
revived after erroneous abandonment.

A preparation for teaching and knowing through schooling and living is partial and imperfect. It does provide some relevant and useful
lessons notwithstanding. And it is *there*, with an inescapable, earthbound

weight. In examining the case for conversion versus continuation in teacher education, it therefore seems impossible and unhelpful to come down on one side or the other. On the one hand, the weight of taken-for-granted understandings in learning to teach makes decisive breaks seem necessary, while unlikely to succeed on all counts. On the other hand, not on all counts can the lessons of personal and collective experience be dismissed. It is no sign of a quasi-religious attitude toward tradition to feel that what has seen people through in school for many generations cannot be all bad. This inconclusive assessment throws doubt, in particular, on breach-making approaches supported by looking over the fence at other professions.

IS THERE EXPERTISE IN TEACHING—AND DOES IT MATTER?

If we order human pursuits on a continuum that marks their permeability to common sense and life experiences—that is, their openness to nonspecialized and extra-professional knowledge—teaching can be placed at the high end, radiology at the low, and the health professions and law somewhere in between. Degrees of relative permeability to common sense and life experiences, in short, vary by one's line of work and are not, in themselves, either good or bad. Instead, they must be judged by reference to task and role requirements.

Illegitimate Evaluations of Knowledge by Source

Roles and activities that are, as it were, close to home are naturally permeable to common sense and life experiences. This fact in itself, to repeat, allows no conclusions about the difficulty of an activity or the worth, validity, and complexity of associated knowledge (conceptual, empirical, moral, and procedural). Take the example of friendship or, more concretely, the question of what is involved in being a friend to someone else. Opening any collection of proverbs or quotations shows that people know a lot about friendship. (The *Oxford Dictionary of Quotations* includes almost 250 items.) Browsing through entries leaves no doubt that it is difficult to be a good friend and that related knowledge is not easy to disentangle and act on in all its bearings. This is almost beside the point, however, for the truth is that one does not have to be literate to know *that*.

Schoolteaching is even more difficult than being someone's friend, for, in schools, teachers have to combine bureaucratic role requirements—at best, those of abstract justice and fairness—with the personally compelling loyalties of friendship (Fried, 1978). When nonspecialized and extra-professional knowledge is being discredited, people may confuse the *source* with the *value* of knowledge—its significance, complexity, coherence, and trustworthiness. As a corollary, where an activity remains relatively impervious to "extraordinary" knowledge (i.e., science, specialized technical knowledge), this permits no conclusions about the difficulty of the activity or the worth and validity of its working knowledge.

Studies of teaching knowledge underscore the conceptual points I have made in this section. The work of Berliner and his associates (Berliner, 1986; Carter, Sabers, Cushing, Pinnegar, & Berliner, 1987) convincingly suggests that—although teachers can have special knowledge—that knowledge is an elaboration and refinement of ordinary good sense. Leinhardt's work (e.g., 1988) shows that a relative imperviousness to knowledge outside of the scope of experience and common sense is consistent with high-powered knowledge and skills in teaching. In principle, many people can gain this special knowledge; in fact, few nonteachers and not all teachers have it, since elaborate and refined teaching knowledge takes time, effort, and what Wordsworth calls a "vital soul" to acquire. Stressing that it is illegitimate to draw negative conclusions about lines of work simply because they are permeable to common sense and life experiences does not rule out other inferences, however.

Invasions of Curricular Arguments by Power Bids

Degrees of relative permeability do tell us something about the extent to which the university ought to be the site of occupational socialization. Importantly, claims will here flow from an impartial analysis of intrinsic characteristics of the line of work rather than being distorted by political aspirations. Such aspirations—as in the call for teacher empowerment—may be justified and helpful when organizational settings and policy environments obstruct the work of teaching. But consider the following fallacious argument, rather widely accepted (see, e.g., Peters, 1964/1977; Garrison, 1988), though not usually spelled out:

> We must empower teachers and/or raise the status of teaching.
> Knowledge is power.
> The status of the knowledge that members of an occupation acquire is related to the social status of the occupation.
> The degree to which a good is in popular possession usually affects perceptions of its value adversely.

Ergo: Teacher education should introduce knowledge remote from common sense and shared traditions.

The general fallacy in this form of practical argument is that it moves from assertions about the existence of a means to the assertion that this means should be used (e.g., I want to have a lot of money. One way to get a lot of money is to rob banks. Therefore I should rob banks.). Its perverse illogic furthermore stems from treating teacher education content—albeit of an elevated nature as knowledge—as a means to prop up a bid for power. The danger is that curricular arguments from political premises may bypass or slight questions of relevance; yet, regardless of its status, it is knowledge bearing on their work that empowers teachers to do it.

No Ideal Sources of Knowledge to Rule Thought and Action

As pretentiousness does not increase the value of something, so unpretentiousness does not decrease it. The key question is how to judge value. Equating social status with knowledge value is wrongheaded. In modern societies, confounding the source with the value of knowledge leads to underrating ordinary good sense and placing too much reliance on science in the conduct of human affairs. Traditional societies tend to refer thought and action to what is sacred—or secured, by religious feeling and social penalties, against violation (which includes questioning). Today, science is often regarded with a respect and reverence similar to that which is attached to holy things. Of course, research knowledge is special. If a knowledge claim is research-based, it is likely to be true over a wider range of circumstances than inferences from personal experience, for instance. At the same time, the scope or focus of scientific studies limits their relevance to people and action; this is where local knowledge derived from common sense and life experiences, though less general and inferentially weaker, is strong.

While both trustworthiness and relevance contribute to the value of knowledge, these—partial—epistemological goods do not oblige by increasing at the same time in the human sciences. Nagel (1979, chap. 14) has cast this problem in terms of a conflict between two coexistent, irreducible points of view: subjective (or internal) and objective (or external). Dismayed by the parochialism and the egocentric, contingent, overly specific nature of the internal point of view, proponents of the second, or external, view claim to have not only a corrective but the one, *right* way to look at the world. It is appealing to have a unified, comprehensive ideal of understanding, but singleness of conception and the abeyance of doubt come at a cost.

When the external view dominates, it ignores the constitutive fact that, for beings such as ourselves, life is rooted, and lived from the inside. Time, place, memory, and other people make experiences out of events. Among philosophers, the attempt to bring everything under one, external description results in the unreasonable moves of reducing the subjective to the objective or denying that it exists. Popper (1962) sees a similar irrationality and incapacity to live with conflict and doubt in the search for the universally best sources of knowledge: "No such ideal sources exist—no more than ideal rulers—and . . . *all* 'sources' are liable to lead us into error at times" (p. 55). This epistemological predicament contributes to the difficulties in what to make of and how to deal with the relationships between transformative education and people's incidental preparation for teaching.

TEACHERS AS INMATES OF THE HUMAN HOUSEHOLD

How can we get from the glazed surface of things as they are to the heights and depths of things as they might be in teaching? The answer does not lie in conversions or simple shifts in what we treat as authoritative knowledge. We must remember that the converted can be singularly incurious and complacent, which is not good for teachers or students. Nor do inappropriate comparisons of teaching with other occupations provide the answer—with a misplaced envy of their professional socialization and greater remoteness from common sense and ordinary experiences. Instead, help may come from looking at teaching deeply and simply, hence also freshly. This is what Wordsworth (1800/1904) does for poetry when he affirms that "the Poet, singing a song in which all human beings join with him, rejoices in the presence of truth as our visible friend and hourly companion" (p. 795). The knowledge and sense of poetry "cleaves to us as a necessary part of our existence, our natural and unalienable inheritance [through which we come by our] habitual and direct sympathy connecting us with our fellow-beings" (p. 795).

And so it is with teaching and learning. As Dewey (1916/1966) writes, "Not only does social life demand teaching and learning for its own permanence, but the very process of living together educates" (p. 6). In his delighted vision of children, he (1900/1959) sees them naturally "running over, spilling over, with activities of all kinds" (p. 54); at least outside of school, the young take a lively interest in talking (communication), finding out things (inquiry), and in making things useful and beautiful. Throughout people's lives, learning that carries these human interests forward naturally involves teaching. We think, learn, teach, tell stories, and dance, Bambrough (1986) points out, because we are human.

> By birthright we are all not only thinkers but also singers and dancers, poets and painters, teachers and story-tellers. This means that the professional

singer or painter, poet or teacher, dancer or story-teller, is a professional in a different way from the solicitor or doctor, physicist or statistician. . . . Like the runner or the writer or the ruler the thinker may become a professional but can never become an *expert*. (p. 60)

The bearing on my argument of Bambrough's distinction between an *expert* and a *professional* is that, while the first concept (*expert*) implies a distinction in kind between people, the second accords with comparative distinctions in terms of knowledge, capacities, and hours spent doing related activities (compare a restaurant chef with a housewife, or a gigolo with a lover, for instance). No doubt there are gray areas where comparative distinctions are so marked and manifold that they may be candidates for differences in kind; judgment will require looking at the case at hand.

The point to hold on to is that the special knowledge of teachers does not derive from their moving in a world of relevances, sensitivities, skills, and dispositions that are separate and remote from the human household. Just as for a poet, however, it matters greatly for a teacher to what extent relevances are seen and connected; sensitivities are keen, vibrant, and refined; skills apposite, ready-to-hand, and malleable; and aims true and just. Taking the larger or species view, even the disciplines of knowledge—arcane as they may become—have grown out of people's thoughts and feelings, trials and errors, the suffering of consequences, and a longing for knowledge and understanding that cannot be stilled. This is the essential connection between the child and the curriculum, which teachers have to see—and to revive in practice.

Hence, whatever we do as researchers and educators, we should not promote tendentious and misleading notions of professionalization or expertise in teaching. Where extraneous knowledge is promoted with a view to raising the status of teachers, we should recall the commonplace of history that greater power or honor alone does not increase people's competence and wisdom. The predicament that puts what is relevant to action and close to people into strained relations with what is generally true and detached should keep us wide awake rather than eager for a final solution. When concerns for teachers' standing in society result in crowding out common sense and local knowledge that is valid, the result is confusion, loss, and harm.

Experience and Expertise

D. C. Phillips

Jean Jacques Rousseau became famous—"notorious" might be a more accurate term—upon winning an essay competition sponsored by a French periodical. He had followed a dangerous strategy, arguing for the unpopular and unexpected side of the proposition that formed the topic of the competition. The judges had chosen their words so that it was clear what position they expected the essayists to adopt, and Rousseau brilliantly went against their expectations. Something similar is true of the three chapters in Part I of the present book: Buchmann, Floden, and Schwille have produced a number of arguments that shock the expectations of their readers by throwing doubt on a number of interrelated popular dogmas in educational theory. In so doing, they exemplify one of the major themes running through their essays—the importance of educators inducing "breaks with experience" in those they are attempting to educate.

The first two chapters attack the notion that education ought to be based upon, or closely relate to, the experience of students. The authors remind us that experience can debilitate and enslave; a person who can deal only with the experiences that are to be had within the immediate geographical and temporal locale is a person who has been disenfranchised from life's rich possibilities. Education should broaden the learner's horizons, and this means that teachers should induce breaks with the imprisoning experience. The third chapter turns to the education of beginning teachers, and, given the theme of the first two chapters, the reader approaches it expecting that the argument will be made that teacher education should break the novice of the habits and beliefs about teaching and learning that he or she already possesses. But once again the reader's expectations are dashed! For, instead, it is argued (half-heartedly, to be sure) that the prior expectations that have their origins in the experience that all of us have had as recipients of education during our own school days possess a great deal of validity and ought not to be broken away from. So, in the case of school-age students, education should break with past and current experience, while for novice teachers education should do the opposite!

In the following discussion, not only will the theme of the first two chapters be endorsed, but an attempt will be made to strengthen it—with an important caveat. The halfhearted argument of the third chapter will be treated with the ambivalence that it so justly deserves.

EXPERIENCE AND ITS CONCEPTUALIZATION

An important principle from epistemology and philosophy of science seems to be relevant to the discussion of the ways in which we can learn from experience: the principle of the underdetermination of theory by evidence. According to this, any finite body of evidence (no matter how extensive) is insufficient to determine fully a unique explanatory theory—many rival theories exist, in principle, all of which can account for exactly the same evidence. So it cannot be argued that because we have discovered *this* evidence, *this particular* theory is correct. (The situation is not quite so stark as this might suggest, for it is likely that many of the possible rival theories that can account for the same evidence are implausible, given other things that we believe; but it is also unlikely that we can rule out *all* of the other possible theories in this way. See Laudan, 1990, for an important discussion of these issues.) An alternative way to make the epistemological point here is to identify *evidence* with *experience*, in which case we get the principle that difference can be conceptualized or categorized in a number of different ways; experience may force itself upon us, as it were, but experience does not carry with it its own conceptualization. A given experience, or sequence of experiences, does not necessitate that a certain conceptualization of it must be adopted. Goodman and Elgin (1988) make the point as follows:

> Sensation [experience] is sometimes supposed to be primarily given. Doesn't a sound present a certain quality or set of qualities even to a person ignorant of its source or musical context? The trouble with saying this is that neither a sensation nor anything else comes already labeled. Our sensations, like everything else, are subject to a variety of characterizations. The range of available alternatives is a function of the conceptual systems we have constructed and mastered. . . . Nothing about a domain favors one faithful characterization of its objects over others. To choose among them requires knowing how the several systems function. (pp. 5–7)

The implications of this epistemological principle for education are very much in line with the points made by Buchmann, Floden, and Schwille. All of us, but especially children, are likely to conceptualize our experience along the lines that are suggested by the significant figures in our immediate vicinity—peers, siblings, fellow gang members, elders in our church, TV personalities, parents, and teachers. And once a framework of conceptualizations and interpretations exists, it will grow like a snowball rolling down a hill—we will become prisoners, as it were, of the first conceptualizations that we make. It would seem that one of the chief functions of education is to provide us with alternative frameworks or categorizations, to suggest new ways of seeing what we have seen before in the old familiar ways, of suggesting liberating alternatives. This, clearly, is what science education is about, but it is also true of education in literature, social studies, and foreign languages. As Dewey (1916/1966) put it,

> The great advantage of immaturity, educationally speaking, is that it enables us to emancipate the young from the need of dwelling in an outgrown past. The business of education is rather to liberate the young from reviving and retraversing the past than to lead them to a recapitulation of it. (p. 73)

It might seem risky to cite Dewey in support of the case that is being made here, for he is famous for insisting upon the need to relate education to the present environment of students—which apparently contradicts the moral that has just been drawn. (Buchmann and her coauthors also note this seemingly contrasting element in Dewey.) But actually there is no deep problem here, for Dewey's notion of the "present environment" is a rather rich one. He includes, as part of the environment in which we all operate and by which we all are influenced, the bodies of knowledge and the cultural forms that have evolved and grown over the ages, the "life of the ancient Greeks and Romans," geographically distant present-day societies, "remote physical energies" and "invisible [physical] structures" (Dewey, 1916/1966, p. 19ff). But because the nature of the influence of these things upon us now "cannot be understood without explicit statement and attention," society establishes schools "to care for such matters" (Dewey, 1916/1966, p. 19). In short, it is the school—and education—that deepens students' understanding of the influences and categories that are operating upon them or that are potentially available to them. Dewey, of course, also insists that exploration of this rich cultural environment should *start* from what students presently know—which is that part of the environment with which they are in direct contact. But at least it is clear that on the broader issues Dewey, Phillips, Buchmann, Floden, and Schwille are all in agreement!

There is another aspect of Dewey's work that is very helpful here, and that builds upon the point just made. In a famous passage in *The Child and the Curriculum*, Dewey (1902/1956) used the analogy of an explorer mapping a new territory, to throw light on the role that codified bodies of knowledge should play in guiding the intellectual explorations of students in schools. Dewey asks, "Of what use is the map?"

> Well, we may first tell what the map is not. The map is not a substitute for a personal experience. The map does not take the place of an actual journey. The logically formulated materials of a science or branch of learning, of a study, is no substitute for the having of individual experiences. . . . But the map, a summary, an arranged and orderly view of previous experiences, serves as a guide to future experience; it gives direction . . . it economizes effort, preventing useless wandering. (p. 20)

Thus, for Dewey, the liberating of the student from the confines of the immediately available environment does not take place at the expense of the student's firsthand experience; rather, it occurs via the directing of this experience into fruitful and liberating areas—such directing being possible because educators have at their disposal maps of the intellectual domain (in the form of the disciplines).

This point leads directly to the important caveat that needs to be registered to the first two chapters by Buchmann, Floden, and Schwille.

A CAVEAT

There is something about the first two chapters that does not sit comfortably. For although the line of argument presented is strong, it seems to go too far: Although experience can be enslaving, it nevertheless seems to be the case that education does have *some* relation to the present experience of the student. Dewey's metaphor of the explorer brings this point out—the fact that other people have gone before as trailblazers does not substitute for *my* having the experience of journeying through the same terrain. The codified experience of the trailblazers—the map, or the structure of the academic disciplines—serves as a guide about what lies ahead, about what the possibilities are for excitement and stimulation on *my* journey. Travelers who do not consult a map or guidebook before leaving home are likely to miss out on a great deal and are likely to return as insular as they were before the trip; and students who never set out on an intellectual journey with a guide (or guidebook) risk remaining forever with unfulfilled intellectual potential.

But, as Dewey stresses, there is no substitute for *actually having first-hand experience.* The issue is, Shall the experience be fruitful and liberating, or shall it be "more of the same," or, worse still, shall it be experience that is forced upon the student who is not yet prepared to benefit from it? (For a person who takes a trip without adequate preparation is also unlikely to gain maximum profit from the adventure.) Furthermore, the metaphor of the map and the journey highlights another important point: A journey always starts from home, from where the potential traveler is already located. A journey where the planning has focused only upon the exotic locale, but has not paid attention to *how* the traveler is to get from home *to* the new terrain, is not going to be a successful venture. And so it is with education.

In arguing for the importance of breaking the student away from the confines of the present environment, Buchmann and her coauthors do not stress enough (and this surely must be simply a sin of omission) the *manner* in which this is to be done, how the student is to be transported to the new domain. For manner or method can be as liberating or as debilitating as can content. Thus, a student being educated deserves to have contact with ideas and subjects that are liberating and empowering, but the student also deserves to have this content presented in such a way that the actual experience of confronting the material is also stimulating and empowering. And there are two aspects to this: Students must be prepared so that they are able to move fruitfully from present experience, and the new material must be presented in an engaging and educationally sound manner. We all know—if from nothing else, from our own school days—that important and potentially liberating material can be presented in a manner that kills interest and motivation; for example, students might not have mastered the prerequisites for learning the new material, or the links between the new and the old may not have been forged, or students might be expected to engage in rote learning, or the material may be delivered via lectures, which often can minimize the extent to which students personally can grapple with the material. Dewey reminds us of both aspects of education, but there is a tendency for Buchmann, Floden, and Schwille to focus on the content and to neglect method—which leads in turn to their giving the impression that education has little to do with the present experience of students. Another way of putting all this is, in short, that educators need to have available a range of techniques for engaging their students *experientially* with the liberating content. And this brings us to the third chapter by Buchmann.

THE THIRD CHAPTER

In this third piece, Margret Buchmann makes a "halfhearted" case for the "folkways of teaching"; she recognizes the wisdom that is often embedded in "common sense," but she also sees that it has a second face—common sense is often in error, and it can choke off questioning. But, nevertheless, she produces a "qualified defense" of commonsense approaches to teaching—which, given the theme of the first two essays, is something of a surprise, as in this third case she argues *against* breaking with everyday experience. Her train of thought is roughly as follows: Common sense is the source of what many of us, even those who are not teachers, know about teaching. For we have had experience of teaching when we ourselves were recipients of it as students in school, and most of us in the course of daily life have to teach or explain matters to colleagues or to family members. Much (although not all) of this commonsense knowledge is sound, and yet teacher education programs regularly adopt the stance that novice teachers need to undergo a radical break with their previous understandings.

I am ambivalent about all this. Certainly it is clear that commonsense views have much going for them: Teachers should be clear in their expositions, they should develop their explanations of a given topic in an orderly way instead of jumping about all over the place, they should try to interest their students, and so forth. These are principles that many laypeople would have no hesitancy in espousing, and there seems to be no good reason why teachers-in-training should have to abandon or even rethink them.

But consider how common sense often fleshes out these principles: If an exposition is clear (and if it is presented in a loud and authoritative tone of voice), then students should have no trouble understanding it and remembering it; if an example or a topic interests the person doing the teaching, then is should interest all students; if a student has not understood, it is the student's fault (and probably lack of effort or plain stubbornness is to blame); all students learn in the same way that the person doing the teaching learns; a student can demonstrate that learning has taken place merely by parroting back the information that has been presented by the teacher; and so on. If common sense is often wise, it is also often foolish. So which should we choose—to guard against the "type one" error or the "type two"? I confess that in the end I come down on the opposite side to Buchmann.

There are two other considerations that sway me here. First, the defense of common sense is conservative, in what is probably a bad sense of the term. Throughout much of the nineteenth and twentieth centuries, in many countries but notably in Britain, in influential circles the view was held that a teacher needed no training at all apart from a very solid grounding in an academic specialty. Thus, all that a person needed in order to become a good teacher of history or literature or science was a quality degree in the appropriate specialty—anything else that was needed would come from common sense. This view, of course, was a hindrance to the development of schools of education in universities, and it helped to ensure that those that were established remained in positions of low status. Now, the fact that the doctrine has had this (negative?) consequence obviously does not serve to *refute* the doctrine, but it is a fact that ought to make us pause and ask ourselves how certain we are of the doctrine before we try to breathe new life into it. (Perhaps Buchmann tends to lean in the opposite direction here?)

The second consideration is more directly to the point. Recent studies of teaching suggest (although they do not, as yet, absolutely make it an open-and-shut case) that good teachers of a subject in schools actually know things that experts in that particular subject matter (e.g., university researchers) do not know: The teachers know how to teach it! A good, experienced teacher of a subject will have a stock of what Lee Shulman has called "subject matter knowledge for teaching"—the teacher will know how to transform the subject so that it gels with the prior knowledge and experience of students; the teacher knows how to introduce a topic in a way that will make the material accessible to the students; the teacher can anticipate places where difficulties or misunderstandings are likely to arise; and so on (Shulman, 1987; see also Phillips, 1988). In short, the teacher of a subject knows how to "psychologize" the material, as Dewey (1902/1956, p. 22) phrased it. Dewey went on:

> Every study or subject thus has two aspects: one for the scientist as a scientist; the other for the teacher as a teacher. These two aspects are in no sense opposed or conflicting. But neither are they immediately identical. . . . The problem of the teacher . . . is the ways in which that subject may become a part of experience; what there is in the child's present that is usable with reference to it; how such elements are to be used; how his own knowledge of the subject-matter may assist in interpreting the child's needs and doings. . . . He is concerned, not with the subject-matter as such, but with the subject-matter as a related factor in a total and growing experience. Thus to see it is to psychologize it. (pp. 22–23)

There is no evidence that knowledge of how to "psychologize" subject matter is a product of unaided common sense. Such knowledge can grow *out* of common sense, if the prospective teacher is educated properly; this is to say that the prospective teacher needs to be liberated from common sense, to be led beyond it—just as, in the first two chapters, Buchmann and her coauthors correctly saw that students needed to grow beyond their present confining experience. What is sauce for the student goose, is also sauce for the novice teacher gander! Subject-matter knowledge for teaching, or the ability to psychologize material, is a core part of a teacher's professional knowledge, and it is the genuine key (as opposed to the spurious ones so rightly condemned by Buchmann) to why teaching ought to be recognized as a profession.

Philosophical Analyses in Contexts

Robert E. Floden and Margret Buchmann

Given our interest in lively second thoughts, we are pleased that our respondent believes we disappoint some reader expectations. D. C. Phillips adduces parallels between our position and arguments from epistemology and philosophy of science that supply further grounds and terms for conversation about the roles of experience in teaching and learning. Returning to Dewey is also helpful in deepening understanding. There always seems to be more to John Dewey's thinking than one realizes.

Still, our respondent is somewhat concerned that our first two chapters ignore students' present experiences altogether, with a consequent neglect of questions about how fruitful breaks with experience might be achieved. We admit to some neglect of method and agree with Phillips that given experiences and teaching manners are important. As Dewey (1916/1966) points out, "manners are but minor morals" (p. 18). Students' current (and past) experiences play diverse roles in determining whether some surprising encounter (with ideas, theorems, people, poems, pictures, vistas . . .) will come to be a salutary, educational break. For guided adventures in learning, the German nineteenth-century notion of "pedagogical tact" (revived by van Manen, 1991) draws together qualities of teacher character and skills relevant to the tangled tasks of protecting, respecting, and challenging learners.

It is important not to allow narrow conceptions of experience to shape considerations of manner, however. Dewey's rich conception of present environment exemplifies an ample breadth of thought in teaching and learning. We agree that students should engage "experientially" with content. (What other kind of engagement might there be?) Yet reconstructing a geometric proof, contemplating a waterfall, and reading poems are all forms of experience. Before his travels in France moved him to a sense of spiritual and emotional cultivation, J. S. Mill's stays at Bentham's country residence, for instance, proved educative.

> The spacious and lofty rooms of this fine old place, so unlike the mean and cramped externals of English middle class life, gave the sentiment of a larger and freer existence and were to me a sort of poetic cultivation aided also by the character of the grounds in which the Abbey stood . . . secluded, umbrageous, and full of the sound of falling waters. (1873/1971, p. 86)

His feelings for nature prepared the young philosopher, in turn, for finding aid during a time of mental anguish in Wordsworth's poems. "In them I seemed to draw from a source of inward joy, of sympathetic and imaginative pleasure, which could be shared in by all human beings" (1873/1971, pp. 131–132).

After wondering whether we have attached too little weight to experience in the first two chapters, Phillips suggests that we may rely too much on experience and common sense in the third. He points out that we change the tenor of our analysis, and it is true that there is a shift in our argument's direction. But our respondent's concern for consistent extension—what is sauce for the goose is also sauce for the gander—may reflect our success in remaining inconclusive, rather than some logical shortcoming. We discuss in several chapters that follow why one cannot account for sensible thought and practice in terms of formal reason and consistency alone.

Throughout the book we take the stance that—because sorting out the roles of experience in education (or the contributions of research to practice, etc.) leaves these issues more clear but unsettled—readers should find and make meaning without inappropriate feelings of resolution. Our analyses implicate differences between seemingly similar ideas, such as reflection and contemplation, coherence and consistency, sociological and moral conceptions of professional roles. We look at some of the associations and values that make concepts scintillate. Separately and in conjunction, our essays highlight energizing tensions, informed by scholarship, common sense, and literature, propelled by moral intuitions and desires for action, based in consideration and felt needs—in a movement toward the endless unknown for both authors and audience.

Thus a great part of readers' possible discomfort with our inconclusive argument about "making new or making do" in teaching may evaporate on reflection. Rather than merely extending the challenge to learning from experience into teacher education, we heighten the tensions that prompted our work on experience, teaching, and learning in the first place. Sharing Phillips's belief that many people take learning from experience for granted, we stress the limits of such learning to begin with. Yet addressing questions of *teacher* education means turning to specific practical and professional contexts, which are also political and rhetorical. In these contexts, we argue, keeping the issues well-aired demands attention to the virtues of learning from experience, and even some adherence to common sense, as a cultural system.

If "the reader's expectations are dashed," again, by the third chapter, this may well show that we have avoided slipping from endorsements of experience into denials of its values for teaching and learning, and that we have duly noticed shifts in analytic contexts. Speaking to philosophers, Dewey (1931/1960) does not pull his punches on the importance of contexts for thought. "The trouble," he stresses, "is not with analysis, but with the philosopher who ignores the context in which and *for the sake of which* [italics added] the analysis occurs" (p. 93). Dewey contends that honoring contexts will teach humility and debar a thinker "from a too unlimited and dogmatic universalization of his conclusions" (p. 100).

Like D. C. Phillips, in sum, we recognize the limits of common sense, and those of philosophy, or of science. We concur with him, too, that schooling should not be an unaided exploration, an adventure without guide (or guidebooks). But, as our respondent notes for other students, the goal for teachers as learners is neither to accept nor to reject all that can be learned from experience, but to organize curriculum so that students can frame liberating, legitimate interpretations in viewing the past and the future, as well as the present. Here, we submit, it is crucial to see that understandings of teaching built into cultures by virtue of long and shared experiences are, at once, "the guardian and avenging angel of every classroom" (Thelen, 1973, p. 195).

Part II

USING KNOWLEDGE IN TEACHING AND TEACHER EDUCATION

CHAPTER 4

What Is Irrational
About Knowledge Utilization?

Margret Buchmann

> Social events do have causes and social institutions effects; but
> it just may be that the road to discovering what we assert in
> asserting this lies less through postulating forces and measuring
> them than through noting expressions and inspecting them.
> —Clifford Geertz, 1980, "Blurred Genres: The Refiguration
> of Social Thought"

In 1835, Tocqueville (cited in Rich, 1981) observed that Americans "have
all a lively faith in the perfectibility of man, they judge that the diffusion
of knowledge must necessarily be advantageous and the consequences
of ignorance fatal" (p. 37). This observation remains telling, as statements
of contemporary social scientists show. Bell (1979/1980), for instance, de-
clares that 'the axial principle of the postindustrial society . . . is the centrality of theoretical knowledge and its new role, when codified, as the
director of social change" (p. 501). Tocqueville implied that he saw the
American faith in knowledge and the advancement of humankind as en-
gagingly naive. But in a book on knowledge utilization, Tocqueville's dry
comments are cited as evidence of his belief "that the possession and
diffusion of knowledge is central to the advancement of mankind" (Rich,
1981, p. 37). This interpretive slip holds a key to the problem of knowledge utilization, attesting to the power of beliefs that ordinarily remain
unexamined.

In *Paradoxes of Education in a Republic,* Brann (1979) describes the roots
in thought and time of the connection of knowledge and utility in the
American republic. The modern notion that knowledge should be useful
is associated with viewing utility as the measure of the good. In a republic "congenitally engaged in instrumental activity" (p. 20), secular in ori-

gin, and scientific in orientation, valuing knowledge for its utility led to a view of commendable action with "an emphasis on pursuing, planning, procuring, producing, and on manufacturing, declaring, demonstrating, projecting" (p. 25). One wonders just how crucial beliefs in the utility of scientific knowledge are to the American ethos, if faith persists in view of an educational reality that Brann (1979) describes as "an enormous, compacted complex of cherished vestiges, trashed experiments, recovered truisms, partial reformations, occasional explosions, compromising accommodations, paths of least resistance, hopeful engraftings, institutional inertia" (p. 4).

I argue that the problem of knowledge utilization in educational practice is not just a problem of creating, diffusing, disseminating, and implementing (scientific) knowledge, but also a *conceptual* problem. Thus I ask, What are people who connect knowledge and utility doing? Why do they pair off knowledge with utilization? What practical or social problems does the connection of (scientific) knowledge and utility appear to solve? What assumptions and beliefs does it imply? To what kinds of imagination does it appeal? What other concepts denoting processes could be associated with knowledge—for instance, conversation, contemplation, or critique?

When one considers the contributions of research knowledge to educational practice, it is important to recall that common sense, personal commitments, and external policies (e.g., legal mandates, curriculum guides) can also be valid bases for action. In general, an overreliance on research knowledge will be inappropriate, for it is time-bound, theory-dependent, and selective. Beyond that, such overreliance is misguided because many problems in the practicing professions do not derive primarily from deficiencies in knowledge. They arise instead because of tensions or deficiencies in the moral framework in which professional practice is embedded.

Lines of thought and action that draw on collective intelligence and are open to its scrutiny will generally be better than idiosyncratic ones. Therefore, it makes sense to require that practicing professionals should attend to public forms of reasonableness. But this does not mean casting scientific knowledge as the guide or means of good practice. Student learning can also be improved by teachers' talking about teaching and looking at their own practice and by school norms that assume that teaching generally can be better than it is. Collegial interaction, reflection, and normative requirements are all based on moral beliefs—specifically, a sense of practical responsibility and professional obligation.

While being grounded in common sense, the connection of knowledge and utility, which includes the notion that the value of knowledge reduces to its utility, misses many of the points of acting and thinking. The commonsense equation of knowledge and certainty relates to absolutist views of knowledge and authoritative advocacy in social science and policy. Elevating these two strands of common sense—connection of knowledge and utility, equation of knowledge and certainty—to a "scientific" view legitimates the quest for knowledge utilization. In consequence, closure and reductionism supplant the openness that marks, in different ways, both common sense and scientific thinking. While common sense is open because of a vital disorganization and elasticity, science is open where it stresses fallibility and critique rather than certainty in the pursuit of knowledge. I argue that knowledge utilization erodes bases for good practice and encourages people to take knowledge as more certain and directly relevant to action than it is.

The concept of knowledge utilization implicitly sets policies urging the use of research knowledge in education. In the following section I will consider by what means these policies are evoked and rendered compelling. I give a brief account of what metaphors do and examine irrational implications surrounding the concept of knowledge utilization. When knowledge is used, it is seen as a good, but only insofar as it contributes to ends outside of itself. Understanding research knowledge in terms of utility is a limited and at times unwarranted view of knowledge. When practical judgment is seen as an exercise in knowledge utilization, the scope of concerns pertinent to educating people has been reduced to knowledge and utility. This reductionist view of practical wisdom captures neither the realities nor the ideals of educational practice.

IF KNOWLEDGE IS A TOOL, WHAT ELSE FOLLOWS?

In his essay, "The Two Cultures," Snow (1959/1963) quotes a scientist "who, when asked what books he read, replied firmly and confidently: 'Books? I prefer to use my books as tools'" (p. 14). Snow comments, "It was very hard not to let the mind wander—what sort of tool would a book make? Perhaps a hammer? A primitive digging instrument?" (p. 14). There is something odd about connecting knowledge and utility, which this anecdote brings out. What sort of utility might knowledge have? And why consider knowledge as a tool in the first place? To think of knowledge as a tool is to think metaphorically.

Metaphors are theory-laden. In fact, it is difficult to make a distinction between metaphors and theories (Scheffler, 1960, 1979). Discourse that is metaphorically structured by expressions that are part of common parlance has a built-in persuasive force (Lakoff & Johnson, 1980; Perelman & Olbrechts-Tyteca, 1969). The analogical material is often not perceived any more; the metaphor has become dormant. Its presuppositions and entailments have been assimilated into the common stock of reason and social practices. Thus the exploratory crossing of categories can take on the appearance of a report on isomorphisms (see Scheffler, 1979, p. 129), relying to some extent on matters of fact—created, in part, under the guidance of metaphors.

The concept of knowledge utilization construes knowledge in terms of utility and draws on the metaphor of knowledge as a tool; thus, the discourse about knowledge utilization is metaphorically structured. This is not of intellectual interest only. To use an example from Lakoff and Johnson (1980), people in Western cultures view arguments as wars. But in a culture where an argument might be seen as a dance, people having an argument would have different experiences and would conduct themselves in different ways. While their goal "is to perform in a balanced and aesthetically pleasing way" (p. 5), our goal is to win. The point is that people not only think and talk but live and act under the guidance of metaphors and other rhetorical evocations. The contentious posture of argument entails and sanctions *ends* and forms of *conduct*. Connecting knowledge and utility assumes that knowledge must be used to be of value.

The Concept of Knowledge Utilization

Utility is a measure of the good—in some ways of thinking, *the* measure of the good. According to the *Oxford Universal Dictionary*, utility is the "fact, quality, or character of being useful; fitness for a purpose; usefulness, serviceableness." More specifically, utility has to do with people's convenience or profit and is attributed to objects that satisfy their needs. To utilize means to make useful, turn to account; utilization signifies related processes or their results. The term *to utilize* and *utilization* similarly carry positive implications of value. As mixed concepts (Wilson, 1963), they do more than describe possible ways of acting. They connote dispositions and actions seen as praiseworthy, not in the sense of being noble or inspired but sensible and down-to-earth.

One's tool should not lie idle: Where knowledge is valued for its instrumental qualities, the charge to use it is almost implied. Only in special cases would using knowledge be wrong, as, say, when doing so could ruin a friend. Although it looks like a neutral term, descriptive of what people do or might do, the concept of knowledge utilization suggests what people *should* be doing and what knowledge *should* be like.

People should use knowledge and, by implication, knowledge should be useful. People ought to put knowledge into practice and operation; hence, knowledge should be constituted so that it could be turned to improving account. The concept of knowledge utilization in much modern usage entails normative theories that anchor action in knowledge and its use, and knowledge in the purposes of action. The expectation is that something good will come of this, exceeding purposes of knowing or understanding: One notes strong economic elements and an expectant emphasis on progress.

William James (1890/1981) saw such expectations as "fringes" (p. 249ff) of words and phrases suffused by a "feeling of tendency" (p. 240ff). Relations and ends, echoes and suggestions are perceived dimly and evoked too readily—habitually and instantaneously—to be noticed. These fringes connect words with past and future in a culture and surround them with a halo that is affectively charged. In this halo, reasons, premises, and conclusions are confounded with one another and with the hopes and fears of people.

Concepts with a neutral appearance that appeal to emotions and hint at what people had better do are tricky. They can bind one unwittingly to assumptions and entailments—in this case, about knowledge, the ends and nature of action, and sources of value. There is nothing wrong with entertaining assumptions, but it is a good thing to know where one makes them, what they are, and what they do. For, first of all, assumptions must be tenable. Second, there may be more than one set of tenable assumptions, with what is taken for granted representing only one possible set. Where a sense of alternatives is fading, given assumptions may go unrecognized while people live with their consequences.

The claims of colloquial reason depend on the taken-for-granted world of common sense. They refer to reality as their author and the authority that confers truth. Yet commonsense tenets surrounding the connection of knowledge and utility do not exhaust what colloquial reason has to say about knowledge and utility as concepts in their own right and in relation to action. I will consider below how common sense manages to be simpleminded about knowledge yet flexible and broadminded about goals.

COMMON SENSE: ENTRENCHMENT AND ELASTICITY

Wittgenstein's (1953) parable about ordinary language and formal symbolic systems provides the terms in which Geertz (1975) discusses common sense. As Geertz renders Wittgenstein's words:

> Our language can be seen as an old city: a maze of little streets and squares, of old and new houses, and of houses with additions from various periods;

and this surrounded by a multitude of modern sections with straight regular streets and uniform houses. (p. 5)

Ideology, epistemology, and quantum mechanics are in the suburbs of language. Common sense is situated somewhere between these suburbs and the maze of the old city; it is "a relatively organized body of considered thought, rather than just what anyone clothed and in his right mind knows" (p. 7). The emphasis is on "relatively organized" and "considered thought," as opposed to, on the one hand, the tight integration of formal systems and, on the other hand, the putative deliverances of direct experience. Common sense is an interpretation of collective experience and a historical system of thought.

But people do not see common sense in this way. They take pride in affirming that the tenets of colloquial reason "are immediate deliverances of experience, not deliberated reflections upon it" (Geertz, 1975, p. 7). That people learn about the way things are by taking experience to be the best teacher, learning the lessons of experience, and going to the school of hard knocks is, of course, a theory of learning, of the relationship of mind to reality, and of people's adaptation to the social world. It represents the commonsense account of learning about the real world—a theoretical account offered imperiously as the plain truth. Fallibility does not come into the picture at all. To cite Geertz (1975) again, the tenets of common sense "are conflated into comprising one large realm of the given and undeniable, a catalog of in-the-grain-of-nature realities so peremptory as to force themselves upon any mind sufficiently unclouded to receive them" (p. 7).

At issue here is not the adequacy or inadequacy of common sense, the degree to which its tenets are worthy or unworthy of belief. Rather, it is the style and general pretensions of commonsense assertions. Common sense objectifies judgment; it takes collective and historical accomplishments in language to be the real thing. Adequate or inadequate, common sense is in a state of entrenchment.

Common sense is entrenched, but not in terra firma. Though not apparent at close range, its grounds are shifting over time. At different times and places, they can be different to begin with. In modern cultures, planning and achieving are behavioral modes of utility that may circumscribe the value of knowledge. But the practicalness of common sense in tribal cultures, for instance, gives a place to knowledge that can be shared and enjoyed.

Ordering Interpretations Are Practical

Anthropologists have been puzzled by the taxonomic achievements of "primitives." American Indians know a lot about reptiles that they do not use for purposes of cooking or for show and display. Pueblans have an elaborate taxonomy of coniferous trees of no discernible use to them, and Pygmies can distinguish the leaf-eating habits of many species of bats. Reviewing this body of work, Geertz (1975) concludes that

> in an environment populated with conifers, or snakes, or leaf-eating bats it is practical to know a good deal about conifers, snakes, or leaf-eating bats, whether or not what one knows is in any strict sense materially useful, because it is of such knowledge that "practicalness" is there composed. (p. 21)

These so-called primitives are not driven by theoretical or material interests. They explore the world around them to make it intelligible. Variations of life and form in nature give people a sense of wonder that feeds on the capacity to name and order things. One never knows, such knowledge may come in handy. Meanwhile, it is a source of pleasure to the individual and part of the lore that gets passed on to the next generation.

Common sense is a system of deliberated thought that grows out of the variety of ends people conceive. It accommodates ideal as well as material interests, and many other things besides. The capacity for containing qualifications and even contradictory principles within its compass is a further sign of its broad-mindedness. This comes out clearly in comparing the utilitarian fascination with planning and achieving with an everyday phenomenon that Leites (1966/1969) terms the *horror of completion* (chap. 5).

Being of More Than One Mind About Things Is Reasonable

Grown-ups oppose a tendency of children not to bring their undertakings to a conclusion. This opposition gives rise to commands and complaints tedious to both sides. The rule of completion applies to work and play alike; its burden is determination, a fixed or settled purpose and the process of arriving at resolute intentions. But everyone knows that there is many a slip between the cup and the lip. And when plans work out as planned, or someone follows through on something, people are often surprised and somewhat awed. One has more sympathy for the waverer, the one who flinches, than for the person who follows through on things to the bitter end.

The following monologue describes the relation in which the impulse for action stands to its consummation or cancellation:

> Even though I am not sure of not wishing to complete an undertaking, I may feel that it is impossible for me to predict just how far I may wish to go before I actually undertake it. It may be only during the actual course of the

enterprise that it will become clear to me whether I intend to complete it or ensure that it miscarries. (Leites, 1966/1969, p. 144)

In the system of common sense, the rule of completion and the horror of completion exist in comfortable vicinity. They are loosely connected by the understanding that intentions may bind one to ends that turn out to be ill-conceived and that reasonable decisions often involve undoing. These insights do not conflict with the rule of completion but balance it, because plans of some moment ought not to be abandoned capriciously or lightly.

Similarly, the word *exploitation* and its connotations delimit and balance what is suggested by the term *utility* and *utilization*. "To exploit" is defined as "to achieve," "to turn to account," but also as "to utilize for selfish purposes." The very concept of exploitation presupposes an idea of conduct *not* dominated by self-regard or utility; and calling conduct "selfish" means to disapprove of it. The single-minded pursuit of utility is bound to miss important points of individual and social action. Purposes that govern thought and action to the exclusion of other concerns tend to be unwise in conception and harmful in their execution. Given the great many errors people are likely to make, unwavering intentions and beliefs are not adaptive. To have common sense means to be of more than one mind about things: about doing or undoing, exploring or exploiting the world, using knowledge or acting on principles and faith.

MORE THAN KNOWLEDGE AND UTILITY

Common sense tends to avoid the assumption that knowledge must be used to be of value (and hence associated problems) by a generalized process of introducing multiple purposes and considering a wide variety of ends. Thus Tribe (1971) concludes in examining the value of mathematical methods for the conduct of trials that—even if mathematical techniques had utility by increasing the accuracy of trial outcomes—a change of legal procedures resulting in a "trial by mathematics" would diminish the range of ideals enacted in the practice of law. For people, outcomes are not all that matters, and the use of knowledge is no good in itself.

Procedure can serve a vital role as conventionalized communication among a trial's participants, and as something like a reminder to the community of the principles it holds important. The presumption of innocence, the rights to counsel . . . , [and] the privilege against self-incrimination . . . matter not only as devices for achieving or avoiding certain kinds of trial outcomes, but also as affirmations of respect for the accused as a human being—affirmations that remind him and the public about the sort of society we want to become and, indeed, about the sort of society we are. (pp. 1391–1392)

The process of law is inspired by ends that we know cannot be achieved; fairness and equality of respect, for instance, are ideals unlikely to be realized in full. They guide the conduct of participants to varying degrees. The maximization of outcome accuracy that a trial by mathematics may advance would probably limit occasions for enacting these ideals in the community. Trials are not simply means to given ends: Their conduct affirms social ends, and changes in the trial process change the scope and specification of these ends, reminding us of who we are and what we want to be.

In general, when people live and think, the scope of their concerns encompasses more than knowledge and utility. It is true that part of the capacity for acting rightly is the habit and ability to give due weight to evidence and the arguments of others who may offer new data, ideas, or alternative explanations. But reducing the scope of concerns inherent to common sense while focusing on knowledge and utility is misleading. It assimilates the use of knowledge to virtue, defining commendable social and personal action as exercises in knowledge use in the pursuit of utility. This rules out as irrational, principled action driven by conviction rather than evidence and ignores the possibility that people may act rightly when inspired by transcendent ideals.

Utilitarian interpretations of the practical are thus unduly limited. The Aristotelian view is that practical wisdom means bringing to bear on a situation the largest number of pertinent concerns. Such concerns are not written into the situation but derive from observation and ideas, norms and commitments, and quiet inward thought. What we regard as known, then, enters into good practice along with other things as only one set of items to be considered. One must take into account that practical reason is exercised, nonrigorously, on the particular circumstances of a concrete case. Lacking severe exactitude and bearing upon singulars, practical reason is twice removed, by method and object, from scientific, theoretical thinking.

Practice is rooted in wanting things and making them happen (Anscombe, 1957). Yet the deliberative search is not, in the first place, a search merely for means but also a search for truly pertinent concerns and the best specification of practical ends. People ask themselves, "What shall I do?" in response to a situation that will make circumstantial demands on their practical and moral perception. All pertinent concerns will not be readily apparent, nor will their order be necessarily hierarchical or, for that matter, fixed (Wiggins, 1975/1978). Particular situations prompt people to reorder their concerns, keeping alive their sense of the many different points of living and acting. Rarely can they all be attended to; therefore, practical decisions tend to leave residues—things that still ought to be done. William James (1891/1969) remarked that "abstract rules indeed can help; but they help the less in proportion as our intuitions are more piercing, and our vocation is the stronger for the moral life" (p. 187).

Sometimes it is admirable to forge ahead in spite of the evidence. Truth claims may have to be subordinated to other concerns and considerations of utility put aside. Consider the example of a warrior. Courage, not foolhardiness, requires that the evil intent of an adversary, the likelihood of being wounded, and past experience of pain shall count for nothing (see McDowell, 1978). It is impossible to give an account of what is, in part, a deliberate failure to reckon with facts as *rational* without reference to virtue—here, the virtue of courage. Teaching also requires at times that what is known for a fact shall count for nothing.

In Teaching, Faith May Override Facts and Create New Realities

Teaching is predicated on a belief that a change for the better can in some way be effected through what a teacher does. An equivalent to the Hippocratic Oath for teachers is a commitment to teaching, whatever the prognosis appears to be. It is logically (and perhaps psychologically) impossible to take on this obligation without some belief that students can learn and teachers teach. Some faith in the possibility of student learning and the efficacy of schoolteaching needs to be upheld, whatever test scores, talk in the teachers' lounge, one's own misgivings, or the opinions of parents may imply to the contrary. In his chapter on the client-processing mentality, Lipsky (1980, chap. 10) makes a similar point. He argues that teachers should maintain a stance of constructive ambiguity with regard to the causes of student learning. For, if certain causal attributions—involving children, their backgrounds, or school resources—are assumed to *settle* questions of student achievement, living with demeaning group stereotypes and deficits in expectations, teaching goals, and student outcomes may become acceptable, perhaps routine, to education professionals.

Here it is instructive to touch on a counterexample, the case of Ms. Allen, one of the teachers studied by Carew and Lightfoot (1979). In the eyes of this teacher, "None of the children in her class were intellectually deficient" (p. 239), despite test scores or the results of psychological assessments. Where test information interfered with Ms. Allen's belief in the capacity of all children to learn, she would ignore it, on occasion spill coffee over it. Part of the point is that Ms. Allen was a very effective teacher by objective measures; her students, for instance, all were good readers. Typically, teachers are encouraged by the school system, test producers, and the media to treat test scores as facts about children. Ms. Allen probably felt that there was something wrong with that. Test scores are imperfect indicators of present and future performance, and the knowledge on which they are based is uncertain. If tests were perfect, however, Ms. Allen would seem foolhardy, not virtuous, to ignore them. Acts of romantic irresponsibility do not always result in happy consequences.

Though honoring facts can support good practice, it can stand in the way of honoring commitments. Of course, honoring commitments can create new facts, such as academic learning in students whose schooling or life experiences have taught them not to expect it. What practicing professionals do with knowledge held to be relevant to their work needs to be judged in light of values beyond truth. Knowledge may appear useful, given certain ends, but it does not follow that it should always be reckoned with.

It is true that a lack of knowledge makes teaching more difficult. Beyond the general imperfections of knowledge, perplexing deficiencies in knowledge include the facts that experience is ambiguous and that things can turn out variously in teaching. But note that the certainty wanting here can usually not be supplied by research knowledge. Accordingly, practical decisions lead people to assume too much and call for revising assumptions in retrospect. Yet what is done is done; only the thought of it can be changed. Hence, what matters is what the act is— what it is like, what it is for, what it changes or leaves as it is, and what comes of it for teachers and students. However, though the point of what people do in teaching is clearly dependent on outcomes, it cannot be accounted for by outcomes alone.

Common sense is properly practical, hence broadminded about goals: Its case for using knowledge is complicated and elastic. In educational research and policy, the connection of knowledge and utility is less casual and the commonsense tendency to temper monomania is less present. But if educational practice is not furthered by reducing its scope of concerns, neither is it advanced by the commonsense equation of knowledge and certainty. I will argue in what follows that both common sense and social science may be too convinced of the certainty of knowledge—a conviction that draws strength from the overarching connection of knowledge with utility.

EQUATING KNOWLEDGE AND CERTAINTY

While common sense may be taken as a starting point for practice and inquiry, this does not mean that it is equally sound on all questions. One would predict that common sense will not excel at reflection on the grounds of belief and the adequacy of knowledge claims. As explained earlier, its very style conveys an endorsement of a theory of mind and knowledge that makes critical probing seem pointless. What comes to mind through the senses is viewed as objectively true, seen as through an undistorting window pane. The commonsense theory of knowledge turns on the notion of immediate experience. But natural scientists regard even sense organs as impregnated with anticipatory theories. And in the philosophy of science, there are rival perspectives to the empiricism of the commonsense theory of knowledge. For example, the work of Popper, Lakatos, and Feyerabend challenges the notion of a simple sensory foundation and stresses the indirect, tentative character of knowledge.

When social scientists succumb to the fallacy of misplaced certainty, they draw on the commonsense theory of knowledge. Yet while the certitude of common sense is provokingly simple, science has elements of self-conscious certainty. Objectivity, abstract generality, and disinterestedness are invoked and function to strengthen scientific credibility. Tending to overestimate the certainty of their conclusions, scientists may lead others into the same error through the rhetoric they use in presenting their findings (Gusfield, 1976, 1981). Thus, according to Frankel (1973),

> Considerable damage has . . . been done by scientists, among whom social scientists are perhaps the most notable, who exaggerate the amount of sound and applicable knowledge they have and who offer confident solutions to social problems—solutions that, when tried, turn out to be only a mixture of pious hope and insular moral judgments. (p. 931; see also Campbell, 1975)

When scientists speak as if their metaphorical, parochial language is the voice of reality, they borrow an authority from common sense that needs to be challenged. Ironically, this authority gets turned against common sense in its flexible understanding of the wellsprings of action and knowledge.

Eroding the Concept of Knowledge

Equating knowledge with claims certified by science relegates to the irrational most everything by which people determine and decide problems of life: values (duty and enjoyment), ends, and commitments. Given this equation, what will drop out of serious consideration is almost all knowledge that ordinary people possess. As Weizenbaum (1979/1980) points out,

> People know a great many things that are neither products of research and scholarship nor materials in textbooks or archives, for example. They know what pleases people they see every day and what offends them. They know their way about their cities and what detours to take when the usual paths are blocked. (p. 555)

The obverse fallacy is to take anything as knowledge on which someone is willing to act, although this relativistic point of view also has its proponents. In their work on knowledge use and social problem solving, Lindblom and Cohen (1979), for instance, assert that 'whether it is true or false, knowledge is knowledge to anyone who takes it as a basis for some commitment or action" (p. 12) and make clear that those who take it as a basis for action will call it knowledge even if it is false.

People do not act on what they believe to be false at the time. However, although it is possible to entertain beliefs that are false, one cannot *know* something if it is false. Something is not true or reasonable just because someone takes it as a basis for action or commitment. Thus, in thinking about knowledge and practical decisions, one should be suitably broad-minded but must maintain requirements for justification. Upholding a belief that children can learn is usually justified. But sticking to what is mere opinion, false, or irrelevant will not support good practice.

The Difference Between Serious Possibility and Incorrigible Certainty

In part, good practice is the art of responding to urgency where perfect certainty is wanting and outcomes are unpredictable. But there is a difference between taking something to be a serious possibility to which one commits oneself in thought and action and *not* changing one's beliefs or policies when practical and epistemic circumstances change (Levi, 1980). The need to assume confidently some things in action does not imply taking for granted their unalterable certainty. Georg Simmel (1906/1950) points out that "confidence is intermediate between knowledge and ignorance" (p. 318).

> The person who knows completely need not trust; while the person who knows nothing can, on no rational grounds, afford even confidence. Epochs, fields of interest, and individuals differ, characteristically, by the measures of knowledge and ignorance which must mix in order that the single, practical decision based on confidence arise. (pp. 318–319)

Nowhere should the difference between serious possibility and incorrigible certainty be more keenly felt than in schools, places that are full of young people and that have change as an institutional mission. The moral import of this distinction derives from teachers in their separate classrooms holding social and epistemic authority in conjunction, having the final say on what is justified belief as an underpinning for classroom procedures and the enacted curriculum. Without a distinction between serious possibility and incorrigible certainty, the concept of knowledge is likely to affect (teaching) practices adversely. Making this distinction acknowledges the practical need for confidence—which also characterizes knowledge use in inquiry—while shifting the grounds of epistemic authority away from privileged sources of knowledge to processes by which beliefs can be probed and revised.

Knowledge must not be confused with the comforts of settled opinion. Trust and doubt are the two faces of knowledge use. For one cannot use knowledge without confidence, and its days as knowledge—justified belief—are numbered where trust is unwavering. The hesitation to trust is realized in observation, speculation, experiment, and revision—second thoughts that, on the whole, tend to be better than first ones.

Making a distinction between knowledge and certainty broadens the scope of valid practical concerns and allows for a more critical and hospitable conception of knowledge. Thus the different ways of being open that characterize common sense and scientific thinking could be brought to work together, increasing amounts and kinds of available wisdom. But reaping the best from both worlds requires distancing oneself from both colloquial and scientific versions of certainty.

GETTING IT WRONG BOTH WAYS

Common sense is sometimes knowledge when science is silent. Yet it seems that social science speaks with authority where it should lean on common sense and leans on common sense where caution would be indicated. There is an odd symmetry in this and a twofold potential for error. For, if social science is to make good its claim as a *social* science, it can ill afford to cut itself off from common sense, on the one hand, as a reliable, though not infallible, guide to the many points of acting and thinking. The commonsense theory of knowledge, on the other hand, "may be said to form the weakest point of common sense" (Popper, 1972, p. 104). Thus if social science is to make good its claim as social *science*, it can ill afford to rely on the commonsense theory of knowledge, either explicitly or implicitly in the rhetoric of implications and conclusions.

The place of knowledge in the scientific ethos explains why the concept of knowledge utilization is compelling to researchers. People whose lives are tied up with knowledge will feel that their preoccupations are important; if they live in a culture in which utility seems the end toward which everything gravitates, researchers may regard—or present—what they know as useful, irrespective of the degree to which that might be true. This is not to say that empirical or logical knowledge *cannot* be useful. But equating value and utility limits definitions of the useful. Useful knowledge could be seen as helpful, and helpful, in turn, as analytically ordering, broadening, or correcting perceptions or perspectives; calling to attention or questioning personal, cultural, and commonsense concepts and beliefs; and clarifying, probing, or refining people's sense of practical ends—their consistency, comprehensiveness, presuppositions, conflicts, and presumable costs and consequences (see Weber, 1904/1963).

Equating value and utility draws on common sense but does not exhaust colloquial understandings about the wellsprings of action and the value of knowledge. Equating knowledge and certainty is consistent with common sense, but disregards scientific acumen and criticism. These lopsided equations can be challenged by common sense and the philosophy or history of science joining forces. But the overarching connection of knowledge and utility—with its emotional accompaniments—supports empirical conditions that reinforce both equations, while masking their troublesome effects.

Empirical Conditions and Side Effects

In general, the concept of knowledge utilization presumes applicability and downplays the fallibility of knowledge. Researchers are no exceptions to the rule that, once asked for advice, people do not like to say that they have no opinion to give. Embedded in the social situation of giving advice are incentives to say something and, having started, to deliver oneself with an air of conviction and well-founded knowledge. Also, who would take or offer knowledge as ready for use that is labeled, "Fragile: Provisional and limited; deteriorates fast; please treat with caution"? Social expectations, the needs and hopes of people, and the pursuit of utility can undercut scientific wariness and tempt researchers to say more than they know—with the style and general pretensions of common sense but without its substance and vital elasticity.

Though better checks against false claims are built into the social system of science, scientists and ordinary people are not so differently placed if knowledge is seen as indirect, based on assumptions, and incompletely corroborated at best. Both groups are, however, differently placed in that, by the definition of their work, practicing professionals cannot avoid situations that will prompt them to overestimate the reliability and applicability of available knowledge. Yet when researchers enter the social situation of giving advice, this is no matter of necessity in the same sense, and it gives researchers a stake in social reality that does not come with their expert territory. In this fashion, the concept of knowledge utilization may encourage abusing the authority of science. Thus Merton (1942/1973) contends that "the possibility of exploiting the credulity, ignorance, and dependence of the layman" (pp. 276–277) is greatly reduced when scientists and the public *stay well apart:* "To the extent that the scientist–layman relation does become paramount, there develop incentives for evading the mores of science. The abuse of expert authority and the creation of pseudo-sciences are called into play when the structure of control exercised by qualified compeers is rendered ineffectual" (p. 277).

The quest for application under the banner of knowledge utilization can turn innocuous theorizing into practical follies. And it creates empirical conditions in which the languages of inquiry and of social authority are confounded with each other. This confusion cements the hierarchy of knowledge claims while working against reiterated knowledge testing. The confusion draws on the faith in knowledge prevalent in the American culture and eventually masks the inappropriateness and inefficacy of policies:

> Each form of language [e.g., language of authority, language of inquiry] performs a distinctive function that an analyst can recognize. But their empirical confusion serves an even more crucial political function. It clouds perception of which policies can be efficacious in achieving desired objectives; for premises, reasons, conclusions, and the affect engendered by widespread fears and hopes are confounded with each other. In this confusion lies a large part of the explanation for a frequent political phenomenon . . . : the continuation indefinitely of public support for policies that do not produce the benefits they promise and that are sometimes counterproductive. (Edelman, 1975, pp. 21–22)

Although it is true that practice and the application of knowledge may indicate needs for new basic knowledge, sharpen and stimulate conceptual development, and provide clues for how and where to pursue these scientific interests, their effective pursuit, then, requires the proper operation of the system of dispositions, incentives, and controls of scientific communities. Scientific mores are institutionalized in methods and procedures as well as in norms for behavior and mental conduct that shape the personal identities of researchers. These mores will loosen their hold on researchers to the extent that they move from the theoretical to the practical realm, thus undermining their principal foothold in society at large.

Many people look upon the distinction between theory and practice as invidious; it is almost bad form to uphold it. However, practitioners may be good at what they are doing, and their success can derive from faith, remembrance, habit, or imitation. Further improvement of practice that does not derive from research or theory is improvement just the same. On the other hand, it is not at all clear that people who are good at theorizing or fashioning ways of knowing are likewise good at improving practice. Actually, this belief can be challenged as a fantasy, an expression of thinking that does not obey the reality principle. In Anthony Powell's (1955) *A Dance to the Music of Time,* a protagonist comments on this propensity:

> Indeed, the illusion that anyone can escape from the marks of his vocation is an aspect of romanticism common to every profession; those occupied with the world of action claiming their true interests to lie in the pleasure of imagination or reflection, while persons principally concerned with reflective or imaginative pursuits are for ever asserting their inalienable right to participation in an active sphere. (p. 38)

Fantasy and egotism are related. T. S. Eliot (1920/1964a) draws attention to this connection while considering the consequences of the fact that people's intelligence—although it may be remarkable in one sphere—is rarely universal. "A brilliant man of science, if he is interested in poetry at all, may conceive grotesque judgments: like one poet because he reminds him of himself, or another because he expresses emotions which he admires; he may use art, in fact, as the outlet for the egotism which is suppressed in his own speciality" (pp. 10–11). Where educational researchers stray outside the boundaries of their expertise with attitudes that are naively self-centered and, in consequence, inept and deleterious, one must be firmly distrustful of their judgments.

The tentativeness of research knowledge is a safety catch that a pretension to usefulness tends to remove. The concept of knowledge utilization may defeat not only purposes of knowing, but purposes of action as well, for it overestimates the certainty of knowledge, underestimates the range of valid practical concerns, and misreads the intelligence of science by appealing to its authority.

CHAPTER 5

Reason and Romance in Argument and Conversation

Margret Buchmann

There is no direct route to knowledge or social action, no route that steers clear of what people say and imagine. Action and knowledge cannot be determined by impartial adherence to rules of evidence and scientific method alone. Talk can bring out the context-bound, partial, and tentative nature of educational knowledge (and this holds for practical, personal, and theoretical knowledge alike); it can make people aware of their various commitments and help them to see that educational research itself often aims to persuade (Floden, 1985).

WHY TALK IN EDUCATION?

People talk because knowledge is uncertain, because the outcomes of action are ambiguous, because their interests and beliefs differ—and because they need to learn. With different stakes in the outcomes of action and some sense that inferences from the data are rarely clear, people speculate on the course of events after the fact, connect and isolate incidents, question supposed proofs, dispute the relevance and value of evidence, and tell each other stories. The discourse approach to knowledge use in education and other areas of public concern fits with both the uncertainties of knowledge and the fact that people's actions proceed from their many differences. If people put aside attempts to eliminate fallibility or bolster their credibility, it seems that everyone can learn (see Cronbach et al., 1980).

Conditions for "Sweetness and Light"

People have ample reason to talk, but words can veil facts and feelings and serve those in power as well as clarify knowledge claims and grounds for action. If discourse is to contribute to greater justice and understanding, "all interested parties must be able to initiate discussion, to establish or influence the rules of conversation, to put forward statements, to request elaboration and clarification, and to call other statements into question" (Cohen & Garet, 1975, pp. 42–43). To meet requirements for a democratic organization of discourse, all participants must distance themselves from *authoritative* views of knowledge and they must *listen*. While the first step toward learning may therefore be silence, requirements for *justification* must also be met. When errors are likely and feelings conflicting, it does not follow that anything goes: A proliferation of delusions is not learning.

In groups with diverse participants, the processes and outcomes of discourse can easily drift away from what is true, right, or better. Where people do not appeal to such standards, talking may simply reinforce existing misconceptions and inequalities. And where interests conflict, there are few incentives for giving up recognized power and status. The cumulative effects of past patterns of participation are also resistant to change; thus, for instance, "the habits developed through past interactions between researchers and teachers will not incline teachers to ask questions. Their expectation is to be told what research has found to be true, not to raise questions about why they should believe research claims" (Floden, 1985, p. 31). Nor can a democratic organization of discourse make people equally good at talking, let alone understanding.

Explaining what one takes for granted is difficult, especially when one's audience is inclined to be puzzled or dismissive. People aiming to learn from each other must therefore have particular strengths and abilities. They need to be honestly attentive, flexible and firm, and somewhat detached from their given states of mind. Over time, participants will have to work out rules about what sorts of talk are appropriate for what purposes. Yet norms of communication are already working and in place; they flow from the life and work of people and the way talk tends to serve their goals. Language works differently in different groups, is about different things, and aims at different outcomes, for instance, either to clarify things—testing logical consistency and entailments—or to get them *done*.

Words With Power?

> The word and silence are incomplete phenomena, only when combined do they represent the true whole, for which there is no name. . . . Light alone and darkness alone, glare and gloom, destroy. But living brightness and living darkness are mutually related. (Guardini, 1965, p. 217)

The notion of improving education by talking depends on a belief that one can do things with words, a belief that not all people share and that is only partially true. Words have limited powers, and expansive articulation has involved relations to morality and knowledge. Quiet attention furthers learning. Tact, caution, and kindness demand that much remain unsaid. On the other hand, spelling out one's underlying sense of the good in clear and descriptive language helps others and oneself to see and examine one's life. On this ancient perspective, logic and linguistic articulacy almost define being human: "We aren't full beings in this perspective until we can say what moves us, what our lives are built around. . . . The central notion here is that articulation can bring us closer to the good as a moral source, can give it power" (Taylor, 1989, p. 92).

Making lucid articulation central to human being and goodness gives a special place to academics. But capacities for analysis do not in themselves enhance one's scope of vision or contribute to what Aristotle termed "greatness of soul": thinking well of others and being hopeful as well as capable of laughter. Moreover, the ability to give precise conceptual utterance—identifying clearly recognizable elements of an idea and tracing the provenance and usages of concepts—will not in itself remove conflict or confusion. One may believe that philosophers, in the words of Rorty (1982),

> know what is going on, in a way in which these people who don't know the genealogy of the terms, or phrases, cannot. This is a *non sequitur.* If a physician is torn between respect for the dignity of her patient and the need to minimize his pain, she is not confused on matters which the philosopher . . . is clear about. Being articulate is a virtue, but it is not the same as eliminating confusion, the attainment of clarity. (p. 223)

The patient's and doctor's troubles are not created by lacks of analytic skills, nor are they susceptible to *logical* resolutions. The dilemma does not yield to explication or learned little lectures. Listening, rather than talking, may help the doctor to find "words with power" and the necessary *silences:* to comfort and be present, consider what is known, discern the needs of the patient, and look into her own heart. No outcomes of articulacy, "being there" and "noticing things" are central to morality and learning.

Trusting reliance on verbal illumination is somewhat naive. Can criticism and public debate, for another instance, be free and *blind* with regard to social authority and personal interest (Popper, 1972)? The willingness to be proven wrong, over and over again, and impartial attention to the merits of a case, no matter where it comes from, presuppose a distinctive purity of motives and capaciousness of mind. J. S. Mill (1840/1962) was not sanguine about the process and outcomes of debate among people who differ: "In truth, a system of consequences from an opinion, drawn by an adversary, is seldom of much worth. Disputants are rarely sufficiently masters of each other's doctrines, to be good judges of what is fairly deducible from them, or how a consequence which seems to flow from one part of the theory may or may not be defeated by another part" (pp. 130–131).

To think of knowledge use as equitable and enlightening discourse may be desirable and inspiring, but how well founded is this conception? I will consider this question by comparing argument and conversation, examining presuppositions, limits, and relations of both approaches to communication.

CONTROL AND PROGRESS THROUGH ARGUMENTS?

When social scientists regard arguments and rationally motivated consensus as the best way to legitimate and successful reforms, they believe that talk can uncover assumptions and values that shape and distort the production and use of knowledge (see Dunn, 1982). I have already mentioned some reasons why talk will not always illuminate; silence as "the other side of language" (Fiumara, 1990) is obviously important. Nor is consensus always rationally motivated, especially in attempts at social change. And does the better argument have a peculiar force? Perhaps, but so have the memories of people and the anecdotes they hear.

Arguments at their best move critically and efficiently in the realm of concepts within systems of deliberated thought. They involve opponents, testable claims, and rules of cool reasoning. Social reforms, however, have to do with "practical imagining," which aims to fill the world with things we both desire and approve (Oakeshott, 1959/1962). Moral sentiments are established by custom and tested by time, while people are supposed to mind them; take care to remember, for instance, the kinds of concerns and dispositions their clients and the public have a right to expect of doctors and teachers. Thus, we cannot account for social improvements by the powers of arguments alone. Good sense and feeling are also necessary.

People determine what to do about problems of individual and social life based on the information available to them, personal beliefs, and traditions. Popper (1962) emphasizes tradition—in point of quality *and* quantity—as "by far the most important source of our knowledge.... Most things we know we have learned by example, by being told, by reading books, by learning how to criticize, how to take and accept criticism, how to respect truth" (p. 56). While this fact makes antitraditionalism futile, it does not entail taking a passive attitude toward tradition. Of all the multitudinous things we have absorbed implicitly, however, only some can be brought to awareness and even fewer tested as to their full and fair grounding. In many ways, people keep each other company, wandering in the dark; as Locke (1690/1959) wrote three centuries ago:

> Who almost is there that hath the leisure, patience, and means to collect together all the proofs concerning most of the opinions he has, so as safely to conclude that he hath a clear and full view; and that there is no more to be alleged for his better information? And yet we are forced to determine ourselves on the one side or other. The conduct of our lives, and the management of our great concerns, will not bear delay: for those depend, for the most part, on the determination of our judgment in points wherein we are not capable of certain and demonstrative knowledge. (p. 371)

Locke concludes that our shared ignorance calls for "friendship, in the diversity of opinions" (p. 372) and "the gentle and fair ways of information" (p. 373). Where people argue, instead, for the sake of winning, arguments can distort the facts and mislead intentions, just as unexamined beliefs can do.

Though some consensus is necessary for social reform, it is not true that arguments make their distinctive contributions to the agreement of people with one another, enabling them to act. Other limitations of argument as a discourse model of knowledge use derive from the influence of argumentative rules on *subject matter* (not everything on people's minds is discussable), from *hierarchical relations* (differences in power and status), and from the *outcomes* one can expect when people are contestants, fighting for different things and wrangling for victory with a certain cold hardness.

Argument is a dress rehearsal of speech with its own dramatic purposes; its performance requirements determine chances of success. Moreover, differences in power, status, and skills count already when people settle what should be discussed; not every group has what it takes to make a social problem an issue of public notice and debate. It is useful to recall that disputation flourished in the Middle Ages, when crucial issues—such as what is true and right or who is entitled to power and rewards—had already been settled, as it were, out of court. Social predestination and unequal patterns of participation are factors still present.

Contemporary philosophers and social theorists nevertheless show faith in the redeeming power of argument. Thus Habermas (1973; Habermas & Luhmann, 1971) posits an ideal speech situation undistorted by power and interests; he makes the strange claim that beliefs capable of legitimating action can be formed *only* under conditions of absolutely free and unlimited debate. If one took this seriously, one would have to write off most things people do as either unjustified or unjustifiable. Neither is public debate likely to expose scientific error. People find it difficult to understand why scientists take only some evidence seriously (Polanyi, 1967), and scientists pay little attention to notions they find lacking in rigor or otherwise distasteful (Boring, 1929/1963).

Argument as an Adversarial Practice

People are more just to their own, whether kith and kin or ideas. A lack of impartiality limits the viability of an argument model of knowledge use when people differ not only in opinions, but in power, status, and the requisite skills. For argumentative fencing depends on verbal agility and vigilance, on guarding oneself while carrying devastation into the enemy's camp by cross-examination and logical blows. The use of mind is strategic and tactical, and the name of the game is war.

> We don't just *talk* about arguments in terms of war. We can actually win or lose arguments. We see the person we are arguing with as an opponent. We attack his positions and we defend our own. We gain and lose ground. We plan and use strategies. If we find a position indefensible, we can abandon it and take a new line of attack. . . . It is in this sense that the ARGUMENT IS WAR metaphor is one that we live by in this culture; it structures the actions we perform in arguing. (Lakoff & Johnson, 1980, p. 4)

Arguments among different people are likely to draw on different kinds of knowledge, yet the party winning the battle may not have the best knowledge or intentions. Distinct from wisdom and sensitivity, levels of sophistication shape argumentative outcomes, and the possession of a special or latinized vocabulary strengthens one's position—regardless of whether its use is informative, ornamental, or coercive. Meehl's (1971) hierarchical example makes this vivid: "The parish priest can refute the theological objections of an unlettered Hausfrau parishioner. The priest, in turn, will lose a debate with the intellectual village atheist. C. S. Lewis will come out ahead of the village atheist. But when C. S. Lewis tangles with Bertrand Russell, it gets pretty difficult to award the prizes" (p. 71). All down the line, rich or well-founded ideas do not guarantee winning the dispute; and someone who maintains an attitude of openness in questioning and seeking truth may come off worse (see Gadamer, 1965/1975, p. 330). Hence, appearing defeated in an argument may not be a good reason to give up practices or beliefs.

We have no reason to assume that warm feelings, buried premises, oblique references, and beliefs that are inarticulate must be associated with indefensible ideas or lines of action. Argument models of knowledge use equate the love of clarity and argument with the pursuit of wisdom—a confusion that stems from the beginnings of philosophy. The continuity of argument models of knowledge use with the classic and medieval tradition of disputation is a genuine continuity, too, in that the way of argument is seldom that of the mother tongue. People can be shrewd and, for that matter, right without mastering argumentative moves or feeling confined by them. While some commitments are too elusive and firmly engrained for debates, they can steady people in their pursuit of truth or goodness. On the other hand, an absence of intellectual curiosity, vigorous sensitivity, and ethical circumspection is compatible with acuteness and success in argument. We cannot equate wanting to say things with wanting to discover them.

Romance and Illusions Surrounding Arguments

Rorty (1982) stresses the difference between the love of argument and the pursuit of wisdom, maintaining that adversarial modes of discourse substitute the goal of winning for that of understanding, while fostering illusions of professorial competence. People whose academic socialization has taught them to despise history as well as stories may take some pride in being keen and clever. Yet the self-esteem and public image of academics must be adjusted to what they actually learn and practice. If philosophy professors, for instance, "were traditionally thought of as wise because they were believed to have read and experienced much, traveled far in the realms of thought, pondered the great problems which have always troubled the human spirit" (p. 221), this contemplative image has vanishing foundations.

In the argumentative mode, thought turns upon itself with little mercy; this is the proof of its incisive quality. "A clear logical conscience," says Peirce (1877/1955), "does cost something—just as any virtue, just as all that we cherish, costs us dear" (p. 21); this notwithstanding,

> the genius of a man's logical method should be loved and reverenced as his bride, whom he has chosen from all the world. . . . She is the one that he has chosen, and *he knows that he was right in making that choice* [italics added]. And having made it, he will work and fight for her . . . and will strive to be the worthy knight and champion of her from the blaze of whose splendours he draws his inspiration and his courage. (pp. 21–22)

Somewhat startling but instructive, Peirce's fervent phrases carry us into realms of chivalry, romance, and noble virtue, in hopes that (pure) logos will be glorious in the end. The story of knights and maidens in their castles—of fearless endurance crowned by the yielding of the (pure) object of desire—has, of course, transcendent and consoling appeal. But it does not follow that this elevating story is true, or that its inspiration and lessons have much of an application to the seeking, gaining, and using of knowledge.

A rapturous monogamy of the mind—being wedded to logic and argumentation as the purifying, right method—may not yield its rewards in terms of good sense or good science. In his historical work on the discipline of psychology, Boring (1929/1963) concludes that people's halting progress toward understanding needs overconfidence and batlike blindness as well as Peirce's clear logical conscience. He warns that a scientist must not "be the judge too often, for then the assured, prejudiced, productive personality might get 'squeezed out,' and science would be the loser" (p. 83). Knowledge in itself and for the social world cannot depend on the aspirations of argument alone. Pure reasoning may not be faultless. While argumentation brings virtues into play, its heroics can be divisive, restrictive, and punitive. Besides, people who seem hardheaded can be obtuse and given to gratifying illusions. What is sacrificed by argument and for its purposes may be central to action and learning. For reason to realize its modest rewards, it must negotiate the dark and unnerving terrain between people.

> This terrain is uneven, full of sudden faults and dangerous passages where accidents can and do happen, and crossing it, or trying to, does little or nothing to smooth it out to a level, safe, unbroken plain, but simply makes visible its clefts and contours. (Geertz, 1986, p. 119)

CONVERSATION, SILENCE, AND THE SPIRIT OF LIFE

If convincing other people is the aim, subduing them by argument is often a poor means. For one cannot convince others of something without knowing their ways of thinking, including how they have reached *their* conclusions. Such matters are found out by listening, not talking, and may require a delayed response or no response at all; thus a young man reflects:

> My education was all a preparation for a certain mental virtuosity, a very hard, clear, reasoned way of thinking, and examining evidence, and de-

fending a logical position. I was taught to regard anybody who didn't bear the hall-mark of this training as wooly-minded and half-educated. It's a useful training in its way as far as it goes.

But.... You can argue the hind leg off a donkey, but that won't teach you any more about donkeys. Whatever method you may have used in forming your own opinions, you must understand other people's methods before you can hope to get anyone to agree with you. You'll never induce a man to change his mind by making him look silly. You merely put his back up. (Kennedy, 1936/1967, p. 300)

Implacable or evasive, silence can increase distance. It can signal boredom, yet also an expectant openness or kinship and affection beyond words. Silence can mean contempt as well as revealing attention. "A person who simply listens is possibly not much, but he is not isolated in the sense that he is connected once again to a network of vivid, moving and complex dynamics" (Fiumara, 1990, p. 61). Martin Buber (1929/1947a) notes that—just as eager talking does not entail communication—so silence can be speaking; and actually finding a listener who matches one's own thoughts tone by tone can paradoxically turn one's own assertions into questions. Hence, attacks are not always needed for boundaries of understanding to recede.

Talkers often delude themselves about the implications of silence. If listeners seem unable to answer or challenge them, this need not mean that the listeners have given way or changed their minds. In being evasive, softness can be unyielding. If one is busy finding holes in what other people are saying or is eager to score a point, what one can learn is restricted by these purposes. Thus, one is also not likely to change one's mind. In either case, if the knowledge being offered is valuable and unequally shared, these outcomes are disappointing. They also throw doubt on the belief that arguments will uniquely contribute to equity and learning.

Far from representing an undistorted speech situation, the concept of argument may be an emblem of group differences. Arguments import their own distortions—adversarial attitude, goal substitution (winning instead of understanding), censorship—into discourse. Fiumara (1990) suggests that these distortions involve dominating and defensive responses to the abundance and unruliness of life; trying to construct a theoretical or conceptual net from which nothing can escape is a "relentless battle ... as an attempt ... to organize everything in the light, or shadow, of the 'best' principles of knowledge: a chronic struggle of territorial conquest" (p. 21). Thus, Wittgenstein (1980) recalls that, in the course of their conversations, Russell would often exclaim: "Logic's hell!":

> I believe our main reason for feeling like this was the following fact: that every time some new linguistic phenomenon occurred to us, it could retrospectively show that our previous explanation was unworkable. (We felt that language could always make new, and impossible, demands; and that this made all explanation futile.) (p. 30e)

This sense of defeat and futility stems from the conquering pretensions of argument: the heroic struggles of logic and lucidity. "In the annals of philosophy the hope of mental control of the Absolute recurs in the euphorias of fearless reason and dies in melancholy skepticism" (Kolakowski, 1972/1989, p. 54). Heroes stand alone, seeing others in their own light.

The Pastoral Romance of Conversation

The move from argument to conversation involves shifting metaphorical grounds from battlefields to country meadows, where disorder need not be rebelliousness. We pass from romances featuring strong (though not silent) heroes to the company of ordinary people, "trivial and irreplaceable," as Martin Buber (1929/1947a, p. 35) calls them. Conversation is no intellectual privilege: "It does not begin in the upper story of humanity. It begins no higher than where humanity begins" (p. 35). Like life, conversation can be busy with many things and vibrant with a sense of different directions. Conversation is close to the comic spirit, which embraces people's frailty and allows for laughter and emotional release.

If conversations are uniting and disarming, they can still inspire apprehension and do not divest communication of its formidable character. Nor is emotional release a deliverance from pain, for we have *feelings* about what we value: things we desire and rightly fear to lose. Hence, emotions such as fear, grief, love, and anger

> are *webs of connection and acknowledgment* [italics added], linking the agent with the worth of the unstable context of objects and persons in which human life is lived. Fear involves the belief that there are big important things that may damage us, and that we are powerless. . . . Love involves the ascription of a very high value to a being who is separate from the subject and not fully controlled. (Nussbaum, 1990, p. 387)

The other is, for us, "a free being in all personal situations: in trust, in love, in hate, in the bitterness of refusal and the disaster of parting, in the risk of fascination, in submission of rapture, in the pangs of disenchantment" (Kolakowski, 1972/1989, p. 55). Lifting restraints on feelings will remind one of being needy, incomplete, and vulnerable in a general sense; it also keeps one open to grief and reproaches. People's hopes are based on experiences of inadequacy and unbearable separation.

As an expression of life and hope, conversation brings to mind a poetic pastoral, where people have mother wit, the setting is natural and simple, and amiability will carry the day. The hero of pastoral romance is no "exceptionally brave or strong person, but only a modest and pleasant young man[,] . . . a shepherd with no social pretensions, except that he is also a poet and a lover" (Frye, 1967, p. 24). Wordsworth (1800/1904) explains that, in such poetry, "humble and rustic life was generally chosen, because in that condition the essential passions of the heart find a better soil in which they can attain their maturity, are less under restraint, and speak a plainer and more emphatic language . . . and, consequently, may be more *accurately* [italics added] contemplated" (p. 791). Related to this, Wordsworth describes the poet as "a more *comprehensive* [italics added], soul, . . . pleased with his own passions and volitions, and . . . rejoic[ing] more than other men in the spirit of life that is in him" (pp. 793–794).

Acknowledgment, comprehensiveness, and accuracy are related to truth and illumination. Otherwise, there is nothing particularly pure or exalted about conversation. Being less guarded, ideas and feelings collide and mingle with one another and are diluted, rounded off, and complicated in the process. Conversational tones are rarely steely. People do not insist that partners follow: It is enough that they enter into conversation.

The Charm and Freedom of Conversation

Conversations can be long, intermittent, inconclusive as in marriage, and continued in the absence of one's partners. Arguments are driven by hopes of coming to rest upon conclusions, but conversations are not driven at all. To some extent following laws of indirection, they begin with differences or notions often vaguely apprehended and, after a while, do not so much end as are abandoned. Arguments favor the here and now, but conversations assign importance to stories and history.

What makes conversations attractive is their enveloping quality and a capacity for surprising turns. Conversations have flexible rules of relevance, evidence, and progression. Condensing fables and finely detailed observations have their place—and so have stretches of argument. Conversations therefore broaden one's conceptual repertoire and moral imagination. They thrive on readiness of speech and language, yet sidelong glances, repeated starts, and arm-waving allusions are all right.

Although they can be elegant rather than awkward, conversational exchanges are thus not disconcerted by ideals of perfection in clarity, parsimony, and coherence. One may get answers to questions one never thought of asking (but ought to have asked) or have one's answers answered in odd, little gusts of inconsecutive thought that interrupt one's plans and preconceptions. The progress of conversation need not be linear: "Like writing, saying might also go from right to left, or even from bottom to top, from forwards backwards, or in still other directions that we are not even able to envisage" (Fiumara, 1990, p. 177). But conversations are not mere talk: they presuppose good faith, *some* common purposes or emergent directions, and the assumptions that people say things they believe to be relevant and will attend (in some fashion) to what others are saying (see Grice, 1975). In short, conversations require being decent and sensible in ways that establish and maintain connections and openness.

While conversations sidestep competition, they are encounters in which the power of mind, good sense, and moral sentiments of a person come to be revealed. As Johnson said, "Men might be very eminent in a profession, without our perceiving any particular power of mind in them in conversation" (Boswell, 1799/1953, p. 1078). In conversation, one listens to persons, not just utterances. Here one comes close to people, to what they know, desire, imagine, and can barely say—and a person who simply listens can be profoundly connected and filled with living force. In the end, silent attention can communicate "the general and surprising apprehension of the precariousness of all language, meaning, knowledge" (Nemerov, 1975/1978, p. 109).

In conversation, people of thought and people of action can please themselves and be true to type, although self-constituted elites or self-impressed individuals will not fare well. One can imagine conversation to be, ideally, like writing at its best, where, as T. S. Eliot (1943/1971) wrote, "every word is at home."

> Taking its place to support the others,
> The word neither diffident nor ostentatious,
> An easy commerce of the old and the new,
> The common word exact without vulgarity,
> The formal word precise but not pedantic,
> The complete consort dancing together. (p. 58, "Little Gidding")

Practice "is recognized not as an isolated activity but as a partner in a conversation, and the final measure of intellectual achievement is in terms of its contribution to the conversation in which all universes of discourse meet" (Oakeshott, 1959/1962, p. 199). Science likewise need not be anything other than itself: It can speak to the mind and about truth with the understanding that meaning in the realm of science is not that of everyday discourse. Conversations accordingly respect not only differences but the *limits* of meaning, knowing, and speaking—realistically including some awareness of their own limitations.

Facile and Erratic Tendencies of Conversation

Conversation can yield insights and astonishing connections; yet it cannot *establish* knowledge. Johnson reminds us that "general principles must be had from books, which, however, must be brought to the test of real life. In conversation, you never get a system" (Boswell, 1799/1953, p. 624). Likewise, if people please themselves and remain true to type, they will be comfortable but vulnerable to denseness and inertia. As Thomas Traherne (1675/1966) put it, "Contentment is a sleepy thing" (p. 146).

Erratic tendencies of conversation are associated with a decline into obscurity and rigidity. If one never examines one's vastly deep convictions, they remain hazy and disconnected; if one never singles out certain things to pursue them, they remain fugitive fancies. Hence, although

> lack of clarity and focus does not preclude useful verbal interchanges, it does make it more difficult to sort the erroneous ideas from the muddled but proper convictions. Doing that requires removing some lack of clarity and filling some gaps in an argument. That takes effort. (Floden, 1985, p. 26)

Tranquil satisfaction with one's doings, thoughts, and feelings can be complacent. If one never presses one's points, one may founder on one's fallacies and expansive vagaries—or do one's partner the disservice of tolerating what is ill-judged or fantastic, though strongly felt. The other side of peaceful acquiescence is passive compliance or submission.

Lack of discrimination verges toward indifference, and in being indifferent, people fail themselves, their partners, and their principles. Differences should *not* always be smoothed out. Geertz (1986) concludes that "'understanding' in the sense of comprehension, perception, and insight needs to be distinguished from 'understanding' in the sense of agreement of opinion, union of sentiment, or commonality of commitment. . . . We must learn to grasp what we cannot embrace" (p. 122). The admirable George Meredith (1879/1947) put it like this in his prelude to *The Egoist*: "Why, to be alive, to be quick in the soul, there should be diversity in the companion-throbs of your pulses. Interrogate them" (p. 3).

To ward off or delimit facile and erratic tendencies of conversation, one must be alert and distinguish between attention and assent or submission, either indiscriminate or insincere. To submit quietly can be quite wrong. One must insist upon the differences between openness, vacuous tolerance, and eventual repression. In other words, one must take recourse to lucid articulation and argumentation, in addition to listening and silence in conversation. Guarded acceptance can be appropriate. As arguments mislead where they remain impoverished communication, so cozily confirming conversations are vulnerable to a capitulation of reason or to its "dispersive flaking away" (Fiumara, 1990, p. 182). While some monitoring is therefore needed, overwhelming logical measures are not required. Instead, we should attempt a conversational posture "both accepting and critical, trusting and diffident, irrepressible and yet consoling" (Fiumara, 1990, p. 90). And a little dryness won't hurt.

THE CANOPY OF CONVERSATION

One might conclude that argument and conversation as discourse models of knowledge use are each equally truncated, each being a view of communication reduced by its better half—the first detached from propensities to receive and listen; the second diminished by a waning of principles: "The grey shades of science, laws and principles . . . vanish like a lifeless mist" (Hegel, 1807/1931, p. 385). On this symmetrical proposition, we have light without sweetness and sweetness without light— and the solution seems an equal partnership, as a modern connubial model primly remote from heroic and pastoral romances.

Yet I cannot give much credence to this model. Its symmetry is wanting in ease and freedom; its abstract conception has a gloss that does not reflect the inexplicable and ominous in ordinary experience. Listening to party talk, a protagonist in Virginia Woolf's (1937) novel, *The Years*, thus slips into a nightmare: "He felt that he had been in the middle of a jungle; in the heart of darkness; cutting his way towards the light; but provided only with broken sentences, single words, with which to break through the briarbush of human bodies, human wills and voices, that bent over him, binding him, blinding him" (p. 411). Pretending that all conversational entries can be sorted out by bright arguments fails to admit of impending darkness and fragility and, accordingly, of the need for miracles and grace in communication.

Areas of meaning, Berger (1967) avers, are "carved out of a vast mass of meaninglessness, a small clearing of lucidity in a formless, dark, always ominous jungle" (p. 24); although talking may hold our world together, the thread of conversation is thin and wavering. In his lyrical poem, "Two in the Campagna," Robert Browning (1855/1895) offers the image of a "floating weft," but he puts his conclusions with a lighter touch, more wonderingly, and with less of a sense of desolation.

> Must I go
>
> Still like the thistle-ball, no bar,
>   Onward, whenever light winds blow,
> Fixed by no friendly star?
>
> Just when I seemed about to learn!
>   Where is the thread now? Off again!
> The old trick! Only I discern—
>   Infinite passion, and the pain
> Of finite hearts that year. (p. 189)

Pitted against the "heart of darkness" is not sheer intellect but hope, not sophistication but a *second* innocence of reason. "The sense of the congenial, of a genuine human communication . . . comes from the innocent vision at the heart of all human creation and the response to it" (Frye, 1990, pp. 88–89). In the consort of communicative modes, argument cannot be an equal partner, for in its refiner's fire, variations become, again, impurities—"divergencies from some ideal, non-idiomatic manner of speaking" (Oakeshott, 1959/1962, p. 206). On the other hand, conversations can accommodate varieties of voices, including judicious passages of argument. Hence I will opt for conversation as a tender romance of reason, where discourse, shining with warmth from within, holds a promise of congeniality and comfort, if not light. Understanding is no trophy of pride. It is in this spirit, I believe, that Buber (1929/1947a) speaks of the "tiny strictness and grace of every day" (p. 36) as the *breakthrough* in dialogue.

Peirce (1877/1955) concedes that people are not, in the main, logical animals, but rather naturally inclined toward being more hopeful and sanguine than experience and logic would warrant; yet "it is probably of more advantage to the animal to have his mind filled with pleasing and encouraging visions, independently of their truth" (p. 8). The yields of conversation are different from those of heroic romances: There are no translucent perfections, no transcendent victories. Like life, conversation grants no irreversible clarification. Under its canopy, gifts and risks are commensurate with the scope and qualities of conversation. They are the promises and dangers of our kind. "The reason why most of us are unaware of this precariousness most of the time is grounded in the continuity of our conversation with significant others. The maintenance of such continuity is one of the most important imperatives of social order" (Berger, 1967, p. 17).

There are good reasons for preferring companionable to warlike visions, fallibilism to perfectionism, the middling to the conquering classes and pretensions, hope and tolerant laughter to the cynicism and destruction induced by raging attempts at controlling the "blooming, buzzing confusion" of life. While conversations cannot make them pure, they can make one's fixed thoughts fluid and permeable to the mystery of difference. Auerbach (1946/1953, p. 13) points out that, in the epics of Homer, we are always reminded of the real world, which means nothing but itself; ordinary life with its shepherds' huts, washing days, feasts, and palaces must be imagined as *enveloping* the heroic struggles. Let argument, likewise, be *nested* in conversation as an encompassing romance of reason, on the understanding that "any story which we tell about ourselves consoles us since it imposes pattern upon something which might otherwise seem intolerably chancy and incomplete" (Murdoch, 1970, p. 87). To close with the words of a German poet:

> It is not good
> To let mortal thoughts
> Empty the soul. But conversation
> Is good, and to say
> What the heart means, to hear
> Much about days of love
> And deeds that have been done.
>   (Hölderlin 1807/1972 "Remembrance," pp. 91, 93)

CHAPTER 6

Dilemmas and Virtues
in Research Communication

Margret Buchmann

> Truth can never be told so as to be understood, and not be believ'd.
>
> —William Blake, 1790/1963, *The Marriage of Heaven and Hell*

In his expansive, many-layered vision, John Dewey brings together communication, experience, art, and learning. Nor are social relations and change left out of the picture. Dewey's (1916/1966) vision of communication as appreciation of meaning and collective growth is my starting point.

> To be a recipient of a communication is to have an enlarged and changed experience.... Nor is the one who communicates left unaffected. Try the experiment of communicating, with fullness and accuracy, some experience to another, especially if it be somewhat complicated, and you will find your own attitude toward your experience changing; otherwise you resort to expletives and ejaculations. The experience has to be formulated in order to be communicated. To formulate requires getting outside of it, seeing it as another would see it, considering what points of contact it has with the life of another so that it may be got into such form that he can appreciate its meaning. Except in dealing with commonplaces and catch phrases one has to assimilate, imaginatively, something of another's experience in order to tell him intelligently of one's own experience. All communication is like art. (pp. 5–6)

Other people are not vessels waiting to be filled by one's overflowing fountain of knowledge. Instead, they are fellow travelers in a world provisionally charted with understandings that collide and move past each other.

Where understandings are shared, expletives and ejaculations can often take the place of searching formulations. This holds for radiologists routinely examining a chest x-ray or mathematicians looking at a dissertation proposal within their specialty. Communicative requirements change when the proposal writer has to be told why her ideas for a thesis are wanting or the patient viewing his x-ray has to grasp the fact that he is doomed. Beyond understanding, the question in such cases is, "What is to be done?" Facts as we know them are consistent with multiple lines of action fashioning futures that are inconsistent with one another: trying out an experimental drug, quietly turning inward, or starting to do all the things for which there never seemed to have been time; revising one's dissertation proposal, changing one's advisors, or giving up on academia with a certain relief.

The task of educational researchers communicating what they believe to have learned to people not in their business resembles these latter cases, including the urgent question of what should be done. Imaginative assimilations of different vantage points and modes of representing what one knows must replace gestures, symbols, and terse allusions born of working conventions and beliefs. When insiders try to look at the familiar from the outside in, they may come to see forgotten limitations and enchanting odd details; outsiders can bring to bear their inconvenient questions. On both sides, the commonplace may become stripped of its protective gray, which makes implicit faith vulnerable. Seeing the familiar with fresh wonder brings an end to smooth sailing, but this loss can be balanced by learning all around.

CURTAILED COMMUNICATION AND PRIVILEGED KNOWLEDGE

Encounters between experts and nonspecialists may, however, foster the invidious parsimony of catch phrases and magisterial opinions, abridged beyond recognition and disconnected from lived understandings—on the comfortable, if not complacent, assumption that the burden of paying attention rests on one side. Social status can rub off on knowledge claims and formulations can shrink to formulas, acquiring the nature of flat prescriptions or of rules to be followed with acquiescence. In curtailed communication, not all participants are treated as potential sources of good ideas or likely errors; knowledge seen as privileged remains sheltered. What is sacrificed by diminishing depth and liveliness, scope of participation, and equality of respect in communication is not only accuracy and comprehensiveness but human connection and opportunities for changing one's mind.

Communication cut off from learning all around may be more typical than practicing the liberal arts of bringing together people and ways of knowing. Of course, the preponderance of curtailed communication does not take away one bit from the power of the more vital, encompassing vision as a means and context for renewing people's lease on learning. Nor does the failure of reality to measure up to the ideal detract from its intrinsic *rightness*, or association with what is good, just, and pleasing in human character and conduct. Conditions of wisdom, liberality, and amiable integrity converge, in short, in Dewey's vision of communication.

My discussion of virtues and dilemmas in research communication visits perennial issues of theory and practice in education in a course informed by ancient concerns for the arts of rhetoric joined to modern, fallibilist understandings of knowledge. The explication of multiplying, tangled dilemmas is meant to clarify what we are up against and what that may require, not to suggest that trying to go beyond the curtailed communication implicit in many attempts at dissemination and improvement is impossible. I propose to outflank dilemmas, with decision, in a Deweyian spirit of exploration, with knowledge conceived as a moving target in the twilight zone of thought *and* action, and learning considered more important than what we take as known.

HOW CAN WE LEARN FROM EDUCATIONAL RESEARCH?

It is not sensible to deny the value of researchers' ability to give meaning to their data or to formulate "results." For there can be little doubt that research findings can best be interpreted by persons who sufficiently master a body of work and methods to be a good judge of what can fairly be made of it or of how insights from different lines of inquiry may or may not be consistent with one another. This is not the same as acting as if everything can safely be left to the authority of science. Accordingly, one must wonder about the notion that practitioners should simply draw their own conclusions from research. Floden and Klinzing (1990) make clear why substituting one authoritative mystique for another—personal experience for research—is not likely to result in collective learning.

> If the validity of research results is supported only by the general authority of research, discussion is closed off. The apparently preferable character of

discussions based on personal experience is undercut, however, by the undesirable criteria likely to be used for resolving such discussions. In an exchange of personal experiences, the one that carries the day will be determined by some combination of persuasive rhetoric and authority. The
decision is no more likely to be based on sound reasoning than that based
on an invocation of the mystique of research. (p. 19)

When one has some reason to be sure, one can make claims that others
have some right to trust. But when are one's judgments good enough to
go on?

Reasonable Conclusions and Open-Mindedness

In theory and practice, a measure of sound conclusions is their reasonableness. What is reasonable is no mere extension of scientific data
or personal experience. Reasonableness involves a host of concerns and
associated goods, as can be demonstrated by sampling from the terms
that may be used to describe a reasonable conclusion, or its reverse—
an unreasonable one: "'rash,' 'well-considered,' 'impulsive,' 'far-sighted,'
'intelligent,' 'sensible,' 'foolish,' 'prudent,' 'wise,' 'dangerous,' 'futile,'
'successful,' 'pointless,' 'inconsiderate,' 'clumsy,' 'clever,' 'imaginative,'
'willful,' 'irresponsible,' 'wicked,' 'vicious,' 'irrational,' and many many
more" (Black, 1972, p. 197). Reasonableness is hence associated with circumspection, due caution and concern for others, skill and know-how,
vision, rationality, effectiveness, responsibility, the exercise of will, common sense and good feeling, and the avoidance of harm and evil.

Though they may seem reasonable enough at the time, one's conclusions often turn out to be wrong or ill-advised; thus, they are not indubitable. Also, available evidence usually allows for more than one reasonable interpretation; thus, most conclusions will have competitors. While
"in its honorable sense, knowledge is distinguished from opinion, guess-
work, speculation, and mere tradition" (Dewey, 1916/1966, p. 188), scientific reasoning does accordingly not move, sternly, by unfailing processes
of inference from unassailable premises to conclusions that are univocal
and indefeasible. Still, researchers are able to suggest things worth believing, discussing, or testing in action by moving from adequately secure
premises, with not so necessarily unfailing processes of reasoning, to conclusions judged warranted at the time. It is useful to recall that

no knowledge is ever absolute. Even experimental analyses are generally
open to more than one reasonable interpretation, particularly when one
wishes to generalize to natural situations and events. Correlative data combined with experiential knowledge and logical reasoning often provide con-

siderable evidence for causal relationships. One should recognize the limitations of such evidence, but not disregard it. (Fisher et al., 1978, p. 4–36)

The fact that will bring revelation will not arrive; the world will not tell us what we are experiencing. But falling short of certainty does not justify obsessive hedging and contortions, as in, "It may not be improbable in view of these exploratory analyses that. . . ." Researchers have to name their findings, thus tentatively committing themselves to their best conjectures, with a view toward moving on—that is, not resting on their laurels. Nor does the absence of irrefutable conclusions entail mindless relativism.

Consider competing perspectives in the arts and sciences. Some critics interpret poems in relation to the artist's biography; others approach them as expressions of "the voice of poetry in the conversation of mankind" (Oakeshott, 1959/1962, pp. 197–247). Some biologists look at an organism as many pairs of fixed and determinate cause–effect connections, but others picture its unity as a vastly complicated feedback mechanism. Dewey (1916/1966) reminds us that possibilities for making meaning, though not arbitrary, are endless: "It all depends upon the context of perceived connections in which [something] is placed; the reach of imagination in realizing connections is inexhaustible" (p. 208). In education, competing perspectives cast higher learning as a useful tool in one's career, as a dusty—racist and sexist—answer to divisive questions of power and entitlement, or as a civilizing treasure of lasting beauty. Again, this variety is not a matter of personal taste and preference; instead, "it reminds us only that different occasions and topics, subjects and contexts, may give us *good reasons* for adopting one standpoint rather than another" (Toulmin, 1982, p. 104).

The coexistence of reasonable perspectives inside and outside of scholarly communities provides grounds (i.e., justification) and substance (i.e., subject matter as conceptual, evidential, and argumentative supplies) for open-mindedness as an intellectual and moral disposition (see Hare, 1985). Open-mindedness is a moral disposition in that it is often easier to live by beliefs that are as comfortable and close to oneself as a well-worn garment. As indicated, this disposition is compatible with judging that, in given circumstances, some things are worth believing and testing, and more so than others. Open-mindedness is not empty-mindedness; as Dewey (1916/1966) makes clear, "To hang out a sign saying 'Come right in; there is no one at home' is not the equivalent of hospitality" (pp. 175–176).

While the tentativeness of knowledge and the inexhaustibility of experience give one good reasons for being open-minded, this stance is not easy to practice. It is perhaps hardest to assume when scholars and researchers turn from their specialized scientific role to their social role, in which they join the ranks of other people in trying to improve the world.

Open-Mindedness and Opinions

People rarely take the world as they find it. When Einstein developed the theory of relativity, however, he was not just fond of his opinions; although when he spoke about politics, he probably was. A trouble with opinions is their entrenchment and crudeness: They are strongholds of belief at the same time that they are usually not thought through or worked out in detail. As Ben Jonson put it in 1641, "Opinion is a light, vain, crude, and imperfect thing, settled in the imagination but never arriving at the understanding, there to obtain the tincture of reason" (1953, p. 63).

Personal opinions need not be self-serving to endanger reasonableness. They can be dogmatic and ill-formed, hotheaded or parochial, and that will do plenty of damage. In reading or listening to a research report, however, it is difficult to tell where the scientist proper stops and the acting, willing person begins talking: Neither page nor speaker suddenly turn pink by way of warning. Perhaps the most vexing difficulty is that, when researchers speak from personal opinions on matters of policy and practice, the "voice of science" seems to become more plain—intelligible and candid—acquiring a straightforwardness it otherwise lacks. This is an agreeable illusion that researchers have every reason (though few incentives) to dispel.

COMING OUT OF THE VALUES CLOSET?

Plainspoken opinions represent what is unscientific in researchers' minds: stipulative assumptions about people, education, and society, which reflect common sense, group membership, or personal experience. They are spoken with the voice of science but without its circumscribed authority. People try to sort out this problem through a disclosure approach, which assumes—along Weberian (1904/1963) lines—that

> (1) . . . any piece of research, any course of study, implies both a selection of subject matter and a selection within the subject matter—a selection of theoretical method as well as a selection of relevant facts.
> (2) . . . This selection will naturally be a function both of the interests

and values of whoever is responsible for it and beyond him, to some greater or lesser extent, of the society or culture of which he is a member. . . . A study whose subject matter was chosen entirely at random, that is, one which might be relevant to no particular interest or which was undertaken in the light of no particular value, need by the same token have no particular importance for anyone.

(3) . . . In order to eliminate any possibility of misunderstanding or of hidden persuasiveness, the [researcher] should start by making an explicit and unreserved declaration of his own values and interests in the subject. (Montefiore, 1975, p. 20)

This approach will go some way toward ensuring that the interests, biases, and personal beliefs of researchers do not remain tacit premises, with the (frequent) result that their arguments unwittingly "pass from bias and opinion in the premiss to the same bias and opinion in the conclusion" (Minkus, 1980, p. 73). In ordinary life, most people know that unreserved declarations are not always helpful. In research communication, the disclosure approach does not go far enough and cannot guard against misunderstandings and manipulation. In fact, while secrecy is bad, sincerity may be a form of hypocrisy.

The Ritual of Frankness

First, it is difficult to be explicit and unreserved, not only due to the frequent conflict of honesty with interests, but because people's minds are psychologically and logically chaotic in a way that poses problems for full disclosure.

Our actual psychological processes are governed by logic in a much slighter degree than their *expressions* make us believe. . . . There is a very great distance between any regulation by rational norms and the characteristics of these conceptions: namely, their flaring up, their zigzag motions, the chaotic whirling of images and ideas which objectively are entirely unrelated to one another. (Simmel, 1906/1950, p. 311)

Excessive honesty makes people contradict themselves. If it is difficult and bewildering to confess all, the second, more interesting question is, What could one get from a full confession of researcher values and interests?

In a provocative paper, Gouldner (1968; see also Shklar, 1984) reinforces the first point and goes straight to the heart of the second one. The "ritual of frankness" (p. 112), as he calls it, is naive, since it assumes that we know the values we have. Beyond that, simple frankness conveys the sense that one's values are good enough, which is smug and assumes that having opened up to the knowledge of others and oneself where one comes from and whose side one is on, one has done all that can be expected. Yet merely declaring values and interests cannot clarify how *having* particular values and interests "affects the worth, the scope, the bite, and the objectivity" (Gouldner, 1968, p. 112) of a particular piece of (educational) research. And exposing the reasons of one's heart does not mean *probing* them. Hence, simple disclosure is vapid—failing to produce any great effect on the understanding—and vacuous, too, for it does not supply a context in which values and interests, with the consequences of having them, can be appraised by analysis and contrast.

Simple frankness about researcher interests and values is a reduction of explanation and examination to sincerity. The ritual of frankness furthermore ignores the fact that not everyone's needs and interests stand on a par in the world we have made. Why else should Nobel laureates, for instance, be called upon to speak about matters of public concern once they receive this prestigious award (see Zuckerman, 1977)? Less exalted researchers declaring their disciplinary affiliations—educational psychologists, sociologists, or anthropologists—do not just provide information that should help the audience to place and qualify their statements; by their declaration, they assert privileged knowledge and status.

The basic, self-assertive hypocrisy in all of this is "the pretense that the ideological needs of the few correspond to the moral and material interests of the many. It is a hypocrisy to which all politically active intellectuals . . . are especially given" (Shklar, 1984, p. 66). The issue of values and interests illustrates the difficulties of helpful and clarifying (rather than manipulative or misleading) communication. For better or worse, the wayward arts of language play a much larger role in research communication than people like to admit.

RHETORICAL ARTS IN RESEARCH COMMUNICATION

> Art is the specific . . . The chief consideration for us is, what particular practice of Art in letters is the best for the perusal of the Book of our common wisdom; so that with clearer minds and livelier manners we may escape, as it were, into daylight and song from a land of foghorns. Shall we read it by the watchmaker's eye in luminous rings eruptive of the infinitesimal, or pointed with examples and types? (Meredith, 1879/1947, p. 2)

Communication misses its point if it simply passes the audience by. Speaking or writing that is unappealing—awkward, tedious, or consistently very abstract—will impede the communication of worthwhile knowledge and sensible conclusions. It was Hume's belief, for instance, that, "because of the remoteness and abstractness and practical irrelevance of some of his results [of investigations in the theory of knowledge], none of his readers would believe in them for more than an hour" (Popper, 1962, p. 43).

Like Dewey, Hexter (1971) argues in his "Rhetoric of History" that more or less apt formulations of knowledge affect understandings on *both* sides: "Even where it is technically accurate, dull history is bad history to the extent to which it is dull.... Dull history blurs [the historian's] findings for himself and for those who read his writing. Those findings then fail to become, or rapidly cease to be part of, the 'workable reserve' ... of the writer and reader" (pp. 45–46). Clarifying what one knows for oneself and other researchers is not the same thing as explaining it to an audience that cannot recapitulate particular processes of scientific work or may not be familiar with them in a general way. Thus, what is wordy, stupefying, or plainly boring depends not only on the rhetorical skills of researchers, but also on the prior knowledge of the audience.

In the social sciences, researchers are caught in a crossfire of norms and expectations. They have to convince fellow researchers of their soundness while also achieving some contact with the public, for people rightly think that they ought to be posted on discoveries concerning their everyday lives—the source of the researchers' data and target of improvements. The technical language of research is not the language of everyday life, however; it serves to communicate specialized meanings in arguments that can be subtle and difficult. This natural language of science is bound to be baffling and sometimes freezes into "overmighty systems of thought" (Ziman, 1968, p. 118).

Researchers rarely have the training or talents for casting their arguments so that general audiences can see how, and to what extent, theoretical and practical conclusions may be authorized and delimited. To attain this educational goal, research communication has to meet three conditions (each of them a potential hitch): those of access, belief, and impact—with *understanding* being the form of impact germane to science. Since one must catch one's hare before one can cook it, the access condition will always have to be met. Catching one's hare can be difficult enough, yet the other conditions are even more tricky.

Issues of Style and Appeal

Meeting the communicative conditions of access, belief, and (defensible) impact involves true rhetorical dilemmas, rather than problems that "linking agents" or popularizers of research can solve. That is, the arts of communication involve multiple goods that may stand in each other's way. Stylistic choices between, for instance, spareness and evidentiary detail, lifelikeness and abstraction, straightforwardness and an involved manner that fits the subject, all have their costs:

> In course of use a defined style becomes its own enemy. If one's writing is abstract, it will accommodate ideas, but it will fatigue the reader. If it is concrete, it will divert and relieve; but it may become cloying, and it will have difficulty in encompassing ideas. If it is spare, it will come to seem abrupt; if it practices a degree of circumlocution, it will first seem elegant but will come to seem inflated. The lucid style is suspected of oversimplifying. (Weaver, 1953, pp. 208–209)

And the dilemmas go on. It is true that there is a relation between the vitality of what one is saying and the appeal of one's style. George Bernard Shaw (1903) put this with style, thus exemplifying his own point: "He who has nothing to assert has no style and can have none: he who has something to assert will go as far in power of style as its momentousness and his conviction will carry him" (p. xxxv). Dryness and pedantry, though potentially tiring, nevertheless reflect some scientific conventions. If research is presented breezily, like a news item on TV, or in the brisk, beguiling fashion of an advertisement, it may appeal to the audience. Yet what is said cannot be given an appraisal that depends on supplying details with cool precision. If detail and precision rule, a research report may fail to get the audience's attention or its point may disappear from view. Since "it is rhetorically much more effective to insinuate the crucial assumptions into the hearer's mind without focusing attention upon them" (Black, 1968, p. 99), keeping suppositions under cover will often promote access and impact, thought not necessarily understanding.

In general, tokens of good faith may weaken chances at having an impact. How convincing are researchers, really, when disclosing all their foibles, together with "the false starts, the mistakes, the unnecessary complications, the difficulties and hesitations" (Ziman, 1969, p. 319) that are part of their work? Scientific writing is a difficult balancing act, for

> it must persuade the reader of the veracity of the observer, his disinterestedness, his logical infallibility, and the complete necessity of his conclusions. . . . [Scientists] favour the passive voice, the impersonal gender, and the latinized circumlocution, because these would seem to permit, in the circumstances, a climate of opinion within which, as it were, one can express relatively positive assertions in a tentative tone. (p. 319)

Although each piece of research is a potential contribution to collective learning, the impersonal style tends, on the one hand, to present scientific work as if its validity were already agreed upon. The remote tone has, on the other hand, its justification, too, for science downplays the emotive and performative uses of language (those uses related to passion and action) in favor of clarifying and informative uses. Scientific knowledge tends to withdraw from the particular, intuitive, and concrete, separating things from the world that is taken for granted. This, in turn, raises problems of communication, for even hardened academics get wearied by incessant abstractions: "Thus the universe of Einstein is represented as 'like' the surface of an orange; or the theory of entropy is illustrated by the figure of a desert on which Arabs are riding their camels hither and thither" (Weaver, 1953, p. 203).

Abstraction can impede communication, and analogies, imagery, stories, and examples can help people understand things while bringing in their baggage of appealing, but partially misleading, associations. "If all communication entails both an assertive, descriptive level and an aesthetic, artistic level then the windowpane is never completely clear; there is always a streak of stained glass to capture our imagination and wonder" (Gusfield, 1976, p. 17). Rhetorical arts help render the incredible worthy of belief. Note, though, that style itself does not discriminate as to the truth of what seems strange. Lies, truth, and half-truths can equally be gilded with happy terms or remain incredible and inaccessible.

Issues of Credibility and Trust

For communication people need, by the first rule of rhetoric, some point of agreement from which a meeting of minds can begin. If they take their communicative task seriously, researchers must somehow accumulate enough belief and trust to get a hearing. Thus, although belief should ideally be earned rather than granted in research reporting, without some *unearned* assent at the outset, the occasion for communicating knowledge never even arises.

What goes down sweetly may be nonsense. But people can believe even something that is warranted, while not coming to believe it for good reasons. In any case, once there is trusting belief, there are few incentives for shaking it, to win it again in earnest. Why endanger assent to claims that seem reasonable enough by drawing attention to their imperfect backing, leaps of judgment in drawing conclusions, and the conflicting perspectives that bear on the matter at hand? Issues of credibility in communication, in short, also involve true dilemmas that are entangled with dilemmas of style. Researchers pay for gaining the confidence of the audience too readily (assent but little understanding); they also pay for trying to ease people too slowly into conviction (diminished access or belief).

The less an audience knows, the greater its need to trust, though trusting reliance is no more justified by greater need. And the smaller the measure of knowledge available to audience or speaker, the more likely it is that confidence born of interaction will be based on irrelevant grounds—having an endearing personality or distinguished looks—while to the eyes of colleagues a researcher may be a plausible fellow but a bit of a fraud. What is irrational and mildly unethical may still be interactionally necessary, for "the efficacy of spoken communications rests in the end upon the transmission of nonverbal signs of credibility" (Black, 1968, p. 96).

If researchers actually say everything that is to be said on both sides of a question or offer advice compassed about by clouds of qualifications, credence may be withheld, for people tend to believe assertions more than arguments. This is particularly true for matters of urgent concern, where at least part of oneself wants to hear "only the voice, the simplicity, the conviction of authority: 'Yes, I understand. It happens. Don't fret. Do this! Believe me! . . .' Or words to that effect—words utterly direct and transparent, words without a hint of prevarication or indirection" (Sacks, 1984, pp. 92–93). Still, the fact that trust will be grounded objectively only in part does not require withholding it or always and totally doubting what others claim to know. There has to be some mutual reliance when people who differ by knowledge, skills, and interests come together—in reality or in postulating an audience in research writing.

Actually, a need to trust not only characterizes relations among researchers and practitioners but applies quite broadly. While "in an ideal free society each person would have perfect access to the truth . . . in science, in art, religion and justice, . . . this is not practicable; each person can know directly very little of truth and must trust others for the rest" (Polanyi, 1959, p. 68). Once there is distrust and misunderstanding, differences shade into suspicion and disregard, eroding bases for communication and learning.

Research communication attending to these tangled dilemmas of access, belief, and impact is highly skilled, even high-minded work. But usually researchers are not very self-conscious writers; sometimes they think that the truth will speak for itself. Nor do these perplexities describe all the difficulties of research communication, especially where it means to affect practice. Then, as I have pointed out earlier, the researcher in her capacity as a self-important human being full of opinions, hopes, and desires comes to the fore. The compulsions and self-compulsions of science will compete with interests and feelings that light up horizons of action.

Issues of Action and Certainty

The wayward arts of rhetoric are involved in helping people understand their world, but persuasion has even more compelling affinities to acting in it. In research communication, persuasion can be seen as a two-edged sword, its scintillating edges corresponding to the different roles of social scientists as acting, willing persons (and, as such, on a par with other people) and as members of scientific communities (Weber, 1904/1963). Rhetorical devices and desires confound these two roles, which are associated with different language uses as well. Research reporting in education is uneasily balanced between informative and performative uses of language, or between imparting and revising knowledge and causing things to happen.

The twofold roles and language uses also involve conflicting pressures with regard to certainty. While researchers like to lay claim to facts, they are well accustomed to modes of eternal doubting. Practice, however, cannot remain in such modes: It requires doing one thing rather than another. While beliefs can be revised, if sometimes with pain and difficulty, actions cannot be undone. Many choices are not subject to revision; thus, a human life seems like "a path picked out, like a tapestry design, upon a canvas of innumerable sacrificed possibilities" (Bell, 1991, p. x). Yet these truths about life and action do not negate truths about knowledge. In sum, the affinity of action and passion to persuasion and the determinacy of practice do not do away with the tentativeness of knowledge. Most certainly, acknowledging that action requires decision is not the same as claiming that knowledge implies action.

Logic Does Not Settle Action

One can understand that people want to believe what they decide to do is the right thing to do, definitely, hoping that their actions will be based on solid, as opposed to shifting and uncertain, grounds. But practical reasons only incline; they do not necessitate. And, strictly speaking, nothing is implied in scientific findings beyond the questions that may be answered by the research and other questions to which particular investigations are related by the intellectual and social traditions of research communities. Supposed implications for practice—as recommendations for action—are neither deducible from nor logically contained in research results. Action and decision depend instead on moral frame-

works and networks of power and authority that affect the work of practitioners, as well as on legal and political knowledge, the resources at
hand, and (importantly) know-how. Practical conclusions are not exten-
sions or culminations of research methods and external data or their highest development and imperative consummation, although their place in
research reports and mode of presentation often suggest just that (Gusfield, 1976).

When researchers cast some of their conclusions as implications for
practice or policy, they gain persuasive force by a terminological suggestion of cogency—a form of compulsion with logical and moral elements,
capable of supplying a *feeling* of certainty. While reasonable people can
disagree, it seems that (logical) implications should be binding. Where
one is sure of one's premises, implications appear to be no mere assertions
or debatable statements, but incontrovertible and hence eminently trustworthy. Appearances do mislead, however. For one can be sure (i.e., convinced) of premises that are false; and one can take issue with logical
consequences, since what is thus involved may well be false. (Falsehoods
have logical consequences, some true, some false.)

The label "implications" may incline one to accept a proposal for
action, because what is offered under this label has the reassuring appeal
of authority. But the rhetoric of implications masks the moral and practical complexity of decisions and the indeterminacy of the logic of action
(see Buchmann, 1988). It is fortunate that language can detect its own
snares and unravel entanglements of beliefs and desires, while bringing
light and air to the issues.

> In being attentive to the elements of language and choice involved in giving
> meanings to data, the analyst calls attention to the singularity and selective
> activity through which policy implications are drawn. In doing this, it be-
> comes more likely that social scientists and others can create, explore and
> develop the potential variety of other interpretations and policies which
> would otherwise remain unnoticed and unavailable. (Gusfield, 1976, p. 32)

OUTFLANKING DILEMMAS WITH VIRTUES?

This analysis has applied Dewey's hopeful vision of communication
as appreciation of meaning and collective growth, indicating also how
social relations, arts and skills, and the diversity of hopes and needs enter
into communicating educational research, especially in writing. I have
assumed that questions of policy and practice are far from irrelevant to
research communication, although I have likewise argued that relevance

must not be construed in a falsely authoritative or uniquely binding manner. It remains to see what this analysis may yield when applied more specifically to practice.

The standard way of thinking about rational action is to consider possibilities and then to choose the one that seems best, acknowledging that the choice is made on imperfect information. If theoretical conclusions are uncertain and practice requires decision, a way out of this quandary may be a partial reversal of this order, that is, confident action with the habit of going back to examine the adequacy of grounds for actions taken, the ramifying consequences, and the normative space that action and consequences help to modify and form (see Scheffler, 1985). For researchers, this suggests making recommendations that have some bite—or that are capable, in style and substance, of taking a grip or hold upon action and imagination—with the habit of going back, alone and with others, to reflect on their reasonableness in the light of emergent or wider understandings.

What Scheffler (1984) describes as the difficult task of entertaining a "double consciousness" (p. 163) in policy making is also required of educational researchers when they consider their conclusions. This double consciousness, resonating with the twofold aspects of the researcher's role, associated language uses, and conflicting pressures with regard to certainty, demands "energetic fulfillment of commitments already undertaken, while at the same time demanding a skeptical reserve vis-à-vis assumptions underlying these very commitments—a deference to accumulating evidence, a willingness to concede, if such evidence so indicates, that these assumptions may, after all, have been mistaken and the policies perhaps therefore wrong" (p. 163).

While moral and mental virtues such as honesty, directness, responsibility, and open-mindedness are, therefore, required in action, communication, and learning, we can conclude that perfection of knowledge, wisdom, and foresight are not. This is a rather cheering thought, recalling, beyond Dewey, the ancient saying that a living dog is better than a dead lion.

Second Thoughts and the Company We Keep

The double-minded, but not dithering, approach to rational action consonant with the maxim, "Resolve it first and keep wondering about it afterward" allows, in its two parts, for the confidence necessary to act and decide. Yet it honors the requirement for "second thoughts" (Buchmann, 1984b, p. 436)—which is essential because of the imperfections of knowledge and indeterminacy of practical conclusions. The confidence that fits with both parts of the maxim is neither overboldness nor presumption. It is an attitude of trust, arising from reliance on oneself (including what one knows and wants), circumstances, and other people. As an expectation so ensured, reliance does not dampen thought. Pushed hard enough, the concept of reliance itself gives way, dissolving from an accomplished fact or condition into life and action: "To talk of reliance is a poor external way of speaking. Speak rather of that which relies because it works and is" (Emerson, 1841/1966, p. 119).

"Wondering about things afterward" can be informed by concerns for truth and rightness, a willingness to test, imagine, and remember— and to listen to others. Thus, the charge to entertain second thoughts carried by the second part of the maxim, brings back the very open-mindedness that its first part ("Resolve it") must suspend in the act of choice, which temporarily ignores the possibility of errors and the shadows of paths not chosen. Open-mindedness justifies confidence because it makes room for learning.

There is no logical difficulty in combining resolute action and commitment under conditions of uncertainty with staying wide awake in the aftermath; still, people do tend to become fond of what they say and do, and tragic losses are real. These psychological difficulties need not keep one from making assertions and choices as long as one stays disposed to turn to the company of others. With some luck, our lives will include a sufficiency of people "who were merry or wise or comforting or revealing, whose presence either heartened the spirit or kindled the mind; people who opened windows instead of shutting them" (Struther, 1940, p. 72).

The Many Uses of Research

Michael Huberman

> "You like to tell stories, don't you?", he asked, and I answered,
> "Yes, I like to tell stories that are true."
>   Then he asked, "After you have finished your true stories
> sometime, why don't you make up a story and the people to go
> with it?"
>   "Only then will you understand what happened and why
> . . ."
>
> —MacLean, *A River Runs through It*, 1976, p. 104

For several years now, Margret Buchmann and I have had an ongoing conversation—shading into moments of debate—about the nature and the functions of research utilization. Now we are taking this conversation public, and I, for one, am enchanted with the opportunity. Our talks over tea—as memorable, almost Proustian, as they have been—were not as demanding as what is called for here: a more textual exegesis, followed by an attempt at reasoned response.

In composing my response, I have first looked across the three chapters for leitmotive critical of research utilization directed at practitioners. After laying out these themes, I shall respond with some countervailing leitmotive, most derived from the empirical literature on research utilization. By the end of this text, I shall try to make the case that the worlds of research and practice—often called the "two communities" or the "two planets"—can be and have been joined in mutually rewarding exchanges and negotiations.

A Naive Belief in Instrumentality

This is the first critical leitmotive spanning the three chapters. Research knowledge is vaunted especially for its "utility," which constitutes a limited often unwarranted view of inquiry: It is "instrumental," "sensible," "down-to-earth," but not "noble or inspired." There is an exaggerated emphasis on linear progress, on the expectation "that something good will come of this." This utilitarian view of knowledge is seen not only as other than but as lesser than "irrational principled action" inspired by "transcendent ideals."

This is not the terrain on which I want to do serious battle—just a short "passe d'armes." First off, we are in a Manicheaen universe here: the Apollonian versus the Dionysiac, the heated debates in Mann's *Magic Mountain* over the rational versus the irrational, the reasoned versus the passionate. Thus scientific research is useful but arid; it will dry out the classroom, rob its practitioners of their passions and convictions.

It's not clear to me why *this* would be the case. If I as a teacher read, say, a piece of research on whole-language instruction while I am experimenting with that approach, I am likely to maintain my conviction in the approach, even if the findings are critical. If the findings are positive, this should presumably strengthen my belief that this is a better approach than, say, phonics or more structural perspectives. Just because the procedures of inquiry in mainstream social-scientific research are rationally derived, neither their findings nor their effects on readers need be artificially rationalized. In effect, what matters is what people *make* of them, and there is little evidence to support an increased pedagogical aridity or a loss of commitment in the classroom on the part of teachers who are greater or lesser consumers of research evidence (Meyers, 1986). Also, many educational researchers are advocates of their domains, passionate advocates, all in being lucid about the validity of their data. Otherwise, they would have been basic scientists.

Also—and I shall return to this—there are species of research utilization that are highly engaged, morally and politically. The obvious example is critical theory. As it happens, however, critical theory, at least the wing derived from Ricoeur and Habermas, is a response to an excessively utilitarian view of research. And Margret Buchmann is right to point out its limits.

The approach under attack is called "research, development, and diffusion" (RD&D), and it has been used widely in education. Its derivation—from the military, engineering, and medical sectors—is also problematic. Basically, it calls for a division of labor between, first, fundamental research (development of basic theory), then applied research (development of prototype materials), then widespread diffusion to a number of "target" publics. We have had ample time to test this hyperrational model and to find it wanting, not least in its creation of separate centers leading from the communities of research to the universe of practice.

Another assumption of the RD&D approach is the top-down nature of the process, as if the research community were able to determine optimal conditions of instruction within the classroom. For several years, we have all known better. But that very premise has created an asymmetrical relationship between the "knowledge-producing community" and the "knowledge-using community," between the research establishment and the educational establishment—as if only one side possessed the requisite "scientific knowledge" and was entrusted to make the subsequent truth claims, whereas the other side could rely only on its reflectiveness wrought from cumulative practice. As Floden (1985) points out in "The Role of Rhetoric in Changing Teachers' Beliefs," teachers' expectations have come to be those of being "told what research has found to be true," not those of raising "questions about why they should believe research claims" (p. 31), and of assuming that, having that requisite knowledge, the research community should then determine policy. In that sense, research utilization becomes not simply an instrumentalist approach to the management of learning and instruction, but also a baldly political act.

RESEARCH KNOWLEDGE DOESN'T ADVANCE PRACTICE AND EVEN ERODES ITS BASES

In part, we will find some of the same arguments here: Scientific work plays down the emotive and the passionate, in favor of informative uses. The sense of wonder is compromised in the products of social science. But then the argument takes what I see as another tack: that scientific knowledge is "not the guide . . . to good practice," owing to its selectiveness, time-boundedness, theory-dependence; that problems in practicing professions don't derive from deficiencies in knowledge, but rather from moral deficiencies. In fact, such knowledge can erode the "bases for good practice."

Each one of these points merits a response, but I would need more background information to do it intelligibly. Scientific knowledge is only one source of information used by practitioners, who themselves have selective, time-bound theories for conducting and explicating what they do. Confronting these theories with research findings has often proved illuminating. Also, deficiencies in knowledge are problematic in school settings, especially at the upper level. Why should more disciplined inquiry about cognition, group management, motivation, physics, literature, and so forth, erode the bases for good practice? Let us not forget that most constructs used in teacher training, incorporated in textbooks and handbooks and exercises inside the classroom, forming the core of professional development, and so on, are virtually all research-originated. When we talk of "constructivism" or "self-efficacy" or "cooperative learning" or "formative evaluation" or "conservation of number" or even "burnout"—all terms familiar to teachers—we are witnessing work in the research community that has bridged successfully to the classroom.

Perhaps Margret Buchmann is getting at something *else* here, something endemic to the research process itself. It may well be that the algorithms of empirical research, not to mention the socialization of educational researchers, bring practitioners to seek meaning in findings where there may be none. The world is a far more unruly, more random, often more squalid place than our research findings let on. Put before data that look genuinely chaotic, we researchers will invariably lay some order and meaning on them. We can contend, I think, with irrational or latent or conspiratorial data—especially since the generalization of critical inquiry and field research—but not with the aleatoric, the purely random or the self-contradictory. There are here, to be sure, so many more things than were dreamt of in our epistemologies and methodologies when we first designed them.

Educational Research Overlooks the Uncertainties of Practice

This is a timeless theme, and Margret Buchmann has some sharp, enlightening things to say about it. Good practice, she tells us, is the "art of responding to urgency where perfect certainty is wanting and outcomes are unpredictable." (Chapter 4, p. 91.) This is the case, of course, in a multitude of classrooms, with their characteristics of immediacy, unpredictability, and the management of simultaneous tasks. Those teachers who fare the best are those who know how to improvise, drawing on patterned recollections and responses to situations they interpret as being analogous to ones they have already faced.

For many years, researchers have been insensitive to these contexts, whether they are the contexts of practice (Huberman, 1983) or the contexts of policy (Bardach, 1984; Lindblom & Cohen, 1979). Researchers have been unable to understand that the knowledge needed by a practitioner is largely *situational* knowledge, as opposed to *propositional* knowledge. They have sought, for far too long, "grand theories" that could account for multiple settings with overarching sets of constructs. In any single natural setting, this work may well have had explanatory value, but only at the most general level; the special configuration of any given class, any children, appeared to be an exception or to present a thicket of interactions. This work did still worse with predictions. As Glass (1979) pointed out, in none of the dozen or so research literatures integrated in the past five years have we accounted for more than a third of the variability in the results of studies. We can predict general tendencies, but not which of several things work well in particular circumstances.

If classroom life is unpredictable to its inhabitants, researchers are unlikely to do better. There are, however, general phenomena having to do with the learning process, the relational and motivational process, and the didactic process that can illuminate, often even *account* for what is happening and for how these events are perceived by the pupils and teachers. This is enlightening knowledge. It provides help without taking the decision away from the professional whose responsibility it is to answer the question, "What is to be done?" It provides background, illustrations, plausible explanations, promising leads, another voice with similar concerns but with some distance from the dizziness of continual interactions.

Also, researchers are increasingly seeking these data up close, in the classroom or school, as participant or nonparticipant observers of the setting over weeks, sometimes months. These data, then, are cemented to the surround. They are not generated, as had usually been the case, through the medium of attitude and achievement batteries taken at several removes from the classroom, then all too often translated into findings exhorting teachers to modify their instructional practices. To be sure, this genre of research utilization has been little more than hubris.

Researchers Have Values, If Not Biases; Their Choice of Topic and Method Is Highly Selective, or Arbitrary; Yet They Are Tempted to Say More than They Know

I think this critique is largely founded, but I would have liked some illustration, some context. I note, too, that it is an *overabundance* of moral commitment that is being skewered here, whereas the arid, utilitarian scholar was put to blame earlier on. Yes—I will come back to this—researchers, like all of us but perhaps more self-consciously than most, operate from a belief in higher-order theoretical principles about the nature of the world (their ontology) and about how this world can be known (their epistemology). These beliefs or concerns then dictate the problems researchers choose to study, the methods they prefer to use, and, if they are not careful, the interpretations they draw from their findings.

I say "not careful" because there are explicit canons for collecting, analyzing, and interpreting research data, and peer review processes to control for abuses or self-delusions. But it is also true that any given research finding lends itself to more than one interpretation—sometimes even to countervailing interpretations. The pull toward bias, however, is this: If one's work has followed a single line of inquiry, and if this particular study is the next step, the "authoritative" interpretation will leap out. Also, philosophers of science (e.g., Quine & Ullian, 1978; Laudan, 1977) have shown that much scientific work does not follow the canon of revising or rejecting one's theories when researchers encounter anomalies. Our Galileos, Newtons, Priestleys, and Einsteins did not abandon their theories in the face of apparently refuting evidence.

The Many Worlds of Research Utilization

Let me now turn to work within the research community itself, with the design of creating another view of the field. That view has the following tenet: Neither research nor practice will evolve unless members of the two communities create "interactive spaces" to negotiate the meaning of classroom life (representing educational professionals) and the interpretation of attempts to account for its constituent parts (representing educational researchers). In other words, although I would consider myself an eclectic post-positivist, I can accept that the meanings of educational phenomena are *products of social negotiation* between theorists of competing schools and between theorists and practitioners. When teachers and educational psychologists identify instances of "aggressiveness" in a classroom, for example, they have not captured the intrinsic properties of the phenomenon, but have developed a community of agreement (Gergen, 1978). The legitimacy of that diagnosis is continuously open to challenge from other psychologists, sociologists, teachers, parents, and peers in the classroom.

Such negotiations seldom take place; a greater number of them would, I think, bring the practice and research communities together, and on a more equal footing. Another spoiler, however, is that there are different ethics with regard to the production and dissemination of knowledge (Deyle, Hess, & Lecompte, 1991). For example, in a *teleological ethic,* the researcher produces knowledge for its own sake, with a general concern for enlightening the public that will find its way to his or her work. A *utilitarian ethic* is more in the logic of the RD&D model examined earlier, but it contains a distant problem-solving component. A *categorical imperative* also imposes obligations to improve social and educational practice and is sometimes tied up with "action research." *Critical theory and advocacy* constitute an emancipatory ideology, an analysis of the social and political forces that sustain the technical or instrumental rationality (Schwandt, 1990). This is the heart of Margret Buchmann's argument. It is here, critical theorists claim, that inquiry, knowledge, and relationships are reified to the point that we no longer discern the distortions of communicative action and language.

The point I am trying to make here is that, when one looks inside "research utilization," one sees a plethora of approaches, each one ontologically and epistemologically justified. Some would enlighten us at a distance; others would work hand in hand with us; still others would emancipate our frames of reference; others would resolve our practical problems in our places. And each would accomplish this by discovering the constants in the uncharted flux of social life, by disclosing the repetitions or regularities in the world. In other words, each—including action research—is making claims to validity or what Dewey felicitously called "warranted assertibility."

Claims to Validity and Conditions of Knowledge Use

In research terms, claims to validity will differ by school of thought. Still, some basic conditions of validity can be considered universal. In qualitative studies (e.g., Maxwell, 1992), we are first concerned with "descriptive validity"—the factual accuracy of an account. There is then "interpretive validity," the meaning of objects, events, and behaviors to people engaged in them, and the inferences drawn from these accounts by researchers. Finally, there is "theoretical validity": the adequacy of the explanation—the validity of the concepts used and the validity of the relationships among them.

The question is this: How is it that research meeting these criteria is no more likely to move beyond the scientific community than work of a lesser robustness? There is, in fact, virtually no study to show that higher-quality research diffuses better outside the social scientific community than does mediocre work (Huberman, 1987). A powerful, elegant piece of research may be simply irrelevant in the field.

The operational criteria of validity must then differ between the two communities. For example, studies with little concern for external validity—the precise range and number of situations and individuals to which findings may be extrapolated—can either delude a public of practitioners or leave them cold. For the classroom practitioner, say, the regnant concerns are local meaning and local use. For these concerns to be met, either the practitioner or the researcher or both must rework the findings or must anticipate, during the conduct of the study, that they will be contending later on with particular contexts of use.

In any event, the transformation of social science knowledge into relevant practice-centered information is often an indirect, complicated process. In this regard, Bardach (1984) makes some telling points about policy research. Its penetration in the policy community is, he says, shallow. It does not "illuminate any particular problem unless it is supplemented by knowledge of the particular context in which the problem exists" (p. 132). As a source of practical guidance, it is probably more useful as a backdrop—an illumination of general principles exemplary of certain kinds of cases. And, of course, dissemination of policy research will depend on which local actors need to use these arguments or to defend themselves against them (Huberman, 1989a). The irony, as Bardach points out, is that when research is contextualized, it comes to be perceived not as social science but as policy argument.

Carol Weiss (1978) makes the same argument, pointing out the extraordinary concatenation of circumstances for research to influence policy decisions directly: a well-defined decision situation, policy actors with real jurisdiction over the decision, a real demand for information, research providing that information in terms matching the circumstances in which choices will be made, findings that are clear-cut and unambiguous and that reach decision makers when they are wrestling with the issues, findings that are comprehensible and that do not run counter to strong political interests (pp. 5–6).

This is a lot to expect. To this may be added, briefly, some other considerations (Huberman & Gather-Thurler, 1991): differences in the terms used to describe the key processes, researchers' hesitations to enter a "political" arena, researchers' fears of "magical" expectations of practitioners, researchers' fears of distortion and oversimplification, many researchers' basic incompetence in the dissemination process. On the practitioner's side, as many restrictions apply: fear of intimidation, antipathy to jargon, researchers' hesitation to "stay" with the situation they have diagnosed, a judgmental tendency on the part of specialists who do not master the context, and so on. And the more generic problem, posed by Cohen and Garet (1975): that much research is focused on the questions academics want to answer, "rather than on the decisions which officials have to make" (p. 25).

All this helps to explain why research findings seldom find their way into a state policy forum or the local schoolhouse. As Cohen and Garet (1975) point out, even large-scale studies, mandated or financed by the government, may affect no single policy decision—at least not initially. These studies may permeate a political climate—or even create one—but they will be one of several sources that, gradually percolating, give rise to the debates that determine the next wave of policy and practice. And these studies will be used, of course, as selective ammunition by partisans on both sides of the aisle. The extreme subtlety of their wording (evenhanded, sober, understated, using the passive voice and conditional forms) will make the findings still more valuable to the protagonists, whose modes of persuasion will otherwise be more impassioned and who can now pepper their arguments with apparently objective data.

Another Perspective

In this section, I try to make three points. First, research utilization is hampered by its multivocal nature; it means many different things to different researchers. For example, "action researchers" have no dissemination problem; they work directly with a group of practitioners to transform their universe, hopefully on terms that the latter have specified. This is not always the case. Second, research utilization has to do with negotiations over the meaning of the world as practitioners know it and researchers attempt to describe, explain, and predict it. In social science, we researchers are on thin ice, because our findings look all too much like elegantly packaged common sense. If we find, for example, no main effects in a program that school people have implemented for 10 years, we will very likely be laughed out of the room.

Next, the cultural and social distance between researchers and practitioners has made the enterprise all the more difficult. In particular, the research community has not mastered the "surround" in which teachers work day to day, the beliefs on which they depend to get through the year, the typical interactions between instructional tasks and learning activities, the ways in which teachers reach outside their classroom for information, expertise, and didactic resources—many of them research-mediated.

This is a constellation of problems at which I have chipped away for several years (Huberman, 1983, 1987, 1989; Huberman & Gather-Thurler, 1991). But let me start with another study (Marsh & Glassick, 1988). Here evaluation findings were converted into recommendations that were subjected all along to negotiations of meaning and import between the parties. These negotiations were intentional, public, and evolutionary. The authors give the example of an evaluator who concluded that the behavior of some special education students constituted being "off task," whereas the program staff interpreted the behavior in different terms. (The evaluator changed his interpretation and recommendation.) Also, users were encouraged to transform the recommendations in ways that optimally fit their home settings. Reported actual use of the recommendations was unusually high, and the authors attribute it to the high levels of interaction throughout the process.

In my own work, I have described this strategy as "sustained inter-activity"—a cumbersome term. What it signifies, basically, is that researchers and practitioners remain in contact through the research process and for some months thereafter. In the initial phase, they determine the degree to which their study can or might answer local questions and they design their sampling form accordingly. During the study, there are contacts (with practitioners or with intermediaries) to detect the emerging findings of greatest interest to practitioners, and to conduct discussions that go beyond the study—which deal with larger issues of instruction or motivation or personality or management.

Note that some interesting things are going on. First, practitioners and researchers are gradually learning one another's contexts, both cognitively and socially. Then, too, there is a mutual "taming" process going on, notably during the informal periods of contact. Also, this process is giving the requisite time to practitioners to master the import of the study and, at the same time, to cast it in a broader perspective. Normally, a study is completed, published, and thrust into the hands of a reader who has not undergone this cognitive journey and who, as a result, is likely to discard the product, to read it selectively, or to distort its findings.

Later still, when it is time to write up findings and craft reports, a dissemination plan can be designed for practitioner publics: "targeted" reports (as opposed to the usual "omnibus" report), more than one channel (visual, written), in-person contacts, readability and attractiveness of written materials, focus on "manipulable" variables (things that can be changed), specificity of conclusions, sensitivity to local contexts and susceptibilities. These are the "dissemination variables" often associated with greater use of research findings on the part of nonresearchers.

There are three more ingredients in the formula. First, follow-up: the presence of researchers in the universe of practitioners well after the study. This corresponds, in fact, to an attempt to advocate the pertinence of the study in particular contexts and obligates the researcher both to master those contexts and to accept a micro-political role in the school or school system. Second, this phase is meant to continue the conversation around the object of study that was begun long ago—not to instruct users on the proper way to exploit these data, but rather to see how they play out locally and what they might signify conceptually. Finally, the researchers go beyond the study, since the study will address so few local issues. They reach into their own background and expertise to answer questions by teachers, help make conjectures, explain mysterious behaviors, illuminate test batteries.

It is true enough that these measures typically result in higher levels of "conceptual use" (new knowledge, perceptions, attitudes, ideas) and, often, of "instrumental use" (changes in everyday practices, new policies; cf. Huberman & Gather-Thurler, 1991; Marsh & Glassick, 1988). In other words, certain ways of bringing research findings to people will result in their greater use. Not because the findings themselves are so convincing, but because researchers have learned how to negotiate the meaning of their findings with others and have learned, above all, that interpersonal contacts and time for practitioners to assimilate the import of a given study are crucial factors.

Two final observations from my own work are, I think, warranted. We found, somewhat to our astonishment, that *researchers were often as affected by these exchanges as were practitioners* (Huberman & Gather-Thurler, 1991). When one stops a moment, the explanation is clear. Researchers report that having their findings contradicted, qualified, and recast in other frameworks all put into question the conceptual bases on which their study was founded. After all, they were carrying on discussions over time with experienced professionals who had seen literally hundreds of cases like those under review in the study findings. The result was that several researchers spoke of reorienting their lines of inquiry next time around, of having been "conceptually affected." What this means—and it is far from trivial—is that researchers have as much to gain from interactive dissemination as do practitioners.

Finally, our data showed that people stayed in touch, not only the research team and the set of practitioners with whom they had worked directly but, gradually, others from the research institute and school system (Huberman, 1990). They stayed in touch and began to initiate collaborative projects together: some training, some more research, some pilot projects, some mutual interventions in another state. This means that, several months after the study, more individuals at different levels from both institutions were doing business together. And this, in turn, signifies that sustained working relationships between the two "planets" are far more desirable than the effects of any given study. If we need the "technology" of research utilization to get to this point, so be it. But there must be faster ways to bridge these two communities in durable ways. Whatever they are, and returning here to T. S. Eliot's "Little Gidding," we have seen that they will cleave closer to mutual attachment than to mutual indifference.

Fragile Communication, Not Utilization

Margret Buchmann and Robert E. Floden

In laying out many uses for research, Michael Huberman provides empirical support and complexity for some of the conceptual arguments in these three chapters. Given its "fringes of meaning," we remain unhappy with the term *use*, yet we concur with our respondent that the virtues of research can be valuable for educational practice (and vice versa), that there are several perspectives on relations between research and practice, and that the most promising approach for both (and all) sides involves sustained, open-minded interactions among concerned participants. With our respondent, we believe that people's differing habits of mind and action require the "canopy of conversation."

We depart from this shared and brightening vista in how we interpret these consecutive chapters and assess the pitfalls of research utilization. Our disagreements arise from divergent understandings of this part's internal progression, of the term *knowledge utilization* itself, and probably also from a tendency to see more that is fragile, paradoxical, and elusive in knowledge and communication. In the seventeenth century, Pascal (1910) spoke to this last point as follows:

> We sail within a vast sphere, ever drifting in uncertainty, driven from end to end. When we think to attach ourselves to any point and to fasten to it, it wavers and leaves us; and if we follow it, it eludes our grasp, slips past us, and vanishes forever. (p. 29)

By singling out themes for his comments across chapters, Michael Huberman's interpretive approach raises issues that relate to this existential and epistemological predicament.

At some points our respondent seems to rebuke us for taking an overly narrow view of research utilization and for casting research as arid and degrading to practice. Given our attention to the passions of researchers and our own commitments to research, Huberman wonders about such positions. There is no inconsistency here. For one thing, as J. S. Mill (1838/1962) makes clear in sympathetically dissecting the strengths and limits of Jeremy Bentham as a thinker, one can be passionately committed to narrow and arid views (of people, the points of their lives, and of thinking). For another thing, our criticisms are leveled not so much at research and researchers as at particular ways in which some researchers relate their work to practice and in which connections between research and practice are conceived, with associated presuppositions and entailments. Suffused by feelings, these interacting conceptions are shaped by history and contexts of culture.

Inclinations to think of relating research and practice in terms of utilization draw upon an ambivalent view of knowledge as a tool and toward an overestimation of the generality, certainty, and applicability of research for policy and practice—with consequent disappointments fostering still greater ambivalence. These observations are not directed against all connections between research and practice. Certainly we reiterate some warnings, based on proverbial human frailties that scholars like Francis Bacon, J. S. Mill, Max Weber, and Robert Merton periodically rediscover. In part, we had hoped that inspecting the concept of knowledge utilization would open readers to more rewarding and mutual connections between research and practice.

Huberman rightly suspects that our overall argument aims to identify inherent tensions, rather than describing fatal flaws in educational research or communication. Just as we highlight vital tensions in teaching and teacher education—holding these tensions steady for consideration and action—so these essays on research and practice aim to remind readers of tensions within communicative relations between researchers and practitioners, within researchers' roles, and within the practice of research. In writing about the perturbing coexistence of detachment and concern as energies of wanting, Hampshire (1967) turns human limits and paradoxes into epistemic advantages. "The vitality of scholarship," he concludes,

> comes precisely from the lack of single-mindedness. It comes from the exploration, conducted in the spirit of objectivity, upon resisting, complex materials, and an *unrelieved concern* [italics added], from an urge to find a definite solution, combined with the recognition that definite solutions are scarcely at all to be found. (pp. 42–43)

We agree with our respondent that "sustained interactivity" provides opportunities for second thoughts and intellectual "tacking" that resonate to multiplying tensions, albeit without resolving them. Indeed, quoting Dewey's thrilling prose on communication, we find ourselves at the beginning of the third chapter in this part where Huberman's response ends: affirming hopes and searching for appropriate techniques, or arts and means of doing. Our stance thus departs from the critical theorists with whom our respondent locates us. We likewise share concerns for improvement with the utilitarian camp, while stressing that people often enjoy knowledge for its own sake.

Can "bridges" between research and practice, however, be faster in the building or more durable than they appear to be? Michael Huberman avers that it must be so; given our sense of shared frailties and fragility in communication, we feel constrained to doubt. Although there is evidence to support Huberman's disappointment that policy is too often uninformed, our tough stand against "utilization" signals, perhaps, greater worries about the incorporation of research into educational policy. The history of research on teaching offers examples of research "findings" that quickly become written into policy requirements, with effects distressing to initial investigators and other parties. When people say "research has shown," they often mean to give others directions for action. Recognizing these political and epistemic problems underscores the need to raise questions about the wisdom of thinking, or saying, that research can be used.

While being protected from sentimentality by the critical tradition, we still adhere to the ideal of conversation. Enlightening avenues and practicable means for relating research and practice thus remain a shared concern. Michael Huberman looked across these chapters, abstracting themes for elaboration and interrogation. Yet purposive switches in the contexts and emphases of this part's analyses—from concepts to forms of interactive discourse to dilemmas of research writing—indicate our attempts to venture beyond critique, with a view toward enabling some confidence in action under conditions of uncertainty and vibrating tensions. This is a leitmotiv, a "figure in the carpet," which we, as authors, foolishly believe to be "as concrete there as a bird in a cage, a bait on a hook, a piece of cheese in a mouse-trap" (James, 1896, p. 18).

Part III

TEACHER THINKING AND TEACHER LEARNING

CHAPTER 7

Role Over Person: Morality and Authenticity in Teaching

Margret Buchmann

What teachers do is neither natural nor necessary but based on choice. Since choice may harden into custom or dissipate into whim, one asks for justification; it is a way of ensuring that teaching will periodically pass muster. In justifying their actions, people give reasons. For teachers, personal reasons can be appropriate when explaining a given action to others, but they carry less weight in considering the wisdom of an action or decision. In other words, some contexts call for explanation and others for justification. When one wants to understand why people did something, one wants to know what actually motivated them; but if one wants to know whether what was done was right, one wants to hear and assess justifications. Here it is important that the reasons be good reasons, and it becomes less important whether they were operating at the time.

RESPONSIBILITY AND REASONS

The question, then, is what counts as good reasons in teaching. I argue that for many teacher actions personal reasons are subordinate to external standards and that the scope of these actions is much broader than is often assumed. Providing acceptable justification requires the existence of a community both to set standards for adequacy and to determine a set of rules for guidance. The role obligations of teachers as members of such a community forge bonds that not only ensure compliance but generate effort and involvement.

Curriculum decisions may be at the top of the list of teacher actions for which one should expect adequate justification, for, as Scheffler (1958/1977b) points out, it is not a matter of indifference or whim just what the educator chooses to teach. Some selections we judge better than others; some we deem positively intolerable. Nor are we content to discuss issues of selection as if they hinged on personal taste alone. We try to convince others; we present ordered arguments; we appeal to custom and principle; we point to relevant consequences and implicit commitments. In short, we consider decisions on educational content to be responsible or justifiable acts with public significance. (p. 497)

But decisions about the social organization of the class, how to deal with parents, and how to treat requests from school administrators are also examples of teacher actions that are responsible acts of public significance. It is useful to recall the root meaning of *responsibility:* Being a respondent has to do with one's answering for things and defending a position.

Personal reasons—centering on one's habits, interests, and opinions—are relevant for considering the wisdom of actions where the question is what the individual *per se* wants to accomplish, but not for professional situations where goals (and perhaps a range of means) are a given. People accepting a professional role are in the latter situation, and one must ask whether their particular actions and general dispositions are enacting and conforming to given standards and goals. Such people have no right to decide whether to act on their clients' behalf and in their interests: It is their obligation to teach school, put a leg in a cast, or appear in a court of law. This is why a professional's most significant choice is whether to take on the role (see Fried, 1978).

What is close to people is always important to them; the personal will take care of itself. But professional aspirations, responsibility, and curricular subjects with their pedagogies must be learned. Tendencies in teacher preparation and staff development to stress individualism, self-realization, and the personal—even idiosyncratic—element in teaching are therefore problematic. This would be true in any case, but such tendencies are extremely questionable in education in the United States, where structural features (e.g., recruitment, induction, rewards) and the ethos of the profession already converge in conservatism, presentism, and individualism. The point is that attention to role is especially important for U.S. teachers because it goes against many potent forces.

An understanding of teacher orientations (role vs. personal) and their effects is particularly important now when there is strong pressure to set policies that will improve schooling in the United States. It is well recognized that teachers have the final word on exactly what will be done in the classroom and what the actual curriculum will be. This implies that making good policy requires knowing how teachers are likely to act in answer to policy initiatives and why (see Wise, 1979). It requires, furthermore, thinking about those competencies and dispositions that teachers as *professionals* should have.

TEACHING AS A ROLE

It is crucial to appreciate the fact that *teacher* is a role word. Roles embody some of our highest aspirations and provide social mechanisms for shaping action in their light. They are parts people play in society and do not describe individuals. Teacher obligations—those behaviors and dispositions that students and the public have a right to expect of teachers—actually have three important aspects that have no personal reference or connection. First, these obligations do not depend on any particular individuals (teachers or students). Second, they apply regardless of personal opinions, likes, or dislikes. Third, they relate to what is taught and learned. In schools, teachers are supposed to help students participate in the "community of subject matter," whose objective contents of thought and experience—systems, theories, ideas—are impersonal because they are distinct from the people who learn or discuss them (Polanyi, 1958/1962).

In an immediate sense, teachers have obligations toward their students; these obligations center on helping them learn worthwhile things in the social contexts of classrooms and schools. The view of students as learners underlies the distinctive obligations of teachers, and role orientation in teaching by definition means taking an interest in student learning. Thus, insofar as teachers are not social workers, career counselors, or simply adults who care for children, their work centers on the curriculum and presupposes knowledge of subject matter. This is not inconsistent with their caring about children or being persons in their role.

Roles also indicate obligations toward more remote communities; in teaching, these communities include the profession, the public, and the disciplines of knowledge. For instance, while it is important to communicate the fact that disciplinary knowledge is not absolute, teachers have to recognize and respect the constraints imposed by the structure of different disciplines on their decisions about what to teach, for, as Schwab (1978a) points out, "if a structure of teaching and learning is alien to the structure of what we propose to teach, the outcome will inevitably be a corruption of that content" (p. 242). Since teachers are supposed to look after the educational interests of children, they have to learn to live with the fact that they are not free to choose methods, content, or classroom organization for psychological, social, or personal reasons alone.

The teacher educator slogans of "finding the technique that works for you," "discovering your own beliefs," "no one right way to teach," and "being creative and unique" are seductive half-truths. They are *seductive* because anyone likes to be told that being oneself and doing one's own thing is all right, even laudable. Conduct sanctioned in this fashion, while consistent with professional discipline for those who already have the necessary dispositions and competencies, allows for both minimal effort and idiosyncrasy in other cases. These slogans are *half*-truths because, although identifying teachers' personal and commonsense beliefs is important, once identified, these beliefs must be appraised as bases and guides for professional conduct and, where necessary, challenged.

Professional socialization marks a turning point in the perception of relevant others and of oneself, yet a reversal of prior conceptions is less clear-cut and typical in teaching than in other professions. Formal socializing mechanisms in teaching are few and short in duration, are not very arduous, and have weak effects. The lengthy, personal experience of being in school as a student, however, provides a repertoire of behaviors, beliefs, and conceptions that teachers draw on. Where it is successful, genuine professional socialization trains attention on the specialized claims that others have on one. Thus the teaching role entails a specific and difficult shift of concern from self to others for which the "apprenticeship of observation" (Lortie, 1975, chap. 3) provides no training. Highet (1950) describes the nature of this shift: "You must think, not what you know, but what they do not know; not what you find hard, but what they will find hard; then, after putting yourself inside their minds, obstinate or puzzled, groping or mistaken as they are, explain what they need to learn" (p. 280).

In general, a shift of concern from self to others comes more from acknowledging "This is the kind of work I am doing" than from stating "This is how I feel" or "This is how I do things." Subjective reasons refer to personal characteristics and preferences. They are permissive rather than stringent, variable rather than uniform. Appraisal requires distance, but detachment is difficult where things are seen simply as part of oneself. Personal beliefs and preferences are often hard to see, let alone analyze or modify. This explains the air of finality that many subjective reasons have. Yet it is not that personal beliefs and preferences must necessarily be misleading or selfish, but that—where such criteria rule—other and more legitimate concerns may become secondary. This reverses the relation in which personal and professional reasons should stand in teaching.

Subjectivity and Reasonableness

When people say, "This is the kind of person I am," they mean to close an issue and put an end to debate, whether or not the issue has been satisfactorily resolved. An emphasis on the self can block the flow of speculation, conversation, and reflection by which people shape habits of action and mind that affect others or the self; it means cutting oneself and the collective off from some of the most valuable human resources. Nor are teachers exceptions to the rule that not everything people want is good. Imperviousness and finality—of feeling, belief, or habit—interfere with learning and with getting better at helping others learn.

Justification is always tied to reason and susceptibility to reason; teaching is special in the sorts of reasons that are acceptable. Professional decisions are tied to the public realm where they are constrained by facts and norms, both forms of public knowledge. Put differently, justification needs to reach beyond the particulars of teachers' own actions and inclinations to consider larger, organized contexts relevant to their work, such as the disciplines of knowledge, laws, and societal issues (Thelen, 1973). And teachers need not be creative to be reasonable. Rather, they must be willing to act in accordance with rules, submit to impersonal judgment, and be open to change for good reasons. To call an action or person reasonable still is praise, for reasonable people are neither inconsiderate nor rash, and their actions are unlikely to be futile or foolish.

Caprice and habit cut teaching off from thought, particularly from its moral roots. In cause and origin, caprice is inherently self-contained; it contrasts with cultivation or improvement by education, training, or attention. Habit is the opposite of impulse, and it confines in a different way. Yet caprice and habit are alike in that they both allow for action without adequate reasons, removing teacher actions and decisions from the realm of criteria for judging appropriateness. Part of reasonableness is the habit and capacity of giving due weight to evidence and the arguments of others who may offer new data or alternative explanations.

Workplace Isolation and Role Orientation

Teaching is lonely work in the United States. Controls are weak and standards low, rewards uncertainly related to achievement, and work success uncertain, often elusive (Lortie, 1975). While an inner transformation from person to teacher may be wanting, one can still get a job teaching school. There is a sense of "easy come, easy go" in teaching; such transiency does not support a sense of community. Tenure and salary are based on years of service rather than competence or commitment. An active interest in student learning does not come with teaching experience, as some teacher development theories seem to suggest (see, e.g., Fuller, 1969). To the contrary, teaching seems to have a calcifying effect on teachers (McLaughlin & Marsh, 1978; Waller, 1932/1961). The teaching career is flat, not providing sufficient opportunities for change in responsibilities or for professional renewal. Together with the uncertainties of teaching, all these things can affect even dedicated teachers. Thus Sizer (1984) describes the feelings of a veteran teacher:

> He is so familiar with the mistakes that ninth-graders make that he can sense them coming even before their utterance. Adverbs are always tougher to teach than adjectives. What frustrates him most are the partly correct answers; Horace worries that if he signals that a reply is somewhat accurate, all the students will think it is entirely accurate. At the same time, if he takes some minutes to sort out the truth from the falsity, the entire train of thought will be lost. He can never pursue any one student's errors to completion without losing all the others. (p. 13)

The organization of public schooling in the United States isolates teachers from one another, and there is a lack of a specialized language and shared workplace experiences. Hence it is difficult to develop a role orientation that one would be able and willing to use in the justification of teaching decisions and actions. And what does the inner self do when left unwatched and deprived of rules? The degree to which one's behavior can be observed and one's beliefs examined by relevant others is crucial in role performance and professional discipline. As Merton (1957) argues, "If all the facts of one's conducts and beliefs were freely available to anyone, social structures could not operate" (p. 115); however, "the teacher or physician who is largely insulated from observability may fail to live up to the minimum requirements of his status" (p. 115).

With increasing size and continuing accumulation of formal policies, schools are becoming public-service bureaucracies (Lipsky, 1980). Teachers adapt to conflicting policies and endemic uncertainties as best they can. These adaptations can result in private, intensely held redefinitions of the nature of teaching and of one's clientele. In resolving the tension between capabilities (often constrained by workplace demands) and objectives, individuals may lower their goals or withdraw from attempts at reaching them. In responding to a diverse clientele, they may reject the norm of universalism and discount some groups as unteachable. Because such private conceptions can help individual professionals placed in difficult situations, they tend to be held rigidly and are not open to discussion. Also, though modifying one's conception of students is private, the content of typical coping responses is likely to reflect prevailing biases.

There is thus a troubling relation between the development and persistence of inappropriate coping strategies in teaching—including racial, cultural, and sexual stereotypes—and the relative likelihood of staying on the job.

Role orientation as a disposition can steady teachers in their separate classrooms, helping them call to mind what their work is about and who is to benefit from it. A disposition is a special kind of orientation. While "to orient oneself" means to bring oneself into defined relations to known facts or principles, a disposition is a bent of mind that, once in place, comes naturally. Dispositions are inclinations relating to the social and moral qualities of one's actions; they are not just habits but intelligent capacities (Scheffler, 1965). With role orientation as a disposition, no extraordinary resolve is necessary to occasionally take a hard look at what one does or believes in teaching. But instead of instilling role orientation as a disposition, teacher educators often focus on the personal concerns of novices and experienced teachers.

Personal Concerns and Teacher Learning

In examining the processes of learning to teach, teacher development, and the adoption of innovations in schools, researchers and educators have identified a shift from personal to "impact" concerns (how is my action or innovation affecting my students?) as crucial. For example, Fuller (1969) identifies the emergence of concern for student learning as a culminating point in teacher development. Yet Fuller's concept of personalized teacher education has been questioned, even as an approach that may lead teachers from self-oriented concerns to other-oriented concerns (Feiman & Floden, 1980). The assumption that earlier concerns must be resolved before later ones can emerge confuses readiness and motivation. Just because some concerns carry more personal and affective charge, it does not follow that other concerns—less immediate, more important—cannot be thought about. Actually, teacher preparation and staff development that focus on personal concerns may have the undesirable effect of communicating to teachers that their own comfort is the most important goal of teacher education.

Zeichner and Teitelbaum (1982) draw attention to the political attitudes that a personalized, concerns-based approach to teacher preparation may promote.

> By advocating the postponement of complex educational questions to a point beyond pre-service training and by focusing attention primarily on meeting the survival-oriented and technical concerns of student teachers,

this approach (while it may make students more comfortable) serves to promote uncritical acceptance of existing distributions of power and resources. (p. 101)

One form of conservatism is to take the given and rest—an attitude that bypasses an important source of learning and change, namely, to take the given and *ask*. An emphasis on personal concerns is unlikely to change the ethos of individualism, conservatism, and presentism in teaching. There is, moreover, empirical evidence that both elementary and secondary teachers base significant curricular decisions on personal preferences. This empirical backing for my claim that role orientation is not getting sufficient emphasis in North American education is discussed below.

Teacher Preferences and the Curriculum

At the elementary level, Schmidt and Buchmann (1983) show that the allocation of time to subjects in six elementary classrooms was associated with teachers' personal beliefs and feelings concerning reading, language arts, mathematics, science, and social studies. Briefly, average daily time allocations went up and down in accordance with (1) teacher judgments on the degree of emphasis subjects should receive and (2) indications (self-reports) of the extent to which teachers enjoyed teaching these curricular areas. When projected over the entire school year, differences in time allocations associated with teacher preferences amounted to significant differences in the curriculum—for example, 45 hours more or less of mathematics instruction, 70 of social studies, and 100 of science.

Researchers also asked teachers to indicate how difficult they found teaching the five areas of the elementary school curriculum. Findings here were mixed and thought-provoking. For instance, in the area of reading, the six teachers studied did not seem to spend less time on reading just because they found it difficult to teach. But some such tendency could be observed in language arts, social studies, mathematics, and science. However, even here the results were less than clear. The mean differences between the teachers who found it difficult to teach social studies or mathematics and those who found either subject easy to teach, for example, were small. It is possible that personal difficulties experienced in teaching a subject may to some extent be neutralized by external policies or a sense of what is an appropriate emphasis on a particular subject. Also, these unclear results may be due to the fact that "finding something difficult to teach" has two alternative senses: the difficulty of the subject for the children, and the difficulty of the subject for the teacher.

In a related exploratory interview study (Buchmann, 1983), 11 out of 20 elementary teachers showed some form of role orientation as they explained the ways they typically organized curricular subjects in their classrooms (integrated vs. nonintegrated). What united the responses of role-oriented teachers was the fact that they placed themselves within a larger picture in which colleagues, the curriculum, and accountability figured in some fashion. They looked outward rather than inward. This is not to say that they had no personal interests or preferences that influenced what they taught and how they taught it. But they felt bound by obligations; the personal element in their responses was framed by a sense of the collective.

Teachers demonstrating a personal orientation in their responses did not go beyond the context of their own activities. Most of them (six out of nine) explained their classroom practices by reference to themselves as persons. Their responses tended toward the proximate: affinity to self, immediate experience, the present characteristics of children. The "language of caprice" (Lortie, 1975) pervaded several of their responses. In cases where they recognized that the needs of some children were unlikely to be met by their approach to teaching, these teachers would still explain what they thought and did by reference to personal inclination or habitual ways of working.

A three-year study of 14 fifth-grade classrooms examining curriculum and learning in science (Smith & Anderson, 1984) concluded that teachers' reliance on personal beliefs and styles hindered student learning. For example, in using a text with an unusual and sophisticated teaching strategy, teachers did not pay attention to critical information provided in the teacher's guide, relying on their previous ideas instead. In general, the researchers distinguished three approaches to teaching science that they identified by observing how teachers used textbooks and materials.

Activity-driven teachers focused on management and student interests rather than on student learning; while following the teacher's guide rather closely, they omitted or curtailed class discussions meant to help students think about the science activities they were doing. Didactic teachers stayed even closer to the text, which they regarded as a repository of the knowledge to be taught; their presentations, however, made little room for children's expression of their naive scientific conceptions, which therefore remained largely unchallenged. By contrast, discovery-oriented teachers avoided giving answers and encouraged students to develop their own ideas from the results of experiments; yet this distorted crucial intents of the text, which required direct instruction at certain points. While the texts were not perfect (failing, for instance, to spell out assumptions about teaching and learning science in the teacher's guide), the fact remains that these teachers relied on personal approaches to science teaching, with the result that the curriculum miscarried.

Cusick (1983) studied two large secondary schools, one predominantly white and suburban, the other racially mixed and located in the central part of a smaller industrial region. Though there were exceptions, a self-oriented and laissez-faire approach to curriculum and student learning was typical in both schools. A U.S. history class with a teacher who had served in World War II became a class on that European war; in a class on speech and forensics, the teacher encouraged students (mostly black) to talk about the seamier side of their personal lives—with no one listening, or teaching about speaking. A premium was put on getting along with kids, and this reward structure, combined with isolation from colleagues, lack of scrutiny, and an open elective system, turned these schools into places where teachers and students did what felt comfortable or what allowed them to get by. Though there was a pattern to these adaptations, they happened privately. These schools were not normative communities.

Cusick concludes that the secondary teachers he studied constructed "egocentric fields": They treated their job as an extension of self. The presumed needs of students accounted for most justifications of teaching practice ("This is the way to teach these kids," "This is what they relate to," or "I'm getting them ready for life"). However, curriculum and student needs were never discussed among teachers in these schools. This raises at least two important problems. First, though the freedom teachers enjoyed may bring high effort in some, other teachers can get by with doing little. Second, while able students with adult guidance may still learn worthwhile things under such conditions, others will pass through high school without learning much of anything.

IN TEACHING, SELF-REALIZATION IS MORAL

Autonomy and self-realization are indisputably personal goods. Schools, however, are for children, and children's autonomy and self-realization depend in part on what they learn in schools. Thus, self-realization in teaching is not a good in itself, but only insofar as pursuing self-realization leads to appropriate student learning. The point is that in professional work reasons of personal preference will usually not do; this applies to nursing, soldiering, and managing a stock portfolio as well as to teaching. The idea of a surgeon keen on self-realization at the operating table is macabre. A nurse who brings up personality and preference in explaining why she or he changed standard procedures in dealing with a seizure would not get very far. There is no reason why such things should be more acceptable in teaching. The fact that we may have come to accept them is certainly no justification.

Everyone likes to be comfortable, free of pain and bother. But the perspectives of psychology and profession are not the same. Things charged with personal meaning may lead nowhere in teaching. Even the integrity of self depends in part on suspending impulse. Simply declaring "where one comes from" makes justified action a matter of taste and preference, which expresses and reinforces a massive moral confusion (MacIntyre, 1981). In general, conscience does not reduce to sincerity: "While the 'heart may have reasons of its own,' when it simply chooses to assert these without critical inspection, then reason must condemn this as complacency" (Gouldner, 1968, p. 112). A deeper analysis of self-realization shows that the self people aim to realize is not, in the words of Bradley (1876/1927), "this or that feeling, or . . . any series of . . . particular feelings" (p. 160); people realize themselves morally "so that not only what ought to be in the world is, but I am what I ought to be, and find so my contentment and satisfaction" (p. 181).

Profession Requires Community

What is characteristically moral presupposes community, on both conceptual and pragmatic grounds. The concept of community is logically prior to the concept of role. The very possibility of the pursuit of an ideal form of life requires membership in a moral community; it is extremely unlikely that minimal social conditions for the pursuit of any ideal people are likely to entertain would in practice be fulfilled except through membership in such communities (Strawson, 1974a). Membership in moral communities is realized in action, conversation, and reflection. As a moral community, a profession "is composed of people who think they are professionals and who seek through the practical inquiry of their lives, both alone and together, to clarify and *live up to* [italics added] what they mean by being a professional" (Thelen, 1973, pp. 200–201). The quality of aspiration—of aiming steadfastly for an ideal—is supported by the normative expectations of others.

Teacher and student learning depend, in particular, on norms of collegiality and experimentation among teachers (Little, 1981). Norms of collegiality can reduce workplace isolation and help develop an orientation toward the teaching role; norms of experimentation are based on a conviction that teaching can always be better than it is. Norms of collegiality and experimentation are moral demands with intellectual substance. They are not matters of individual preference but are based, instead, on a shared understanding of the kinds of behaviors and dispositions that people have a right to expect of teachers. These norms require detachment—a willingness to stand back from personal habits, interests, and opinions. What one does or believes in is not considered as part of oneself but as something *other*—it becomes a potential exemplar of good (or not so good) ways of working, or of more or less justified beliefs.

Community provides not only constraints and guidance but succor. Collegiality, however, also depends on the degree to which another person is deserving and one's equal in deserts; it is not just loyalty and mutual help, but the enjoyment of competence in other people. Essential to collegiality in teaching is the degree to which its practitioners are good at talking with one another about their work and can be confident about their own ability, and that of others, as teachers and partners in the improvement of teaching. Without mental, social, and role competence, norms of collegiality and experimentation cannot take hold.

Morality and Authenticity in Teaching

Of course, teachers are persons. But being oneself in teaching is not enough. As Thelen (1973) emphasizes, authenticity must be paired with legitimacy as opposed to impulse and inflexible habit and with productivity as a reasoned sense of purpose and consequences:

> An activity is legitimated by reason, as distinguished from capricious-seeming teacher demand, acting-out impulse, mere availability, or impenetrable habit. An activity may be legitimated by group purposes, disciplines of knowledge, career demands, test objectives, requirements, societal issues, laws, or by any other larger, organized context that enables the activity to go beyond its own particulars. . . .
> An activity is productive to the extent that it is effective for some purpose. . . . It is awareness of purpose that makes means–ends thinking possible, allows consciousness and self-direction, tests self-concepts against reality, and makes practice add up to capability. (p. 213)

Legitimacy and productivity are entwined, capturing social expectations and aspirations central to teaching and to learning from teaching. People's ordinary conception of morality describes this interplay between ideals and the rule requirements of social organizations (see Strawson, 1974a).

To the extent that roles have moral content, their impersonality is not inhuman or uninspired. But rules, norms, and external standards alone cannot account for moral action in teaching. Role orientation must be lodged concretely in someone's head and heart. Where one's solid and full response to obligations is withheld, the claims of others are not acknowledged livingly. As Dewey (1933) stressed, thoughtful action does not depend only on open-mindedness and responsibility; wholeheartedness is also part of it. To the extent, then, that the content of role has been absorbed into the self, role becomes a personal project—shaping the inner self and the self as it appears to others. Thus, moral aspirations cannot be separated from the question of personal identity, but conversely, responsibility for oneself as a person does not mean that anything goes (Taylor, 1970).

In sum, the moral nature of teaching—which also requires being genuinely oneself—does not remove the need for role orientation. Instead, a proper understanding of authenticity in teaching builds in the idea of external standards within which teachers make authentic choices. The need for authenticity hence supplies no argument against role orientation, but suggests that there are some teacher decisions that will be completely determined by role, some that are constrained but not determined by role, and some—not many—for which role does not and should not provide guidance. The self has a peculiar place in teaching as a form of moral action; it is at once subdued and vital as a source of courage, spirit, and kindliness.

CHAPTER 8

The Practicality of Contemplative Attention: Devoted Thought That Is Not Deluded

Margret Buchmann

The painter's vision is not a lens,
it trembles to caress the light.

* * *

Yet why not say what happened?
Pray for the grace of accuracy
Vermeer gave to the sun's illumination
stealing like the tide across a map
to his girl solid with yearning.
—Robert Lowell, 1977, *Day by Day,* "Epilogue"

To speak of contemplation and practicality in one breath is to be guilty of a contradiction in terms, or so it seems. Practicality is associated with usefulness and action, while the careful vision of contemplation suspends wanting and doing in favor of a wonder-struck beholding. What, then, makes contemplation desirable in teaching, and what might such thinking require? How can its receptive stance be for the sake of practice? What should teachers contemplate? To address such questions, there has to be some understanding of practice and contemplation as a kind of thinking defined by many negations: absences, oppositions, surrenders, or repudiations.

Contemplation is "non-utilitarian, non-volitional, non-emotional, non-analytical . . . , an act of unselfish almost impersonal concentration" (Haezrahi, 1956, p. 36). Schopenhauer (1844/1956) similarly argues that conditions for coming to know exist if a person *relinquishes* the common way of looking at things, gives up tracing . . . their relations to each other, the final goal of which is always a relation to his own will; if he thus ceases to consider the where, the when, the why, and the whither of things, and looks simply and solely at the *what;* if, further, he does not allow abstract thought, the concepts of the reason, to take possession of his consciousness, but, instead of all this, gives the whole power of his mind to perception, sinks himself entirely in this and lets his whole consciousness be filled with the quiet contemplation of the . . . object actually present, . . . whatever it may be. (p. 147)

A common way of looking at teacher thinking is to regard it as planning or decision making, based, at its best, on research and scholarship. Yet people think about a great many things they can never know, and—in its search for meaning—the need to think is different from the need to act. To perceive teacher thinking rather than preconceive it, we need to look at some contexts in which people talk about thinking. To get clearer about the practicality of any kind of thinking, we must consider the concept of practice. I will show, then, how the moral discipline of quietly receptive attention expands notions of valuable thinking in teaching as one of the helping professions, while indicating an answer to the question of what more busy and controlling processes of thought may themselves refer to for support and guidance.

WHEN DO WE TALK ABOUT THINKING?

One might stand before a seventeenth-century Dutch painting, thinking, "The young woman sits at a table, pen in hand, gorgeous in her yellow jacket; a servant, waiting to carry her letter, smiles rather slyly: her mistress is wrapped in thoughts of her lover." Confronted with a puzzling situation, one turns it over in the mind, hoping to make some sense of it. In thinking, people often relive the past. When one asks a friend, "What is your thinking on that?" her answer may detail ambiguities of experience and feelings.

Thinking is an ordinary activity. We think because we are human, and if someone tells us to think, we do not ask a specialist, "How do I do that?" As "a natural need of human life," Hannah Arendt (1977/1978a) concludes, thinking "is not a prerogative of the few but an ever-present faculty in everybody; by the same token, inability to think is not a failing of the many who lack brain power but an ever-present possibility for everybody—scientists, scholars, and other specialists in mental enterprises not excluded" (p. 191).

The Many Faces of Thinking

More or less conscious of what they are doing, people think as they inhabit their world. To think means "to form or have in mind as an idea"; "to consider, mediate on, ponder"; "to have, or make, a train of ideas pass through the mind," which itself can be reviewed. In forming ideas, thinking is imagining or conceiving. Thinking may require effort, as when one applies one's mind to something, giving it a steady mental attention that aims at comprehension. Thoughts can thus be fixed in the mind and worked out in detail. Judgment comes to the fore when thinking involves situations that require forming an opinion, good or bad, valuing or esteeming something or someone, highly or otherwise. And poets have associated thinking with the heart; as Wordsworth (1833/1904) wrote, "'Tis the still hour of thinking, feeling, loving" (p. 705).

Some thoughts have their beginning and end in a wonder that is "neither puzzlement nor surprise nor perplexity; it is an *admiring* wonder" (Arendt, 1977/1978a, p. 143). Holding someone in regard (as the young woman in the Dutch painting does) is not just looking at a person but being drawn to what may be visible only to the inward eye. But thinking can also lead to solving a problem or eventuate in a project whose likely outcomes are considered. Consideration recedes into memory in the senses of "to think" as "to call to mind, bear in mind, recollect or remember." "Remembrance has a natural affinity to thought. . . . Thought-trains rise naturally, almost automatically, out of remembering, without any break" (Arendt, 1978b, p. 37).

Thinking plays havoc with the restrictions of life. It can recall the past, make the future present, and move people through time and space. Thoughts are intangible, elastic, light in movement, even fanciful. But innocence is also lost in thought. Hence, thinking is not void of effects. Once one has started a nontrifling argument with oneself, one cannot always abandon it. Literature and experience testify to the disclosing and disturbing powers of thought. And mind's suspension of natural laws coexists with people's belief that there is often a duty to think.

Thinking Attention and Goodness

What can one learn about thinking when considering the *absence* of thought? First, thoughtlessness is less a lack of mental prowess than a missing disposition or capacity for being mindful of things and people. Second, *thoughtlessness* is no purely descriptive term, nor is it considered a mere mistake. One's failure to acknowledge "the claim on our thinking attention that all events and facts make by virtue of their existence" (Arendt, 1977/1978a, p. 4) is also a moral failure. We describe someone as thoughtless who, being heedless, ignores what calls for attention. An assumption is that, with due attention, people can hardly fail to see the import of some particular thing or things, including other people's needs and feelings, and their own obligations. Considering how people regard the absence of thought qualifies the airy freedom of thinking.

Iris Murdoch (1970) contends, accordingly, that "the idea of a really good man living in a private dream world seems unacceptable."

> Of course a good man may be infinitely eccentric, but he must know certain things about his surroundings, most obviously the existence of other people and their claims. The chief enemy of excellence in morality . . . is personal fantasy: the tissue of self-aggrandizing and consoling wishes and dreams which prevents one from seeing what is there outside one. (p. 59)

It is a mistake to assume that what is most personal is also most profound and most reliable as a source of energies; the self often moves in a vain circle. Detached *and* concerned, thoughtful persons are valued for their attachment to the right objects of thought. Note that objects of thought are not necessarily things but simply that toward which one's attention is directed; their kinds and relations vary by contexts of thought and practice.

IS PRACTICE PRACTICAL?

Good carpenters have patience and skill, understand the purposes of their craft, and see more in their work over time. While practice means the habitual carrying on of something—customary or constant action— it also implies ideals of perfection. Comparative imperfections stem from people's shortcomings, the vulnerability of aspirations to chance and circumstance, and the multiplicity of conflicting goods attached to any action. If, in the ordinary case of failure of attention to some good, we are "open to the voice of complaint," William James (1891/1969) observes, the "good which we have wounded returns to plague us with interminable crops of consequential damages, compunctions, and regrets" (p. 188).

Due to the assumption of special knowledge and skill, and an associated power over others, participants in a practice should be (in the sense of having a duty to be) people others can trust: trust to do their best, to be honest and fair, to be concerned about the effects of their actions, and to acknowledge the particular claims which their work makes on its practitioners. What sets the professional apart from the chiseler (the person who gets by with minimal efforts, looking out for the self as "number one"), as well as the amateur, has some commonalities across different endeavors. Take a musician's reflections on her performance, for instance.

> I did not expect praise, for that is the prerogative of amateurs, who have a limited objective in view. Once one is a professional musician one's goal is set in infinity.... All that one can hope from a professional (even if that be oneself) is an admission that one is in a state of motion, and when this admission is respectful it often takes the paradoxical form of a complaint that one is not moving fast enough. This seems inconsistent, but then to be a professional musician one must ... [have] a split mind, half of which knows it is impossible to play perfectly, while the other half believes that to play perfectly is only a matter of time and devotion. (West, 1984, p. 124)

What matters in being a professional, she concludes, is walking with others in a "procession that would gloriously never arrive at its destination" (pp. 124–125) and, in so doing, affirming a community of evolving craft.

When people speak of a practice, they have more in mind than a sum of activities, skilled capacities, or the modes and outcomes of typical work. They imagine configurations of goods and excellences that are anchored collectively. This normative concept of practice indicates that human flourishing—acting, thinking, and living well—is not just single or solitary, nor simply a skilled production. Weeding the flower beds or checking student tests are not practices in this sense, but playing the piano, teaching, and cultivating one's garden are, though there are many different ways of going about these complex, patterned endeavors (see MacIntyre, 1981). Yet each of these ways has a quality of relatedness that, depending on attention, resonates to the possibilities of what one is working with. The learning of a cabinetmaker, like that of a poet, Heidegger (1954/1968) argues,

> is not mere practice, to gain facility in the use of tools. Nor does he merely gather knowledge about the customary forms of the things he is to build. If he is to become a true cabinetmaker, *he makes himself answer and respond above all* [italics added] to the different kinds of wood and to the shapes slumbering within wood.... In fact, this relatedness to wood is what maintains the whole craft. (pp. 14–15)

Thus, showing a new employee around the shop, a seasoned carpenter gives "his usual speech about the importance of choosing your wood."

> "Me, I always go for cherry if I can," he said. "It's the friendliest, you could put it. The most obedient."

"Cherry," the man said, nodding.

"It's very nearly *alive*. It changes color over time and it even changes shape and it breathes." (Tyler, 1991, p. 250)

Hearing Secret Harmonies

Attention vibrates, deepens, and spreads as understandings and skills develop. If this is true for working with words and wood, it is true in even more compelling ways for people-work, where responsiveness and relatedness take on a special meaning. People relating to others are already related; they make themselves answer to their own kind and must not assume, for instance, that what is best in themselves is, therefore, peculiar to themselves, or that what gives them most pain is due solely to their own precious sensibilities. Responsiveness that assumes congruence, however, must be leavened and made perspicacious by a thrilling sense of irreducible uniqueness in the person confronting one.

While the other person has her own urgencies, one can apprehend them only if one has felt them, somehow, oneself; nevertheless, they are not one's own urgencies. These matters become even more perplexing when other people—friends, students, patients—cannot or will not reveal what is urgent to them or what is an impelling, prompting, or constraining force in what they think, feel, and do. So one must learn to hear secret harmonies, but one must hear them accurately and also resonate to them. Hence Canetti (1973/1978) asks:

> But what is urgent? What he feels and recognizes in others and what they cannot say. He must first have felt and recognized it and then found it again in others. The congruence creates the urgency. He has to be capable of two things: to feel strongly and to think; and to *hear* the others and take them seriously in a never-ending passion. The impression of congruence must be sincere, undimmed by any vanity. . . . He must be able to keep it upright when it threatens to crumble, he has to nourish it incessantly through new experience and effort. (p. 276)

Virtues and Their Obstructions

One cannot take part, in association with others, in some form of human striving if one is mean-spirited, dishonest, unfeeling, or vain, or heedless of the goods and excellences that a normative practice embodies and extends. All people are almost compelled by what they *can* see, but these considerations have a particular moral force for doctors, social workers, and teachers. In these helping professions, practitioners must look beyond the dense, sprawling self to cultivate virtues such as generosity and kindness, sobriety and gentleness, hope and courage in the service of others.

> If someone says that he cares for some individual, community or cause, but is unwilling to risk harm or danger in his, her or its own behalf, he puts in question the genuineness of his care and concern. Courage, the capacity to risk harm or danger to oneself, has its role in human life because of this connection with care and concern. (MacIntyre, 1981, p. 179)

Virtues alone cannot account for human flourishing, however. Thinking of activities as like rivers, one can see how the fulfillment of their potentials can be obstructed from the outside: "One way they can be impeded is to be dammed up and prevented from reaching a destination. Another way would be to be filled up with sludge so that their channel would become cramped and muddy, their continuous flow slower, the purity of their waters defiled" (Nussbaum, 1986, p. 327). In teaching, bureaucratization and "legislated learning" are instances of the second kind of obstruction (see Wise, 1979). Since not only external factors but misguided ideas and feelings can obstruct any activity that is the bearer of human goods, improving practice requires that people interrupt the flow of everyday cognitions and activities and hold their attention steady in really looking at their work and listening to the people it may affect. Karl Barth (1961) warns:

> Neither the people among whom we have to work, nor things, relations and problems in their everyday form, are waiting for the man who is ready to sacrifice himself for them with some heroism and excitement. On the contrary, men want to be seen and understood as they are. They want to be considered in their situation and from their own point of view, and addressed and treated as such. . . . They are not there as mere objects of our zeal or good intentions or will-power, which must adjust themselves to us as such. Rather, we are there . . . to take to ourselves their need and worth and purpose, and on these presuppositions to give them of our best. (pp. 642–643)

Contemplation sets aside ties to self-involved willing and feeling, to given ways of thinking and schemes of action, making room for the quietly receptive attention that any dedicated work requires.

DEVOTED THOUGHT THAT IS NOT DELUDED

Participation in the contemplative life—rather than preoccupation with utility, desires, abstractions, or immediate circumstances—may be the spring from which the meaning and increasing worth of many actions and decisions originate. Contemplation requires serenity and clarity of vision. It engages the emotions and the will only insofar as these dispose one toward peace and purity of heart and help one direct one's attention to worthy objects. Importantly, it is less those objects than oneself and one's thinking that get changed in the continuing process of contemplation. *Via* fidelity—faithfulness to others (see Noddings, 1986) and to what there is—truth and goodness converge in a contemplative experience that is not otherworldly.

Aquinas (1966) discusses the active life and the contemplative life in *Summa Theologiæ*, where he also examines the question to which form of life teaching might belong (2a2æ. 179–182). In the active life, people aim to affect things or other people and are often ruffled by their recalcitrance. The life of contemplation may involve a kind of application in cogitation or meditation. But contemplation is the point where activity comes to rest; its essential qualities are those of a wonder-struck beholding, in attending to some desirable or lovable good—including any truth whatever. And the goods intrinsic to a practice can be contemplated "not just by dedicated experts but by ordinary people: [in] an attention which is not just the planning of particular good actions but an attempt to look right away from self towards a distant transcendent perfection" (Murdoch, 1970, p. 101).

The Priority of Contemplation

Though the active and the contemplative lives can be distinguished, both are forms of human life, and in an actual existence now the one, now the other form, will predominate. And it is possible for action to lead to contemplation and for contemplation to lead to action: Both forms of life are complementary. In accordance with most medieval authors, however, Aquinas (1966) maintains that the contemplative is superior to the active life. He stresses that the "return to the active life from the contemplative is by way of *direction* [italics added], in that the active life is guided by the contemplative" (p. 83); divorced from contemplation, the active life would be cut off from its source of value (see Thomas Aquinas, 1966, Appendix 6).

If action is shown the way by contemplation, to which action, as a derivative, must refer, we can conclude that normative practices begin and end in contemplative thought. It is not difficult to apply these claims to work in the helping professions. In teaching, for instance, thought and action need to flow from—and return to—raising one's sights to people (primarily students) and teaching subjects, and thought and action without reference to the ultimate good of learning would be without rudder. Inducting people into teaching entails helping them attend to ideals of perfection relating to their work and its distinctive goods, fostering dispositions to think and be concerned about those goods and the people affected by one's work, and upholding—as well as feeling the import of—general human virtues such as truthfulness, sobriety, gentleness, and courage.

Contemplative attention assumes telling force and sustaining energy, for "our ability to act well 'when the time comes' depends partly, perhaps largely, upon the quality of our habitual objects of attention" (Murdoch, 1970, p. 56). It is not only the stance of contemplation and its revealing quality but the *worth* of the objects to which it attaches itself that accounts for the priority of contemplation, since what people thus hold in regard is, by function and affection, the substance of their comprehensive practical life. Action, to quote Murdoch again, "tends to confirm, for better or worse, the background of attachment from which it issues" (p. 71).

LEARNING TO ATTEND IN THE HELPING PROFESSIONS

> Human life is inexhaustible in all its branches. We have to lay hold of it even to find it interesting, let alone to like it. . . . The greatest reward of faithfulness to vocation is to be able to devote ourselves to our concern not only with interest but with desire and love. . . . But this is a reward which we cannot expect nor demand, and at which we are not to aim. (Barth, 1961, p. 642)

In their vital imprecision, professional ideals provide a growing sense of order, direction, and deepening meaning. They attach people to their best selves and to worthy objects of attention, illuminate the real and desirable, and supply ways to distinguish the passable from what is excellent. Teachers, doctors, and nurses, therefore, are people who make decisions, but there are stringent limits to their freedom, which consists more in choosing activities so that one will encounter opportunities and can cultivate abilities for *acting on* ideals than in discovering them—like some newly found islands—or causing them to exist (see Schwartz, 1979). As Martin Buber (1926/1947b) says, "Every form of relation in which the spirit's service of life is realized has its special objectivity, its structure of proportions and limits which in no way resists the fervour of personal comprehension and penetration, though it does resist any confusion with the person's own spheres" (p. 95).

Helping people become attached to ideals of perfection in their work is hence a crucial *practical* task, which depends on recalling what a practice is about in the first place. "Meaningful devotion," as Barth (1961, p. 643) calls it, must be well guided and closely informed. What keeps doctors, nurses, social workers, and teachers from seeing other people with accuracy and kindness is not just their private blind spots, however, but also the categories and theories in terms of which professionals may think of their clients. To clarify the meaning and development of contemplative attention in teaching and other helping professions, I will relate several stories.

Letting Go of Protective Theories

Going back to the beginnings of his life as a psychiatrist, Robert Coles (1989) describes his professional learning in terms of developing a certain direction and quality of attention, concluding that the issue "was not only whether a doctor trained in pediatrics and child psychiatry might help a child going through a great deal of social and racial stress, but what the nature of my attention ought to be" (p. 25). How, in short, was he to use his mind?

As a novice, Coles was aware of his lack of knowledge, a strong command of various theories and classification schemes notwithstanding. His first response to the demands of dealing with patients was mobilizing social authority: Whatever his shortcomings in maturity and competence, he could get a nurse to bring a patient to *him*. His second response, encouraged by a supervisor admired as a brilliant theorist, was to establish (rapidly and almost aggressively) conceptual control of the situation. Yet Coles was quick to sense the "protective function of theory." He writes that, having acquired an "intellectual fix" on what happened during "therapeutic" sessions,

> I often found myself feeling less afraid for myself, if not for the patient. I now "knew" her, and I could look forward to yet another chance to listen, to inquire, to *hear confirmed what I'd been taught* [italics added]. As for the occasional moments of doubt and worry (Why isn't she getting any better?), my supervisor had some analgesic words. (Coles, 1989, p. 9)

Less inclined to soothe the young doctor's pains, another supervisor "encouraged a gentler tone, a slower pace, a different use of the mind" (Coles, 1989, p. 14). Listening to the novice more than talking himself—although not hesitant to teach pointedly at times—this older doctor encouraged a shift from theories and patient classifications to concrete persons and their stories. He asked questions like "Do you *see* her in your *mind?*" or "Did you stop and wonder what he's *now* going through?"

Implicitly, this supervisor was asking whose words mattered, *who* was to appropriate the word "interesting."

Throughout his career, Coles recalled his teacher's words that "the people who come to see us bring us their stories. They hope they tell them well enough so that we understand the truth of their lives. They hope we know how to interpret their stories correctly. We have to remember that what we hear is *their story*" (p. 7). The doctor struggling to learn began to discover the mind-opening power of listening to his patients "with a minimum of conceptual static" (p. 19). This shift in the quality and direction of professional thinking brought a partial reversal of roles, for people troubled in mind became the doctor's teachers, enabling him to help them.

The professional knowledge of the second supervisor in Coles's story centrally includes an understanding of the value of the pretheoretical— an understanding that, among other things, implies turning one's back on any controlling or defensive uses of expert knowledge. These psychiatrists accomplished a movement of return in the service of profession: recognizing and enacting a shared humanity in the form and content of stories, and the occasion for telling and listening to them with revealing attention.

Mind-Opening Attention in Teaching

In moving from psychiatry to teaching, much remains the same. There are still professional learners needing to pay attention to people as concrete persons and to transcendent ideals that embody and extend a practice. The distinctive learning teachers are supposed to advance, however, is primarily children's learning of school subjects. Teaching differs from other helping professions in having subject matter as its *first* object of contemplation. Teaching subjects and students can be known neither altogether, nor once and for all. The more they really look at their students, the more teachers recognize that their knowledge of learners is imperfect, a fallible vision also because youngsters change, and are supposed to change, in school. The more teachers think about their subjects, the less they are sure of their ground, becoming clearer about the limits of given understandings.

Contemplating teaching subjects. In accordance with Aquinas, the first object of contemplation in teaching is the unending consideration and love of knowledge in all of its forms, with the teacher taking delight in that love and consideration. Referring to Aristotle, Aquinas (1966) argues that the ability to teach is an indication of learning (p. 59). Since wisdom and truth belong to the contemplative life, he concludes that teaching belongs to the contemplative life. The implicit connections here seem as follows: One can teach because one has learned something; ultimately, learning is oriented toward truth and wisdom, involving, therefore, continuing contemplation.

Compared with other activities of thinking in teaching, contemplative attention to teaching subjects has logical, though not necessarily temporal, priority in teaching (see Buchmann, 1984a). One needs to have a sense of the concept of number and enjoy wondering about that idea—thus complicating one's understanding and sensing its limits—in order to help others think about what a number may be. Without knowing how to look at a painting and recognizing an artistic creation for what it is, what can a teacher say about a child's drawing except that it is "nice" or "true to life"?

When one manages to look with observant wonder, one will often become dissatisfied with conventional answers—whether based on common sense, textbooks, or science. This means that one becomes teachable again; Hawkins (1967/1974) tells a pertinent story about a young and very learned physicist:

> My wife was asking him to explain something to her about two coupled pendulums. He said, "Well, now, you can see that there's a conservation of. . . . Well, there's really a conservation of angle here." She looked at him. "Well, you see, in the transfer of energy from one pendulum to the other there is . . ." and so on and so on. And she said, "No, I don't mean that. I want you to notice this and tell me what's happening." Finally, he looked at the pendulums and he saw what she was asking. He looked at *it*, and he looked at *her*, and he grinned and said, "Well, I know the right words but I don't understand it either." This confession, wrung from a potential teacher, I've always valued very much. It proves that we're all in *it* together. (p. 62)

It is essential that teachers share, with their students, in an authentic and renewing engagement in looking at the world, at what there is outside one.

Wonder has its place as well in literary learning. Consider a poem. That it is patterned writing, arranged in lines, metrical and often rhyming, indicates something, but not all that much. To say that it is "poetic" or "the work of a poet" begs the question, while to claim that a poem is concerned with feelings or the imagination may be a falsehood—or a truism. After a lifetime as a poet, Robert Lowell (1977) asked in his "Epilogue' to *Day by Day,* What is a poem for? What is a poet supposed to do—remember or create? His concluding lines draw reader and poet, together, into contemplation.

> We are poor passing facts,
> warned by that to give
> each figure in the photograph
> his living name. (p. 127)

When they are inside their subjects, teachers, like poets, obviously know many things outsiders do not know. They are aware of major, often divergent perspectives, know how to work with specialized terms and symbols, and know that language should be arranged in certain ways: essays, proofs, or sonnets. In this they will be different from their students. But if teachers go beyond the surface of terms and forms and begin asking where concepts and patterns come from—or what they may *mean*—smooth answers will give way, leaving things to marvel at. This is true for everyday objects as well as for poems and pendulums. In looking at a teacup, a woman reflects:

> How little she knew about anything. Take this cup for instance; she held it out in front of her. What was it made of? Atoms? And what were atoms, and how did they stick together? The smooth hard surface of the china with its red flowers seemed to her for a second a marvellous mystery. (Woolf, 1937, p. 155)

Seeing concrete persons in teaching. If subject matter is the first object of contemplation in teaching, its *second* object are students. "Object," again, must not be confused with "thing"; it means "that toward which attention is directed" and does not imply any reified conception of people. Aquinas (1966) connects contemplation to the active life in teaching by stating that "it seems an office of the contemplative life to impart to another by teaching, truth that has been contemplated" (p. 61). Office here has the meaning of good office, a kindness or attention in the service of others; Aquinas (1973) also points out, "Just as it is better to illumine than merely to shine, so it is better to give to others the things contemplated than simply to contemplate" (p. 205).

Genuine relatedness *in teaching* depends on being attached to one's teaching subjects in the first place, while also caring for others in helping them to learn. That teachers' attention is urged on toward others also follows from the relation that exists in human life between what one most delights in and the wish to share it with others, particularly one's friends. To the extent that teaching involves other people—aiming to enlighten and perfect them as learners—the helping profession of teaching belongs to the active life and requires its skillful and well-informed exertions in the spirit of fellowship and kindness. Aquinas therefore concludes that teaching sometimes belongs to the active and sometimes to the contemplative life. Yet in moving from contemplation to action we do not subtract the contemplative but add the active dimension: The active life in teaching "proceeds from the fullness of contemplation" (1973, p. 205). To drive this point home, I have adapted a story from Iris Murdoch (1970).

Suppose that a secondary English teacher, Miss Jacobs, notices her hostility toward a new student. From the first day of school, John grates on his teacher's feelings. He seems uncouth in behavior and raw in intellect, overfamiliar and moody—always tiresomely adolescent. Miss Jacobs herself is a quiet person, a bit severe but intelligent and well intentioned. She knows that she is not at her best with boys of that age; in general, she cannot say that she *likes* adolescents. A term passes. Yet the teacher does not perfect her view of John as an impossible boy, firming it up in outline and elaborating it in detail; that is, she does not make her aversive picture of this student more impenetrable and solid.

Miss Jacobs has instead come to see John as endearingly awkward; his raw intellect now seems an untutored intelligence that calls for teaching. John appears to be not overfamiliar and excitable but trusting and emotional, to the point of being vulnerable. Protective, almost tender feelings supplant the earlier hostility. What has happened? John has not changed; he is still a rather pestilential adolescent. Nor has Miss Jacobs been busy in any external sense or drawn up plans to change him. On the surface, the teacher has substituted one set of (moral) words for another, with positive instead of negative meaning. But deep down she has been thinking, attentively, until she could give John, as Lowell put it, his "living name."

A change of vision can be a delusion, but let us further suppose that his teacher has *looked* at John (and beyond the stereotype); she has concentrated her attention on *him* (and away from her own sensitivities and limitations), achieving an inward stance and progress of intrinsic worth and attraction that does student *and* teacher good. Part of this progress stems from setting aside self-centered feelings together with conventional and self-protective modes of classification; yet the greater part stems from seeing John not just with accuracy but with kindness as a concrete person. In this fashion, Miss Jacobs has come to see much more of John's traits and aspirations, many of which are repeated in other adolescents, but which the teacher attends to "not as pieces of something homogeneous that turns up in many places in the universe, but as forming the essential core of what that concrete person is" (Nussbaum, 1986, p. 357). There is John's generosity of heart and his painful desire to see the world set right, which surface in awkwardness and mood swings.

Why do adults, who act so godlike and knowing, make such a mess of things, between famines, wars, and divorces?

As Miss Jacobs feels John's accusing eyes on herself, she has to admit that she does not understand it either. The teacher also knows that she would prefer to be seen less as a member of the pretentious and floundering tribe of adults and more as herself: imperfect but real. Still, she realizes that it may not be in John's power, now, to fulfill that wish, nor is it his duty to do so. Through thinking, Miss Jacobs prepares herself to be loyal to John in her professional role, becoming attached to what is most excellent in him and choosing to make his good as a learner her own.

Contemplative attention is one's corrigible vision of other people and the response to *their* reality, the careful vision of their truth, which is their individuality, separate and distinct from oneself. Such attentive thinking involves a personal application that is not willing; it is a modifying and disclosing force that works by progressive inward operation. In this way of looking, "the soul empties itself of all its own contents in order to receive into itself the being it is looking at, just as he is, in all his truth" (Weil, 1950/1951, p. 115).

FROM DECISION TO CLEAR-SIGHTED, CAREFUL VISION

What the ideal and the unknown demand is infinitely perfectible, attentive thought. In focusing on planning and decision making, scholars and educators have only partially comprehended the thinking that teaching requires. In general, it is difficult to lead an excellent life if its basic activities are not seen fully and clearly. Scholarly failure converts into practical failure through policy, and also in its support of popular misconceptions. The quietly receptive attention I have associated with both objects of contemplation in teaching is inherently appealing, self-renewing, and a rich source of professional development. There can, however, be no genuine relatedness in teaching, no resonating to people's possibilities as learners, without intelligent care and concern for teaching subjects.

Teaching is structured by a generative background of attachments that hold no matter what; this normative concept of practice appeals to a concept of teaching as a virtuous activity that is a bearer of human goods and has a distinctive scope, proper energies, and ends. Thus teaching calls for contemplation as a kind of devoted thinking in which one is not deluded or possessed by one's will or ideas: "a refined and honest perception of what is really the case, a patient and just discernment and exploration of what confronts one, which is the result not simply of opening one's eyes but of a certainly perfectly familiar kind of moral discipline" (Murdoch, 1970, p. 38). In carefully attending to subject matter, learners, and professional ideals, teachers maintain and perfect their singularly vibrant craft and themselves, while enlightening and perfecting others.

CHAPTER 9

Figuring in the Past:
Thinking About Teacher Memories

Margret Buchmann

> We do not have too much intellect and too little soul, but too
> little intellect in matters of the soul.
> —Robert Musil, 1990, "Helpless Europe"

Having lately returned from Norway, I am full of memories. Landscapes, tapestries, Viking ships, the lilt of the language, the hospitality and kindness of friends, much talking and more thinking. I have also learned a bit about Ibsen and his times.

IBSEN AND COMPANY

In 1879, the playwright wrote to a friend, "There are at present not as many as 25 free and independent spirits in the whole of Norway. Nor *could* they possibly exist" (cited in Keel, 1991, p. 122, author's translation). Ibsen then executes a familiar and customary turn, which one might call the pedagogical turn in social and political arguments; without further ado, he posits an implicit explanation for how people's lacks of freedom and autonomy are caused: "I have tried to see and feel from the inside the daily life of schools—modes of instruction, curriculum policies, the content of subject areas, the plans that regulate every hour" (cited in Keel, 1991, p. 122, author's translation).

Ibsen's writer-friend, Bjørnstjerne Bjørnson, wrote in the same year: "In our times, in our country, it is *utterly impossible* to be an intellectual without seeing everything in relation to society; and it is impossible, in turn, to do that without assuming a political or religious standpoint" (cited in Keel, 1991, pp. 122–123, author's translation). In modern countries today, these *pedagogical* turns in the critique of society and *political* turns among people devoted to the life of the mind are still taken for granted. Note that these turns assume quite a lot about the sources and causes of desirable change, as well as about human freedom and perfectibility. In general, these turns overestimate the role of schools and intellectuals.

RESEARCHER THINKING: DIVISIONS IN TONALITIES AND POLITICS

Research on teachers and teacher thinking can be seen against this background of pedagogy, perfectibility, politics, and faith. As the Norwegian context is suffused by somber and earnest features, so this variegated body of research and researchers has some peculiarities. Distinct tonalities in researcher thinking remind one of two great *narrative* moments: one, taking an alarming view of things, involves reactive myths of progress; the other, inclining toward romanticism, is associated with pastoral myths (Frye, 1967). Thus, some researchers recoil from much of what goes on in teachers' minds, because teacher thinking seems rarely transformative, being instead conservative, idiosyncratic, oriented toward the present, and narrowly practical (see, e.g., Lortie, 1975; Jackson, 1986). From an ironic or cynical point of view, mimesis appears to be the nemesis of teaching. Veering from vindication to defense, other researchers attach themselves to teachers' thoughts, even calling them theories, just because those thoughts are personal and grown in "their own gardens" (e.g., Elbaz, 1983; Connelly & Clandinin, 1985, 1987).

Each camp is affected by a version of "holy terror." The first ponders the contents and workings of teachers' minds with exasperated fascination and an almost superstitious dread; the other tries to spell those contents out with piety and reverential awe. While the second camp pronounces its defiance, "And we saw what teachers thought and did, and it was *good*," the first reverses valuations, rifled by the deflating ordinariness and mundanity of teaching. The queer logic of their factious opposition incapacitates both sides, rendering each motionless. In one camp, researchers do not wish to meddle with teacher thinking, whose expressive truth is sacred; in the other, they are transfixed by a metaphysical refusal to explore truth and rightness as residing *in* the world, defined as profane.

These fixations translate into politics with disagreements about *who* are the keepers of the faith and the gatekeepers of change. Those who feel baffled by the stolid immovability of schools (and society) are frustrated precisely because they cast teachers as agents of change, heralds of a new and better order envisioned by intellectuals. Where teacher thinking is valued just because it is what it is, issues of empowerment and self-determination for a (mostly female) profession, often not accorded much status or "voice," are not far below the surface and sometimes pointedly up front (see, e.g., Elbaz, 1990; Belenky, Clinchy, Goldberger, & Tarule, 1986; Delpit, 1988).

TEACHER MEMORIES: RAINBOW OR GRANITE?

On either side of this divide in tonalities and politics, I see the presence of myth with its normative and meaning-generating content (see Kolakowski, 1972/1989, 1990); opposing views of teachers and teacher thinking come down to conflicting mythologies. I develop a critique of this divide and its implications for teacher education and researcher thinking by looking at issues of memory and learning, interpreting memory, broadly, as the primordial stuff of being and thinking, feeling and acting, suffused with personal and collective elements. While, to some, teacher memories seem but a heavy, repressive dead hand of the past, whose weight accounts for the persistence of unambitious teaching and oppressive social evils, they appear to others as uplifting—a luminous thread of life and personal meaning.

Contrasting mythical pictures of teacher memories implicate the dichotomies of structure and development, individual and society, tradition and imagination, memory and reason, interiority and externality. Associated oppositions grow out of anxieties and concerns: fears of a "deadly" real world, hopes for a transforming—saving—vision above action, and conflicting commitments to the source of that vision and of human *progress*, whose stimulus and direction derive, in turn, from comparisons of the actual and the ideal.

Opposing views of teachers and teacher thinking thus appear to be rooted in acts of faith; their underlying structure of concern is part of the *religious* impulse. "Being religious" referred originally to one's being part of an order and state of life spiritually and practically bound by vows; not unrelated, more general and transferred senses imply envisioning some higher powers or purposes that give meaning and direction to human destiny. Bjørnstjerne Bjørnson may be more up-to-date than it might at first have seemed.

As Northrop Frye (1967) explains, "The language of concern is the language of myth, the total vision of the human situation, human destiny, human aspirations and fears" (p. 16). The question is whether the growing point of concern—researchers' heartfelt, generative commitments to preserving or fostering human freedom, life, and happiness—is also a growing point of knowledge. Is concern for improvement, like detachment, a precondition for learning? I will approach this tough question, indirectly, by sorting out researcher perspectives on teacher memories (broadly construed) with their entailments and ramifications.

Motley Aspects of Memory

In attempting to sidestep conflicting mythologies and contrary affiliations in research on teachers and teacher thinking, I have chosen something similarly deep down and powerful, namely, the poetic truth of a prose passage in Virginia Woolf's (1928/1956) *Orlando*. Orlando thinks about human nature, mind, action, uncertainty, and continuity, with memory busy at the center of it all:

> Nature, who has played so many queer tricks upon us, making us so unequally of clay and diamonds, of rainbow and granite . . . ; nature . . . has further complicated her task and added to our confusion by providing not only a *perfect rag-bag* [italics added] of odds and ends within us . . . but has contrived that the whole assortment shall be lightly stitched together by a single thread. *Memory is the seamstress, and a capricious one at that* [italics added]. Memory runs her needle in and out, up and down, hither and thither. . . . Thus, the most ordinary movement in the world . . . may agitate a thousand odd, disconnected fragments, now bright, now dim. . . . Instead of being a single, downright, bluff piece of work . . . , our commonest deeds are set about with a fluttering and flickering of wings, a rising and falling of lights. (pp. 50–51)

Clay *and* diamonds; rainbow *and* granite: There is a great deal in this passage which is evocative, justly observed, and poignant. Consider the last sentence, depicting *ordinary actions* as taking wing, but uncertainly, half in light, half in darkness: Are they winged, soaring messengers or birds hopelessly caught? Let us turn to the "capricious seamstress."

By giving memory this paradoxical name, Woolf has unsettled our thinking, though with a light touch. She does the same in calling human nature a "perfect rag-bag": odds and ends go into it, and who knows where they come from or go? A tendency to be capricious conflicts with one's notions of a patient needlewoman sewing straight seams and neat hems, following a given pattern with regular suitable stitches, bent on having no frayed or unraveling pieces. A seamstress sticks to a task whose outcome and purpose are no mystery—except, of course, where she is capricious.

The homeliness and humor inherent in Woolf's metaphors for human nature and memory provide some relief from their darker sides. A ragbag may attain perfection, but its state of completion and greatest excellence is still one of its own, rather ill-assorted and disreputable kind. Yet caprice recalls the remote and smiling unconcern of marvelous Greek gods. It is a state of self-reliant energy and bliss in which justice, good judgment, true need, or the facts of the matter do not count for much. It is a state of youth.

To be capricious is to be lighthearted rather than solemn. It can mean being willful, disorderly, imperious, wayward, and inconstant, but, in any event, moving, changeable, doing and being the unexpected—thus escaping prediction and control. Being subject to sudden, irregular changes will affect others as being unreliable and intractable. However, one can also see remoteness and fancy as forms of release, and capriciousness as a positive power. Elusiveness and animation are appealing. Caprice engenders the unique and surprising. There is a generous and jubilant quality in its freedom.

What do these explorations suggest for the contents and workings of teacher memories? Remembrances are put together from many things, somehow, but they are no objective records, cold, clear, and immovable. Memory, instead, is dense, shifting, sprawling—a kind of "spiritual capital," peculiar to a person, whose income, "in the form of reviewed experience, is merged with the incoming experiences of her continuing life in the present" (Hampshire, 1989, pp. 120–121). As the primordial stuff of being and meaning, feeling and knowing, teacher memories are, to some extent, inventive and—though often deeply rooted—no stranger to flux and fantasy. There is no simply bleak or rosy scenario here: Cynicism and celebration seem equally inadequate.

Often, however, researchers do not consider the motley aspects of memory, evenly and jointly, in their unquiet, paradoxical union. Rather, they appear drawn to either a gloomy or rosy view of the nature and effects of teacher memories on teacher and pupil learning, as well as on society at large. I question the starkness of these views—their tendency to be unmitigated—as well as their partiality in the descriptive and evaluative senses of the term. In both, partiality contributes to the tyranny of illusions.

PARTIALITY IN VISION AND POLITICS

The *Oxford English Dictionary* defines partiality in its evaluative sense as the quality or character of prejudgment, or of being "inclined antecedently to favour one party in a cause, or one side of the question more than another; prejudiced, biased, interested, unfair": Its opposite, then, is being impartial. There is a weaker evaluative sense in which partiality indicates one's being sympathetic or feeling kindly toward a cause, group of people, or side of a question. (Mature concern, of course, is no gush of kindly or sympathetic feeling.) Descriptively, as in the example of an insurance policy covering only a part of one's total loss of property or other damages, something's being partial means simply that it is incomplete, that it constitutes a part only, rather than the total.

In research on teachers and teacher thinking, conflicting perspectives on teacher memories are partial in *taking sides* and in representing only *part* of the picture. We should try to recognize and rectify these matters because partial pictures of memory—views that are fundamentally incomplete as well as a matter of bias and partisanship—eventuate in misleading beliefs and ill-founded practices in teacher preparation and professional development. Yet the attractions of partial, divided views are potent: They rest on their comparative starkness and a feeling of being on the right side. Dwelling underground are myths with normative and meaning-generating content: products of the spiritual life and constitutive elements of culture. Partial, divided views, moreover, lead to exciting programs of (educational) inquiry and action, programs that fire people with a sense that they have found a key to things (how they are caused) and recipes for action (what ought to be done). True in general, this applies to views of teacher memories as follows.

Ramifications and Implications of Partial, Divided Researcher Views

If the contents and workings of teachers' minds are viewed, gloomily, as unhallowed obstructions to progress, as idiosyncratic, conservative, disorderly, and intractable, a central goal of teacher education—if it is not to be doomed—must be their revision, control, extinction—or different recruitment patterns for the profession. On the rosy view of teacher memories as interior luminescence, we must, by contrast, stand back respectfully as teachers accomplish and recount their personal journeys of development and discovery, perhaps helping them to bring out what is hidden, muffled, and indistinct, "within," as their tacit knowledge. Researcher perspectives must be a bit off the mark where they portray teachers as either superstitious primitives (waiting for "the word": for our repair of *their* false consciousness) or noble savages (better off left alone, and better for *all* of us); chances are that neither one-eyed description fits most members of that mass occupation.

Several connected conceptual issues call for attention here. First, of course, the facts are neither good nor bad: It is people's reasoning that makes them so. Second, the dark view of teachers and their memories comes with a reactive sense of cause as external, technological control, whereas the rosy view places implicit trust in agent causation, with teachers center stage. Again, senses of causation are not written into the world. Third, although we must often sort out things and their aspects to understand them, distinction is not division. There are indeed dampening and transcendent aspects to people's memories, but it does not follow that diverse aspects do not mingle or that they materialize as separate existences—each, as it were, of one color or *reducible* to either drabness or irradiating light.

Fourth, researchers' partial views of teachers and their memories are implicitly divided in their attachments to an external versus an internal perspective, equating this analytic, descriptive distinction, in turn, with the evaluative one of good versus bad—although, on opposite sides, valuations continue to be inverted. Finally, the concept of progress featured by the rosy, internal view likewise confounds descriptive and evaluative meanings: "progress" as the movement, in time, through one's professional and life cycles and "progress" as positive advance or improvement; one can, however, simply get on in years or decline, with age, in hope and generosity (Buchmann, 1990, pp. 481–508).

Overcoming Partiality Through Metaphor

Faced with conceptual problems so sturdy in their entanglements with each other and with needs and feelings, a fresh, more lively, and more integrated view of memory might help in providing a new approach and sifting the issues. This was my idea in introducing Woolf's passage, although I judged that offering an antecedent explanation of my strategy might blunt its effects. Hampshire (1989) contends that the nature of memory almost *requires* the use of metaphor. Literal descriptions delineate and mark off parts of the involved aspects of memory, thus fostering partial pictures, at least in the descriptive sense. He furthermore argues for using particular kinds of metaphors, which "have to convey the unmechanical and confused connections which intimately link our memories, conscious and unconscious, to each other and which 'colour' all our later experiences and which form the constantly changing and enriched 'background' to later experiences" (p. 121).

In contrast to Leibniz's image of a heap of stones, Hampshire (1989) compares memory to "a compost heap, in which all the organic elements, one after another as they are added, interpenetrate each other and help to form a mixture in which the original ingredients are scarcely distinguishable, each ingredient being at least modified, even transformed by later ingredients" (p. 121). With its earthy, organic—partly subterranean (i.e., inaccessible)—subject matter, this metaphor adds to Woolf's image featuring memory's wayward maker. Compost heaps contain a lot of rot and some unconvertible residue, but they are also places of slow disintegration and productive transformation; this point leads into the discussion of teacher memories and learning.

MEMORY AS STRUCTURE AND QUEST

Personal memories combine impressive idiosyncratic elements with equally authoritative elements that are shared; Thelen (1973) calls these "archetypes"—typical views and experiences of teachers, subject matters, and schooling that are anchored in a culture. What is personally meaningful, typically the case, and affirmative of given cultures shapes ineluctably what people think, feel, and do. Teachers are no exception to these rules of common sense, psychology, and sociology. Memories outside the scope of professional education are relentlessly present and unquestionably compelling. That there is rule-governed behavior does little to lighten up the bleak picture, for those patterns are viewed from an external vantage point that *contrasts* (social) structure and (individual) development, memory and reason, tradition and imagination, and so on—which makes personal patterns idiosyncratic and cultural patterns conservative.

Against this bad news, consider the fact that memories—conquering time that conquers all—do also provide light and warmth, giving one heart and direction, while supplying a sense of community as well as cherished images of rightness ("This is what I ought to do!") and of mastery in life and action ("This is what doing it well looks like!"). What is illuminating, inspiring, and, at least, alive about teacher memories is left out of their inert picture. The roots of childhood, for instance, may be "impacted, interwoven, scrubby, interlocked, fibrous, cankerous, tuberous, ancient, matted" (Drabble, 1980, p. 132). Still they twist and turn, inside, and help provide for life, if not growth.

From Past to Future, Vision to Intention

In considering memory's relations to learning, we are assuming a modified internal perspective involving valuations: One does not consider just any change as evidence of learning. John Donne's *Devotions upon Emergent Occasions* are relevant here as guided exercises in using the visionary powers of contemporary experience and memory, or in giving those powers practical effect in spiritual improvement. In the words of a commentator, "By forcing his reader to use his memories . . . , Donne's *Devotions* made him probe the eternal; by engaging his understanding, it inspired deep comprehension of spiritual things; such comprehension, in turn, invariably led the reader to the exercise of the will for love" (Raspa, 1975, p. xl).

To illustrate relations of memory to intentions, I will quote from a poem by Coleridge (1817/1951), as he addresses himself to William Wordsworth:

> And when—O Friend! my comforter and guide!
> Strong in thyself, and powerful to give strength!—
> Thy long sustainéd Song finally closed,
> And thy deep voice had ceased—yet thou thyself
> Wert still before my eyes, and round us both
> That happy vision of belovéd faces—
> Scarce conscious, and yet conscious of its close
> I sate, my being blended in one thought
> (Thought was it? or aspiration? or resolve?). (p. 77)

Coleridge and Donne do not claim only that memories have visionary powers but that those powers are formative, beyond thought. Remembrance shapes inclinations for feeling and doing. The blending of being and thinking in a steadfast desire or longing for something at present above one—"resolve" suggesting both firmness of purpose and a process of clearing away doubts and obscurities—is the anticipatory movement toward a union of good sense and feeling that prefigures action by living memory.

Coleridge's parenthesis—"(Thought was it? or aspiration? or resolve?)"—inserts abrupt, stirring questions into the flow of yearning memories, which are no self-indulgent musings. The unexpected movement from elegy to inquiry is no digression. It redirects attention, from the past to present and future, from reflection to resolution and a living, breathing desire for the good. The fact that Donne fashioned exercises to be followed—read and imitated—implies a belief that desirable fruits of memory do not come naturally or without care and increasingly perceptive attention. Instead, they require proper observances, some suitable detachment, time, and recollection.

From Experience to Knowledge Through Memories Reviewed

Some intimations of these matters came to me when I first read a wonderful novel by Rebecca West (1966), *The Birds Fall Down*. In this story of espionage, revolution, conflict of cultures, and love, a mother's joyfully giving a hat to another woman is a memory around which crystallizes a daughter's acquiring wisdom and understanding—in an extended process of revelation and formation that is both systematic and of a quirky randomness. The woman receiving the gift is the father's mistress, and that fact is unknown, at the time, to the mother and observing child. When first drawn to revisit the event, the daughter is deeply impressed by her mother in her radiant generosity: loved, and the needed image of safety and love. The other woman seems but her mother's foil, not beautiful to the child, yet disturbing in her complacency and nameless fascination.

Over time, a gesture that commanded love and admiration, a gesture of overflowing, self-assured kindness, becomes an emblem of pity and betrayal. With experience, remembrance becomes more aching and detailed, and the passive actors in the past—recipient, onlooker—are invested with more active, significant roles. Chance events precipitate connections: Vague, fragmentary notions fall into place. Remembrance comes at irregular intervals; indirectly, it refashions the daughter's sense of who her parents are, who she is, and where she, and they, stand. The event set in motion a roundabout process of imagination and investigation that corresponds with memories and knowledge and creates memories and knowledge, while preparing the ground for actions and decisions.

In this example, I have outlined a process of fictional learning, that is, the growth of juster sensibilities, questioning and comprehending powers in a person imagined. At the same time, I have rendered an account of my own movement from the flat, though gripping, surface of experience to more lucid and many-sided understandings in the course of repeated passes through a text. T. S. Eliot's (1920/1964a) description of how one grows as a literary critic is clarifying for both of these cases of learning from memory.

> There is not merely an increase of understanding, leaving the original acute impression unchanged. The new impressions *modify* [italics added] the impressions received from the objects already known. An impression needs to be constantly refreshed by new impressions in order that it may persist at all; it needs to take its place in a *system of impressions* [italics added]. (p. 14)

Yields of Texts and Lives in Shifting Perspectives

The movement from experience to knowledge in serious reading is an iterative process similar to learning from memory reviewed. Barely formed, unexamined feelings, by way of first response, are followed by another reading, in perspective. This term rewards analysis. Perspective, first, denotes the act of viewing, as in its meaning of a visible scene or mental view; originally, it signified the science of sight. Perspective also implies a relative position that need not be fixed, hence, a particular point of view in relation to objects, including imaginary or abstract ones. With a true change of perspective, one's views follow suit. The relations of perspective to time are open, since a mental view or outlook can be applied to any extent of time, real or imagined, past or future: Perspective can be a *pro*spect.

As viewing in a literal and metaphorical sense, perspectives require a living, thinking, feeling person and some *externalizing* movement; only comparative remoteness makes close inspection possible, even on the internal view. Perspectives can be broad in mental grasp and sympathies, yet they cannot be all-encompassing or neutral. A specified and limited perspective, however, is not the same as a decided view, a settled or unquestionable position. As Dewey (1931/1960) said, outlooks can themselves be looked at: "One can only see from a certain standpoint, but this fact does not make all standpoints of equal value. . . . One may have affection for a standpoint which gives a rich and ordered landscape rather than for one from which things are seen confusedly and meagerly" (p. 102).

Dewey implies that pairing richness and confusion is as unsatisfactory as joining meagerness to order in perceptions. In evaluating standpoints, he proposes joining generative substantive criteria (diversity, elaboration) to logical ones (structure, direction). A map is well wrought, for example, if it lays out an abundance of well-marked routes and places to go; proper specification provides means for further explorations. Importantly, Dewey suggests that one can become attached to rich and orderly maps or develop a preference and fondness for them.

In responding to text, Frye (1990) argues that initial readings, which follow the narrative, are a mere "collecting of data for understanding" (p. 74), whereas secondary stages of response (not necessarily obligating one to pick up the book again) take the perspective of a whole structure and turn the "wandering through a maze of words into a directed quest" (pp. 74–75). This staged process, Frye concludes, "is the result of living in time, where experiences comes first and the consciousness of having had the experience comes later, and sometimes does not come at all" (p. 89). Memories of text and life provide for learning that balances investigation and imagination, being controlled by a respect for the data that are held, and highlighted, in some comprehensive view, itself capable of review. A difference between text and life is that one's existence is animate: Although it does end, life does not stay put—nor, as it seems, do its memories.

In *The Beloved Returns,* Thomas Mann (1939/1982) supplies a summary of these reflections on (teacher) memories as structure *and* quest. Picture Goethe's Lotte, the beloved of young Werther, returning to Weimar in her middle age. As she rests from her journey, shimmering images of youth and summer came crowding into her mind.

> Yet the strange thing was that all these images and memories had not obtained their extraordinary pointedness and luminosity, their precise fullness of detail, at first hand, so to say. To begin with, mind had by no means been so keen on keeping them in all their particulars; instead, it had been compelled to yield them up only later, piece by piece, word for word, out of its very depths. They had been investigated, restored, painstakingly brought to the surface again with all their appurtenances, varnished brightly and placed, as it were, between candles—for the sake of the meaning they had gained after the fact, against all expectations. (pp. 34–35, *author's translation*)

We may, in short, be under the spell of memories but their import is not spelled out for us. In an account that lightly moves across centuries, Orlando's life and learning show how there can be a "multitude of things which call for explanation and imprint their message without leaving any hint as to their meaning upon the mind" (Woolf, 1928/1956, p. 115). For her, or him, however, "the image with all its associations," ultimately, "[gives] place to the truth" (Woolf, 1928/1956, p. 107).

UNEASY ACTS OF EVALUATION

Let me set the tone for this section by quoting from Primo Levi's (1975/1984) third memoir, *The Periodic Table.*

> There are the so-called inert gases in the air we breathe. They bear curious Greek names of erudite derivation which mean "the New," "the Hidden," "the Inactive," and "the Alien." . . . They are also called the noble gases— and here there's room for discussion as to whether all noble gases are really inert and all inert gases are noble. (p. 3)

If teacher memories are to be retained and restored for successive viewings, their presence had better be importunate. Hence, there are virtues even to the vices of capricious memory. What does not follow from my revision of memory's inert picture is that all memories are illustrious icons or that all instances of looking back will impart a higher character, more refined perceptions, or nobler intentions to teachers. Not all fidelities accord with purposes of learning. And some memories elude meaning.

So as to procure learning for teachers, memories must satisfy differentiating criteria of value concerning inherent qualities of remembrance as well as qualities of mind's likely response. Both kinds of qualitative features are related, in that a quality of teacher response may affect the yields of texts and experiences, while substantive characteristics of teacher memories may engender responses more or less productive. I will illustrate these points in Northrop Frye's (1990) discussion of "magical lines" (see pp. 64–66) in poetry. The question is what makes particular passages of life and text not only compelling but fruitful.

Magical Passages: Transports Across Boundaries

In reading a poem, a line or part may detach itself from the whole and stick in memory. Although this is a personal experience, great poetry is public in ways that other memories are not. Many people get caught in the magic of Marvell's "To a green thought in a green shade," or remember Keats's lines in "Ode to a Nightingale" that tell us how the bird's song has

> Charmed magic casements, opening on the foam
>   Of perilous seas, in faery lands forlorn.

We can look at these culminating lines for what they suggest about the power of the poet's song, or of our words, to open up vistas. In fact, T. S. Eliot (1920/1964b) maintains that "the ode of Keats contains a number of feelings which have nothing particular to do with the nightingale, but which the nightingale, partly perhaps, because of its attractive name, and partly because of its reputation, served to bring together" (p. 56).

While it brings a widening from within, the mental gaze is framed, as by a window or embrasure in a fortification. It yields some of its sheltered containment to the enchantment of language, however, in which the lure of many hidden, perhaps unconscious, implications of words—including shadows of earlier usages—contradict their apparent inertia. What is thus hidden, alien, and inactive is "precisely what permit[s everyday language] to be used as an instrument of human freedom, as a way of introducing new ideas, new attitudes" (Passmore, 1970, p. 272). Unfortunately, lacks of clarity and closure also make room for bewitchment and dangerous allure, since "these very same 'imperfections' allow men to talk nonsense, to confuse, to deceive, to corrupt" (Passmore, 1970, p. 273).

Although there is the poem as a coherent whole, Frye (1990) observes that Keat's couplet "seems to burst through that unity to suggest different orders of existence" (p. 66); he goes on to propose a principle of response that applies to the issue of memory and teacher learning: "The inference is that there may be something potentially unlimited or infinite in the response to poetry, something that turns on a light in the psyche, so that instead of the darkness of the unknown we see something of the shadows of other kinds of emerging being" (p. 66). A principle of response *to* memory can be analyzed in its own right, yet its coming into play is made more likely by teachers' good fortune in encountering "magical" passages or by qualitative features *of* memory. With time and attention, one's response to particular passages of life or text may extend indefinitely beyond its context and given orderings of reality—perhaps approaching regions where meaning found is lost again.

Thus, in the shelter of night, a student is settling down to read *Antigone*, surrounded by books. "When the lamp was turned higher," Woolf (1937) writes in *The Years*, "he saw his work cut out in a sharp circle of bright light from the surrounding dimness" (p. 49); reading, frowning, he perceived at first nothing but the Greek characters before him—yet slowly

> he caught phrase after phrase exactly, firmly, more exactly, he noted, making a brief note in the margin, than the night before. Little negligible words now revealed shades of meaning, which altered the meaning. He made another note; *that* was the meaning. His own dexterity in catching the phrase plumb in the middle gave him a thrill of excitement. There it was, clean and entire. But he must be precise; exact; even his little scribbled notes must be clear as print. He turned to this book; then that book. Then he leant back to see, with his eyes shut. . . . He felt as if he had thrown himself down on the turf after running a race. But for a moment it seemed to him that he was still running; his mind went on without the book. It travelled by itself without impediments through a world of pure meaning; but gradually it lost its meaning. (p. 50)

The passage communicates personal effort and excitement in making meaning, the striving for precision and exactitude, as well as the fragility of process and results. If this fictional reader studied *Antigone* in the original, we must remember that, in a sense, all experience is Greek to us and—briefly incandescent—may revert to darkness and dull surface: Woolf's "rising and falling of lights."

Remembrance is, with text, on a continuum of meaning-making and conserving retention involving systems of interpretable signs. Signs whose meaning is capable of being made out are embedded in multiform contexts. Still, there are transports of thought and feeling across boundaries. Every instance of making meaning implies the opportunity, power, and liberty of a crossing, or some traveling from one place, condition, or form of being to another. Transition and difference are part of the meaning of passage; a corollary is that the strange, although it may be hidden, is never far away.

Meanings Fashioned in Diverse Regions

Picking texts for interpretation and illustration in this chapter, I made choices, some involving languages and artistic forms. I could have looked at Rilke's letters or essays by Musil instead of considering verses by Coleridge and Keats; I could have drawn on Goethe's autobiography, *Poetry and Truth,* instead of the fictional creation, *Orlando.* Choices of text, form, and language are not just ornamental but affect one's points and meanings. Translating the passage from *Lotte in Weimar,* I spent days with dictionaries and etymologies, trying to catch the charm and meaning with which the German original sparkles. The fascinating thing was that, moving between languages—word choices, variant renderings of phrases and their dependencies—meanings were found as well as lost. As a native speaker, I had not noticed that two German words for "memory"—*Erinnerung; Gedächtnis*—also signify "inwardness" and "thinking," respectively, as process and result. Sorting out fringes of meaning increased my conscious repertoire, on both sides. I compared light effects, ambiguous overtones, and earthbound strains, yet literal representations rarely succeeded as communication.

Clifford Geertz (1986) puts the point that meanings are fashioned by people in places as follows: "Meaning, in the form of interpretable signs—sounds, images, feelings, artefacts, gestures—comes to exist only within language games, communities of discourse, . . . ways of world making; . . . it arises within the frame of concrete social interaction in which something is a something for a you and a me, and *not in some secret grotto in the head* [italics added]" (pp. 112–113). And culture is no matter of select pretentions or time-honored verities but, in the pointed words of Oakeshott (1975/1989a), "a contingent flow of intellectual and emotional adventures, a mixture of old and new where the new is often a backward swerve to pick up what has been temporarily forgotten; a mixture of the emergent and the recessive; of the substantial and the somewhat flimsy, of the commonplace, the refined and the magnificent" (p. 29). Culture seems just as motley in character as personal memories.

Looking at cultures as collective memories, Dewey (1931/1960) distinguishes between "blind customs" and traditions with their intellectual qualities: "Traditions are ways of interpretation and of observation, of valuation, of everything explicitly thought of. They are the circumambient atmosphere which thought must breathe; no one ever had an idea except as he inhaled some of this atmosphere" (p. 100). Oakeshott's variegated list of cultural characteristics and Dewey's firm distinction drive home the need for discriminations, or the drawing of distinctions in making and responding to meaning, so as to determine when teacher memories may eventuate in learning.

The Vitality of Distinctions and Evaluations

Distinctions enshrine the conceptual order of languages and cultures, supporting and expressing forms of life, probably with some universal, species-related underpinnings. To that extent, conceptual distinctions have permanence and act as a conservative force. At the same time, distinctions supply conditions for learning. Knowing and questioning things depends on their being differentiated, in some illuminating way, and on granting that there are possibilities for faulty differentiation.

From the assertion that everything is what it is and not something else—tradition is not blind custom, structure not the same as quest, beliefs not mere wishes—it does not follow that opposites have no connections or mutual dependencies: People must often distinguish where they cannot divide. Objections against dichotomies are therefore not justified by their being cases of faulty differentiation but invoke their built-in refusal to admit of relations between paired opposites. Nor does the presence of troubling tensions—between the actual and the ideal, rigidity and the forces of change—imply that final, harmonious resolutions are possible.

Maintaining that distinctions are vital is not to say that facts and values, for example, are not often entangled. They are. We are not equally interested in all facts. We consider truth to be better than falsehood. Yet from the likelihood of matters being tangled, it does not follow that they are homogeneous or that they can be confounded with one another. In particular, it will not do to confuse descriptive distinctions, such as that between internal and external points of view, with the evaluative distinctions of good and bad or right and wrong. Where conversions of distinctions into divisions go hand in hand with failures to uphold appropriate distinctions, fantasies and misconceptions are the result, while myths turn into ideologies, or tendentiously twisted tales.

Dialectical Value Judgments

Frye's concept of magical lines dramatizes issues of memory and (teacher) learning and exemplifies evaluative considerations bearing on substantive qualities of memory and qualities of response. If magical passages of text and life are special, they are so in a positive or, at least, appealing sense. Of course, something can be an exception to the rule and located at the negative end of the evaluative spectrum; such placements, too, are acts affirming value. The point is not only that valuations are diverse and consequential, that such determinations have to be made and learned, but that their diversity is structured in terms of degrees and kinds, as well as complicated by interrelations, including issues of truth and rightness.

In trying to determine how poetic assent may be conditioned—do we have to agree with Shakespeare's renderings of differences between men and women, for instance, to appreciate *Antony and Cleopatra?*— Heller (1988) considers the absence of what is valuable. Involved are, again, both inherent poetic qualities and qualities of people's response. The interplay of text and response characteristics is mediated by readers' attention to epistemological criteria, or the degree to which what is asserted or implied seems worthy of belief. Heller concludes that epistemological value is required not only for appreciation but for poetic production itself: "There are ideas and beliefs so prosaic, outlandish or perverse at their core that no great or good poetry can come from them. . . . It is this *negative* consideration that to me finally proves the intimate *positive* relation between belief, thought and poetry" (p. 112, footnote).

There remains room for doubt, however, for, as Wittgenstein (1980) notes in *Culture and Value,*

> Nietzsche writes somewhere that the best poets and thinkers, too, have written things that are mediocre or bad, yet that they have set aside what is good. But it's not altogether like that. In his garden, a gardener does not only keep roses, of course, but manure, rubbish and straw; what makes here for difference, however, is not (inherent) goodness but, above all, function in the garden. (p. 59, author's translation)

Interminably complex and demanding, though not without groundings, acts of evaluation in making meaning ought not to come easy to teachers or researchers. "How much less burdensome," Oakeshott (1975/1989a) comments, "to be incapable of error, of stupidity, of hatred and of wrongdoing, even if this meant the surrender of truth, wisdom, love and virtue" (p. 20). Yet there is no escape. Thus Strawson (1962/1974b) observes in "Freedom and Resentment":

> It is an exaggerrated horror, itself suspect, which would make us unable to acknowledge the facts because of the seamy side of the facts. . . . We have to take account of the facts in *all* their bearings. . . . This is in no way to deny the possibility and desirability of redirection and modification. . . . But we

may reasonably think it unlikely that our progressively greater understanding of certain aspects of ourselves will lead to the total disappearance of those aspects. (p. 25)

Conflicts and limitations do not distort but express human nature.

MYTH AND DETACHMENT IN THEIR RIGHT PLACE

By care, pains, chance, and nameless fascination, memory may procure learning. But, if teacher memories beat back change, that need not always be fatal. Nor does it follow that, if memories are irrefragable, teachers are refractory: obstinate or perverse. In research on teachers and teacher thinking, in sum, we need searching acts of appraisal that confront memory's conflicting aspects as structure and quest, as well as researcher needs and fantasies.

Tempering partial, divided views of teachers and their memories should lead to sensibilities that are more just, dispelling some gloom and purple haze without diminishing inherent tensions. For all parties, gaining keen awareness and emotional consciousness will entail paying attention to the internal point of view but not letting it go unexamined, thus heeding the external point of view, while not letting it swallow up everything (see Nagel, 1979, chap. 14). Mutually necessary, these opposing perspectives do not furnish grounds for partisanship and political faction; instead, each is, in itself, simply what it is—vindicating neither teachers' rights nor scientific utopias.

Neither anxiety nor indifference, the proper attitude toward teacher memories is *concern*. In being concerned, one has a commitment to well-being but no blind attachment to the given contents of teachers' minds, the social setting, or one's hopes and ideals. The imperfections one ought to expect all around prompt careful efforts at understanding and improvement, not rejection or denial. Moreover, one's respect for the integrity of truth and people forbids transforming facts and meanings to meet one's own wishes and needs. Detachment is thus involved in being concerned and in coming to know, both of which presuppose some selfless attention and a recognition of independence.

Distinguishing truth and rightness from fantasy and epistemological from political fervor is consistent with giving the proper place to myth, faith, and concern. Yet in research and scholarship, the question is not "Whose side are you on?" but what makes conceptual, empirical, and ethical sense—which seem to be self-renewing questions grounded in traditions and myths. What is true for philosophy is also true for educational research; as Kolakowski (1990) reminds us, it is "the spirit of truth" itself that requires that we never "forget that there are questions that lie beyond the legitimate horizon of science and are nonetheless crucially important to the survival of humanity as we know it" (p. 135).

> All the most traditional worries of philosophers—how to tell good from evil, true from false, real from unreal, being from nothingness, just from unjust . . . , or how to find order in chaos, providence in absurdity, timelessness in time, laws in facts, God in the world, world in language—all of them boil down to the *quest for meaning* [italics added]; and they presuppose that in dissecting such questions we may employ the instruments of reason, even if the ultimate outcome is the dismissal of reason or its defeat. (p. 135)

It is no good to deny mythologies or to annex them to reason. Instead, educational researchers and scholars should make their mythologies clearer and see them for what they are: neither more, nor less, than varieties of meaning-generating faith.

Moral and Intellectual, Personal and Professional: Restitching Practice

Deborah Loewenberg Ball

Buchmann's tracing of the web of moral and intellectual, personal and professional threads of practice reveals fundamental tensions inherent to teaching. Three stand out: the dual commitments of respect for students and for knowledge; the absence of shared standards and the compelling power of personal experiences; the struggles for appropriate balance of external authority and teacher autonomy. A story from my own teaching of third-grade mathematics[1] provides a context for considering Buchmann's analyses and the attendant tensions of practice.

Problems in Cookie-Sharing

One day in April, I gave the following problem to my third graders[2]:

You have a dozen cookies and you want to share them with the other people in your family. If you want to share them all equally, how many cookies will each person in your family get?

I knew enough about my students' families to know that, in our discussion of the problem, we would have to reckon with fifths, sevenths, and probably both halves and eighths. I also knew that students would be inclined to divide the leftover cookies, but would not necessarily know what to *call* the pieces they produced. I expected that some children

---

1. I teach mathematics daily to a class of third graders in a local public elementary school. My aim is to learn about trying to teach for understanding, investigating dilemmas that arise in this kind of teaching (see, for example, Ball, 1993a, 1993b).
2. A more extended discussion and analysis of this story appears in Ball (1993a).

would call fifths and sevenths simply "pieces." But I thought that the children would probably see fifths and halves as clearly different in amount, and I hoped that we could use their intuitions to name these pieces in meaningful ways. I anticipated that this problem would launch us into an extended exploration of fractions, building on what they already knew and moving beyond that. What had concerned me were "the ways in which the subject may become part of experience; what there is in the child's present that is usable in reference to it; [and to] determine the medium in which the child should be placed in order that growth might be properly directed" (Dewey, 1902, p. 23). However, I did not anticipate some of the problems I would face as we began to try to work with this situation.

Problem #1: Who "counts"? We started by figuring out how many cookies everyone in *my* family—with four members—would get. Then students worked independently or in pairs or threes to figure out how the dozen cookies would be shared in *their* families. I heard some discussion about whom one should count as a member of one's family. Keith wondered aloud if he should count his about-to-be-born baby brother or sister while Riba decided *not* to count her new baby sister ("She can't *eat* cookies!"). Sean noted that "my dad doesn't like cookies" and did not include him. I was uncomfortable when I overheard some students questioning other students' ways of counting family members. Mei asked Lucy with characteristic directness, "Who's the fourth person? You only have *three* people in your family." Lucy responded matter-of-factly that she was counting her mother's boyfriend who was living with them. Someone else challenged Lindiwe's counting his father since his parents were divorced and his dad was currently living in Washington, D.C.

These conversations seemed intrusively personal and I found myself questioning the way I had decided to contextualize the problem. I had used families as the context because the divisor would vary nicely among the students, allowing for a range of interesting solutions, some simpler than others. I knew we would end up discussing division of 12 by 2, 3, 4, 5, 6, and 7—and that 5 and 7 would lead us into fractions, my destination. This was exactly where I now wanted to move from our work with division and multiplication. Yet, as I listened, I grew uneasy about my choice, for the goodness of an instructional context depends on its social and cultural appropriateness as well as on content and learning factors. I decided to discuss the issue with the class the next day—to ask them what *they* thought about the problem and the surrounding interactions.

The next day, many children said that the problem seemed okay to them, that they had not minded the questions that came up around it. Betsy, however, empathized with how some students might have felt: "Well, for some people I think it would be sort of being nosy, because if somebody really missed their dad and they didn't want people talking about it, that would make them feel even sad or something like that, so it might not be such a good idea." Tory agreed. At this, Lindiwe spoke up and said that many people kept arguing with him, saying that he only had four people in his family while he kept explaining that he was counting his dad. I asked how he felt about that and he said that he liked the discussion of the problem but that he thought people should let him decide whom he wanted to count in his family: "I think that people shouldn't really be saying how much you have in your family. They don't know because they've never been to your house. So, they shouldn't really tell you stuff that they don't even know."

After listening to the children's comments and thinking about the problem myself, I wondered whether I would use this problem again in exactly this form—at least in this particular context. Despite the fact that, in this school, families vary widely and children do not assume that others' families are just like their own, the problem now seemed to me intrusive, pressing children into explaining their family situations and defending their method of counting family members. One alternative might be to pose the problem as sharing cookies among "the people who ate supper at your house last night."[3] Another might be to have the children identify a group of relatives, friends, or neighbors with whom they would each like to share their cookies and then to share the dozen cookies among those people. Yet another alternative would be to continue to use the family problem, as is, but preface it with a discussion about respect for others' situations and methods of counting.

Problem #2: Cassandra's solution: 12 ÷ 5 = 4. Cassandra, a tall African-American girl with five people in her family, was working at the chalkboard and was eager to show me her work on the problem. She had drawn a chart as a tool for and display of her reasoning.

Ch	C	J	P	Ce

The letters in the columns, she explained, were the first initials of her family's names. Then she distributed 10 of the cookies by making hash

---

3. This possibility was suggested to me by Helen Featherstone.

marks across the columns until each member of the family had two hash marks, representing two cookies.

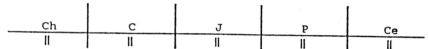

Ch	c	J	P	Ce
II	II	II	II	II

Cassandra: Um, I would have two cookies left over so I figured what I would do with those two cookies? I would split them in half or either just throw them away. She drew two circles on the board.

Cassandra: So here's two.

She drew lines in the circles, cutting them first in half and then in quarters and described what she was doing.

Cassandra: I cut them in half and then in half again and so there's four.

Cassandra: But I have 5 people in my family (adding another line to each cookie), so there's one more.

And Cassandra added two more lines for each person on her chart.

Ch	c	J	P	Ce
IIII	IIII	IIII	IIII	IIII

Then I asked how many cookies she would give each person in her family. Cassandra counted the hash marks: 1, 2, 3, 4.

Cassandra's solution was intriguing. On one hand, she got a close approximation of a "right" answer—(2-⅖). On the other hand, she reported it as 4, counting *pieces* irrespective of size. In most classrooms, Cassandra's solution would be judged to be wrong. After all, her conclusion in writing was 12 ÷ 5 = 4. Even after looking at her cookie drawings—which may, in fact, represent 2-⅖—questions remain about Cassandra's intuitive understanding of fractions. She realized that the five pieces (inside each of the two leftover cookies) are not the same size. Did she mean them to be equal but just did not know how to *draw* fifths properly? Dividing a circle into five equal parts is no easy task. Or did Cassandra not recognize that equal size is a crucial aspect of dividing something like cookies equally? Was she focused only on coming up with the same number of *pieces?*

I debated about how to respond to Cassandra. Should I question her further about her solution? She was not at all dissatisfied with it and it made sense in many ways. Our time was almost up. I could tell from scraps of conversation around us that we were ready for a group discussion of the problem. Should I ask Cassandra to present the solution that seemed so compelling to her, but which would undoubtedly invite challenge from some of the other students? Those challenges would likely be productive and useful to the group's evolving understanding of fractions and division, but was Cassandra up to being on the spot—and, perhaps, to feeling that her solution was less good than fractional interpretation? Worrying about these issues is both a personal matter—can Cassandra deal today with this particular problem?—and a pedagogical one—is this the best avenue for her learning and for the group's collective deliberations?

Respect for Students, Respect for Knowledge

Balancing the dual commitment to students and to knowledge is never easy. Respect for students as knowers comes frequently into conflict with respect for knowledge. Buchmann characterizes the aim of teachers' work: "In schools, teachers are supposed to help students participate in the 'community of subject matter,' whose objective contents of thought and experience—systems, theories, ideas—are impersonal because they are distinct from the people who learn or discuss them." To characterize knowledge as impersonal is puzzling in the context of the work of teaching, for students' investigations are intensely personal. To steer students' investigations in ways that are at once responsive and responsible is to act on the basic commitments of teaching: care for knowledge and for students. This caring is not detached.

Noddings (1984) refers to teaching as the "prototypical caring relation: "The one-caring as teacher, then, has two major tasks: to stretch the
student's world by presenting an effective selection of that world with
which she is in contact, and to work cooperatively with the student in his
struggle toward competence in that world" (p. 178). Dewey (1902), too,
argued that we should think much more fluidly about the links between
the lives and minds of children and the notion of "knowledge." We
should, he claimed,

> abandon the notion of subject-matter as something fixed and ready-made in
> itself, outside the child's experience; cease thinking of the child's experience
> as also something hard and fast; see it as something fluent, embryonic, vital;
> and we realize that the child and the curriculum are simply two limits that
> define a single process. Just as two points define a straight line, so the pres-
> ent standpoint of the child and the facts and truths of studies define instruc-
> tion. It is continuous reconstruction, moving from the child's present experi-
> ence out into that represented by the organized bodies of truth that we call
> studies. (p. 11)

Cassandra's solution to the cookie problem illustrates the deep tensions inherent in trying to help students extend what they know. She had
solved the problem to her satisfaction. Each member of her family would
receive four cookie-pieces. Her solution was functional, and might well
suffice around the supper table. Still, I had created this problem as a
context for stimulating students' capacity to discriminate and name fractional quantities, which Cassandra's solution averted. Instead of concerning herself with the relative *size* of each piece, she concerned herself with
the *number* of pieces. Her solution suggests that $12 \div 5 = 4$, a conclusion
that causes the next teacher to worry about Cassandra's knowledge—and
perhaps about Cassandra.

Awareness of issues related to race and class added to my sense of
tensions as a teacher. Cognizant of Delpit's (1988) argument that teachers
must make sure minority and poor students acquire the conventional
knowledge that can give them access to power and opportunity, I worried
about my choices. I knew that, before she came to this school, Cassandra
was retained in at least one grade, and that she was consequently over
a year older than most of the other children. Delpit (1988) argues that
pedagogies emphasizing process at the expense of content (e.g., the writing process approach) disadvantage minority and poor students because
these children often will be less likely to acquire the conventional knowledge on their own outside of school. This knowledge constitutes a code
of power and cultural capital necessary for success in our schools and
society. Knowing that mathematics problems that involve division are as-

sumed to be solved in equal parts, or how to name and write fractional quantities—these constituted some of the conventional mathematics knowledge that Cassandra would need. Making her own reasonable but nonfractional solution would be seen by many merely as evidence that she lacked basic mathematical skills.

Concerns for gender issues—that Cassandra is a girl—pulled me in other directions. Knowing that many girls experience school mathematics as senseless and defeating of their own intuitions, I wanted to reinforce Cassandra's sense that she can think, that she can reason sensibly about mathematics. I did not want her only school experiences to be ones where her ways of thinking, her knowledge, were somehow wrong.

I was pulled between respecting Cassandra's sensible solution on the one hand, and feeling responsible to help her develop a more conventional mathematical solution on the other, one that appropriately uses fractions as a means of denoting quantity. It would be an abdication of my responsibility to allow Cassandra to think that $12 \div 5 = 4$. But not to respect her reasonable strategy would be equally irresponsible.

How could I do both—honor my commitments to both students and knowledge? Possibly I could ask Cassandra to present her solution to the class. Maybe there is a way to value what she has done and yet also create an occasion to examine it alongside a fractional solution, which would undoubtedly be offered by another student. But what does it take to manage to respect genuinely, and also to extend helpfully? Tall and older, Cassandra sometimes is self-conscious in front of the others. But at other times she takes—and revels in being—center stage.

The connection between myself, Cassandra and her classmates, and the mathematics of division is not impersonal and not objective. Close up, the obligations of the teacher's role are tangled and elusive. To avoid compromising either my respect for Cassandra or my respect for mathematics means seeking ways to care about Cassandra's *learning*—and this is about Cassandra, about who she is, what she knows, feels, and values, as well as about what she has a right to have access to. As Buchmann writes,

> In teaching . . . thought and action need to flow from—and return to—raising one's sights to people (primarily students) and teaching subjects, and thought and action without reference to the *ultimate good* [italics added] of learning would be without rudder.

The "ultimate good" of learning is incontestable but elusive as a compass for teacher thought and action.

Understanding that this central task of teaching is at once fundamentally moral and intellectual is crucial. For how to assist and contribute to students' learning in right ways entails unending puzzles and uncertainties. My concerns for the original cookie-sharing problem itself reveal this. Should I create and shape the context so that we can sensitively use the family-centered problem? Or should one avoid this problem? What does this mean if some of my students do not live in conventional "families"? Should the space be ensured to talk about these sorts of issues in school, and should it happen during mathematics instruction? Or should children be encouraged to respect one another's private lives, and *not* to question one another? To characterize my struggles over how to respond to Cassandra—or what to do about the cookie problem—as merely about "subject matter" would miss the point. To characterize them as simply expressing concerns for students' emotional well-being and social relationships would be equally off the mark. In practice, the moral and intellectual are inseparable and serving professional aims is a deeply personal matter. How, then, to address Buchmann's concern for defensible *professional* action?

Absence of Shared Standards and the Compelling Power of Personal Experiences

Where could I go to find out what would constitute best practice in the case of either of the problems I was facing? With whom could I confer? Buchmann asserts the importance of justification in teaching. She argues that the expectation that teachers can justify what they do with students ensures a standard different from personal idiosyncrasy. The question of what this standard is, or where to learn it, is elusive. That teachers are accountable to do what is right for their students hardly settles the question. Who can determine for a given teacher what is "right" for her students? If we ask that teachers be responsive to the individual students' needs, are we forced to acknowledge that teachers' pedagogical interpretations and choices will of necessity be particular and not general? Or that individual interpretations make shared standards unfeasible?

Not necessarily. Although the specific contexts and work conditions matter, having standards does not preclude individual interpretations of practice. Having standards for any kind of work seems not only worthwhile but necessary. As Buchmann argues, people who take on a professional role do not have the "right to decide whether to act on their clients' behalf" or their own. Teachers' decisions and actions are not personal and private, but matters "of public significance." Teachers are responsible for acting in the public trust to educate young people in ways that are responsive to their needs and responsible to a collective sense of what is worthwhile to learn.

However, two tensions exist within the logical argument for standards of practice. First, despite its pervasive sameness (Cohen, 1989; Goodlad, 1984; Waller, 1932/1961), teaching is colored with a rhetoric of individual style. In general, Americans are deeply ambivalent about the idea of "standards." In a society that values individualism, standards ring of standardization and control. Nowhere has the desire to codify expectations and ensure results confronted the fear of sameness and control as it has in education, where the mottoes of finding one's own way and figuring out what works for oneself are embedded in the very culture of teaching. Statements such as "there's no right way to teach" even work against the notion of shared standards.

The second tension in the debate about standards for teaching practice grows from the first and lies in the noncommunal nature of the profession. In any formal organizational sense, such standards do *not* exist in teaching as they do for other professional communities to which teaching might be compared.[4] In most other professions, there are codes of ethics, standards boards, and review processes set and enforced by the professionals themselves. When accountants perform in ways that do not comply with established agreements for ethical practice, it is possible to challenge and judge their decisions against a set of agreed-upon standards. When doctors wrestle with specific moral and scientific dilemmas of their practice, they have standards, guidelines, and codes to which they refer for guidance. Not so in teaching. Teaching is not a formally organized community, or discipline, with explicit standards for what counts as proper action, good reasons, or adequate evidence.

Buchmann is not necessarily making a claim for organized professional community. She argues that teachers are, by virtue of the work they do, members of a "moral community" whose obligation it is to help students learn. This is a difficult notion of standard. Some possible teacher decisions are quite clearly inconsistent with the obligations of the role. Self-satisfaction and personal preference are no justification for pedagogical choice. Deliberately advantaging some students, withholding opportunities to learn to others, teaching falsehoods, or treating children cruelly—no one would argue that such activities are somehow just matters of individual style, and thereby permissible. But whereas some

---

4. Some recent exceptions include: The National Board for Professional Teaching Standards and the National Council of Teachers of Mathematics *Curriculum and Evaluation Standards for School Mathematics* and *Professional Standards for Teaching Mathematics*.

activities may be judged to be immoral, or inappropriate in teaching, what counts as good or right cannot automatically be found in the remaining options. In thinking through how best to treat Cassandra's solution to 12 ÷ 5, no standard exists to guide my deliberations or to judge the appropriateness of my decision. In fact, the imperatives to which I must respond are in conflict (Lampert, 1985). For example, on the one hand, connecting academic learning to students' everyday lives is good; on the other hand, sheltering children from aspects of the realities of life outside of school is also appropriate. Teachers ought to take seriously students' knowledge and ways of reasoning; teachers are also obligated to give students access to knowledge that students have not developed on their own. To reason about the competing goods inherent in the alternatives apparent in a particular situation, teachers are left to figure out what is right on their own.

The commonly held view that "each teacher has to find his or her own style" results from working within a professional community that has been inhibited from defining from the inside out what it stands for and where its disagreements are, and the bases for managing among discrepant claims. Because teachers are left on their own to develop standards for choosing and inventing their pedagogy, their learning is often idiosyncratic. Consequently, being responsible to the moral imperatives of practice remains a highly individual and personal matter, lodged within the person of the teacher.

Authority and Autonomy

If role obligation is indeed lodged within the person of the teacher, then new puzzles arise in evaluating the appropriateness of teacher actions. In exploring the extent to which role orientation guides practice, Buchmann criticizes the frequency with which it appears that teachers disregard their obligations to the established school curriculum. For example, some teachers teach merely what interests them (Cusick, 1983). Other teachers disregard information given to them in innovative curriculum materials (Smith & Anderson, 1984). Teachers justified their departures from established guidelines by talking about their knowledge of what works and by what their students "need." Buchmann lauds those teachers who, in contrast, "looked outward rather than inward. . . . [who] felt bound by obligations" external to their own sense of what to do. On the face of it, these teachers' work, compliant with guidelines, seems more defensible than that of their colleagues. And, in many cases, the researchers' interpretations may well be correct. But what of the teachers whose professional judgment leads them to decide that a particular topic, method, material, or regulation is inappropriate for their students? What of teachers whose knowledge of the subject matter leads them to judge that a particular textbook is intellectually immoral? What of teachers whose knowledge of their students leads them to decide that a particular mode of working will engage and interest their learners more than the "required" approach?

To hold as one standard for justifiable professional practice compliance with others' stipulations seems problematic. On the one hand, lack of compliance may signify abdication of professional responsibility by reducing pedagogical choice to matters of personal preference. On the other hand, compliance with external guidelines can also interfere with teachers' essential obligations to their students' learning of worthwhile material. If all teachers were to comply with requirements of schools as they currently exist, they would merely reproduce the practices of schooling with all their inequities and poverties of intellectual opportunity. To be an agent of change, congruent with the moral imperatives of teaching, may mean allowing personal judgment to override obligation.

Buchmann points out that bureaucratization and "legislated learning" can obstruct the exercise of pedagogical virtue. As such, devotion to professional ideals of perfection means learning to hold in abeyance those things that obstruct one's capacity to contemplate either subject matter or students. This means thinking past convenient categories and comfortable habits, beyond directions solidified as policy. It does not mean abandoning such structures capriciously. The requirement that teachers be able to justify their choices holds, and herein lies the difficulty.

Suppose a teacher, like myself, claims to have abandoned the textbook because the mathematics that it includes distorts the content, thus compromising unreasonably students' opportunities to learn. My cookie problem came from no text or formal program. How can we determine whether my decision to abandon external curriculum programs is right? We have no way to discriminate among well-intentioned but flawed attempts to improve what students learn, personal whim, and preferable approaches to helping students learn worthwhile content. Substitutions or omissions in content or approach are relatively inappraisable, for we lack standards for justifying such decisions. We lack forums for adjudicating their wisdom and integrity, for deciding whether they constitute adherence to the ideals of our work or violate them.

To make professional orientation synonymous with compliance with all the good and bad institutionalized requirements of schools is to doom any possibility for the improvement of student learning. But to allow that wise practitioners must, at times, deviate from those requirements is risky. It is risky due to the lack of ways to judge these deviations. Irresponsible and capricious departures will be mixed in with proper and defensible ones, although our ability to discriminate one from the other is very rough and our opportunities to do so at all are infrequent.

The three chapters paint a rich portrait of the intertwining of the person and the role, the necessary connectedness and detachment between the moral and the intellectual aspects of the practice. Teachers must give reasons from within the role, and yet they will inevitably see and act from within the examined and unexamined experiences of their personal lives. They must be committed to subjects and students, learning to listen to both openly, unfettered by conceptual baggage, and yet their own experiences and judgments cannot help but shape their perceptions. Buchmann's work on teacher thinking and practice offers ways of reconceiving the relationships between teachers' selves and professional roles, as they negotiate their obligations to the moral and intellectual demands of the work. The story of Cassandra and her classmates highlights the profound and difficult tensions that teachers face in responding to the moral obligation to help students learn worthwhile content. Neither subject matter nor professional role can dominate practice. Concern for students and personal commitments are equally problematic if made central to the work of teaching. It is the striving for a justifiable balance of knowledge and learner, obligation and autonomy, common standards and personal style that makes teaching a virtuous—and very difficult—activity.

Detachment for the Sake of Concern and Learning

Robert E. Floden and Margret Buchmann

Deborah Ball's vignettes illuminate tensions inherent to teaching. As she points out, no single goal can be a guiding star for teacher judgments and choices. Teachers live with urgent obligations, but these do themselves conflict. Obligations, by the way, are engagements of oneself, having to do with mutuality and ties, not just of bounden duties but of gratitude, civility, and kindness. One's compliance with obligations, therefore, does not entail a pliability in sinister or denigrating senses. As with the other issues addressed in this book, rather than coming to rest upon single-minded solutions, we ask readers to recognize that unfolding dilemmas require (and requires) engagement in second thoughts—periodic, attentive inspections of one's assumptions, actions, and ramifying consequences. As we argue in the preceding sections, this engagement is rarely solitary, but depends on the mind-opening presence of others, real or imagined.

In her concluding paragraph, our respondent describes the generative tension between detachment and concern that runs through this book. Yet elsewhere in her response, Deborah Ball seems either to force a choice between the two stances or to criticize us for favoring detachment. Because some such interpretation of our position may occur to other readers, we welcome this chance to revisit the terms and their convergence in the mental and moral discipline of attention.

We agree that no single goal, as, for instance, accurate representation of subject matter, can guide a teacher in decisions about how to act in response to emergent understandings of Cassandra. To begin with, teachers should, though acting in the instant, also take a long view in seeing to it that (all) students learn. Here many will take into account the possible effects of their responses on Cassandra's motivation and on other students' aptitude and willingness to venture and defend mathematical explanations, and mind the likelihood that anything teachers do and visibly feel can affect the classroom as a place for communication and learning. A professional obligation to teach content in accordance with evolving disciplines of knowledge hence remains an overarching concern, not an overriding rule.

To clarify the fundamental tension between detachment and concern it is important to note that detachment is not an absolute term; instead, the concept is both relational and relative. That is, detachment presupposes something to which one is attached by feeling, habit, or belief, and it denotes a distance that is incomplete and variable. Every effort at seeing involves forms of distance and relation. Just as the knowledge-producing distinction of self and nonself is consistent with intensifying human interest, so growing professional concern requires unwinding some coils of self. Detachment and concern flourish together as conditions of human learning that one can distinguish but not separate.

Note similarly that, contrary to our respondent's portrayal of the intellectual and moral domains as competing (and also contrary to our reading of the title of her response), the obligation to promote worthwhile student learning is itself *moral,* "or pertaining," as the *Oxford English Dictionary* sums it up, "to the distinction between right and wrong, or good and evil, in relation to the actions, volitions, or character of responsible beings." Accordingly, Ball's vignettes bring out concerns for student distress, inclinations to learn and participate, congruence of transacted content with fruitful formulations of mathematics—perhaps also for the teacher's sense of who she is and wants to be as a pedagogue and person. Detachment is important in teaching in large part *because of* concern for students. Concern for people's well-being encompasses an interest in their learning things that are worthwhile in themselves and for what they allow participants to become.

Deborah Ball stresses that lacking forums for discussing teaching standards, let alone for agreeing upon standards themselves, makes it difficult for teachers to evaluate their choices. But she jumps from this difficulty to the assertion that teachers are left with the options of acting on personal preference or following the mandates provided by external authorities, such as school districts or textbook publishers. She seems to see us as defenders of compliance in a rather objectionable sense. To sort out these issues, it will be helpful to recall a few facts about people and morality.

It is a home truth in more than one way that we first learn about the moral life through external authorities, such as parents, playmates, teachers, precepts, and so on; this may surround considerations of right and wrong with an aura of imposed restraint and compulsion. Rightness, however, is no derivative of externality and power or, for that matter, of internality and rebellion as mere reactions. Slipping from questions of rightness to considerations of ancestry (genesis and source) confuses the issues. The emphasis in Chapter 7 on teachers' "looking outward" therefore can mislead readers. Emphasizing contemplative attention and personal memories, the other chapters in this part develop and balance the "role over person" argument by reviewing varieties of inwardness in teacher thinking.

Our argument that teachers should "look outward" in making decisions was no endorsement of blind obedience, which mutes concern and arrests learning. Looking to the nearest available administrator has many of the drawbacks that relying on personal preferences has. It isn't looking outward far and freely enough. Our point was that, in making decisions, teachers should be mindful of student learning and their own obligations to ideal and real communities (including those of the subject-matter disciplines, the teaching profession, society, and humanity), rather than relying on self-centered criteria, such as the teacher's enjoyment of a topic or the ease with which instruction can be managed. If considerations are legitimate and productive, it is primarily because they contribute to growth and learning.

Quite likely, conceptual ambiguities got in the way of communication, for "standards" can be looked upon as authoritative, definite exemplars or measures of correctness, implying unreasoning force and dreary sameness. We assumed, however, a meaning of standards as principles or means of judgment and estimation. It is true that communities relevant to teaching could not be imagined without *human* language and relations, but this does not reduce them to playgrounds for power or idiosyncrasy. Again, our argument would have been more clear had we been more explicit about the difference between the personal and the subjective. Polanyi (1958/1962) distinguishes the subjective from the personal in acts of knowing; in their personal participation, people "can transcend [their] own subjectivity by striving passionately to fulfil [their] personal obligations to universal standards" (p. 17).

Our respondent points our correctly that teachers have not reached consensus on what is most likely to promote their goals, or even how professional goals should be formulated. Yet that does not mean that it is impossible to discriminate between better and worse criteria for teacher attention and choices. Although people have not reached consensus on moral action in general, it does not follow that all relevant arguments are equally good. Things are not black and white. In what Dewey (1916/1966) called "the twilight zone of inquiry" (p. 148), holding on to significant shades of meaning allows for learning. If questions of truth and rightness do not contract to certainties, it does not follow that we are absolutely ignorant or that means of judgment, communication, and education are absent. It all depends on grasping "the live nettle."

Part IV

PURPOSE AND DESIGN IN PROFESSIONAL PROGRAMS

CHAPTER 10

Between Routines and Anarchy: Preparing Teachers for Uncertainty

Robert E. Floden and Margret Buchmann

Certain: 1. Determined, fixed, settled; not variable or fluctuating, unfailing. 2. Sure, unerring, not liable to fail; to be depended upon; wholly trustworthy or reliable. 3. Established as a truth or fact to be absolutely received, . . . not to be doubted, disputed or called in question; indubitable; sure. 4. Of persons: Fully confident upon the ground of knowledge, or other evidence believed to be infallible; having no doubt; assured; sure.

—The Oxford English Dictionary, 2nd Edition

Teaching is evidently and inevitably uncertain. No teacher can be sure how a lesson will go or exactly what a student will learn. No one can know which teaching approach will guarantee success for particular groups of students. While casual observation and systematic research indicate the importance of multiform uncertainties to the ways teachers think and feel about their work, little has been published about the stance teacher educators should take toward uncertainty. Writings about teacher education stress how much teachers can learn. Reviews of the literature describe the "knowledge bases" of teaching. Essays advocate knowledge and skills for effective instruction or working with diverse students. Because residual uncertainties of teaching are largely neglected in teacher education, we explore what it would mean to prepare teachers for uncertainty.

UNCERTAINTIES IN TEACHING

Since academic learning is a primary goal of teaching, it is especially troubling that teachers are seldom sure about what their students know and what they are learning (Jackson, 1986, chap. 3). Uncertainty about student understanding results both from people's variable interpretations of subject-matter concepts and from the limits of educational measurement.

Uncertain Assessments of Student Learning

Drawing on their personal—sometimes idiosyncratic—beliefs and experiences, individuals construct meanings. Usually, these meanings are comparable enough to permit interaction, but their significant variations make teachers unsure about what students learn. Studies of student conceptions provide dramatic examples of misassessments that stem from these difficulties. Take the case of a student named Benny (Erlwanger, 1973): Benny's classroom used a system of individualized instruction in which students worked through a set of written materials on each topic, then took an exam on that topic. If they did poorly, students could inspect the answers given in the key, then take an alternate version of the test. This cycle could be repeated until the student's answers matched a high proportion of those in the key. Only answers that matched the key exactly were acceptable, however. If the answer was given as "1–1/2," "1.5" would be marked wrong.

Benny made sense of this instructional environment by seeing mathematics as a wild goose chase in which he had to find rules for getting acceptable answers. The system's insistence on an exact match to the answer key supported his conviction that his rules might be right, even if answers were initially marked wrong. When he or the teacher's aide checked his unit tests against the answer book, for example, Benny reconciled differences between his own understandings and the book's solutions by an expanded idea of which numbers are equivalent. Just as 1/2 is equivalent to 2/4, he reasoned, his answer (1.5) was probably the same as that given in the answer book (1/5). Despite regular testing, Benny's misunderstandings remained invisible; in fact, he experienced consistent success within this system of instruction.

Classroom tests are a means for ranking students and assigning grades. But because no test is perfectly reliable and valid, any nontrivial inference people draw from test performance is open to error. A mistake may stem from carelessness or fatigue rather than a lack of knowledge. A correct answer may be no more than a lucky guess or a fortunate misunderstanding of the question. Test results might also depend more on vocabulary than on students' knowledge of American history. Though themselves imperfect means of assessment, clinical interviews can probe the limits and distortions of other test formats. Discussions can reveal degrees and kinds of understanding that differ from those an essay or multiple-choice exam indicates.

Uncertainty is compounded when teachers have responsibility for teaching many things to many students. Moreover, some areas of knowledge are easier to assess than others (Frederiksen, 1984). Recall of facts and mastery of simple skills may be relatively easy to assess; still, results are not indubitable. A clinical interview may clarify one child's understanding of photosynthesis, but no teacher can spend an hour interviewing each student on every major concept. Important areas—such as the ability to respond to complex, changing situations (like those that teachers face)—probably require elaborate individual assessments difficult to implement and to interpret. Limitations of time, energy, and measurement expertise imply that teachers must get by on general indicators of student learning and reasonable guesses.

Uncertainties in testing and grading can surprise and trouble novices. Their own teachers appeared firm and confident—even inflexible—about the grades they assigned; but when these beginners give tests or read essays, they see that the common means of assessing understanding are far from fail-proof. The impersonality, importance, and finality of grading make teachers feel especially uncomfortable about this source of their uncertainty.

Uncertain Teaching Effects

Even if teachers had a good idea of how much students know, they would remain uncertain about links between teaching and learning. The belief that students will grasp focal concepts if teachers provide clear explanations and engage students in tasks closely tied to the content is often disappointed. Students' behavioral, emotional, and cognitive responses are affected by the contexts in which they live, of which school is only one (albeit, for some, an important one). The child whose creative writing suddenly improves may have been inspired by a parent's comment, not by the teacher's language arts unit. The student who has never completed her homework can turn in a carefully composed essay. The lesson that has always excited students can miscarry with this year's class. Although experienced teachers have some sense of how students will react to a lesson or assignment, some uncertainty remains.

Research on teaching and learning can contribute to understanding teaching effects, but it cannot provide means to engineer classroom success. Research offers illuminating concepts and pointers toward the relative overall merits of different teaching approaches. It does not, and will probably never, permit accurate predictions of what *this* child will learn from *this* lesson taught in *this* way by *this* teacher in *this* school. Certainty decreases even further when one considers a person's education over 10 or 20 years. The long-term effects of teaching are variable and surprising. This is driven home to teachers whenever someone testifies to the importance of a lesson or comment that seemed insignificant to the teacher at the time.

Uncertainties About Instructional Content

Though often taken for granted, the instructional content teachers hope to get across—mathematics, history, or language arts—harbors several uncertainties. Bounds for content choices may (or may not) be set by guidelines, materials, and collegial agreements. Each teacher, however, faces significant, difficult decisions about coverage and emphasis (Schwille et al., 1983). Some decisions are global, such as how much to emphasize facts and rules and how much to stress relationships among concepts and broad understanding; other decisions are more specific, such as how much time to spend studying the Spanish-American War. Teachers must plan what to cover today, how to structure this week's unit, and what units to include this year.

Uncertainties springing from teachers' own imperfect subject-matter understandings are added to uncertainties about what to cover. It is no scandal that high school teachers probably know less than Nobel laureates or that elementary school teachers probably know less about ecosystems than do high school biology teachers. Although degrees of imperfection in content knowledge are understandable, they still leave teachers uncertain about the concepts to teach, especially for topics that seemed elusive when they were in college. The range of content in schools, coupled with the comparative brevity of teachers' content studies, implies that teachers can expect to teach many things about which their understanding falls short of the best scholarship.

Further studying, however, will not bring certainty. The deeper one goes into a subject, the more one gets insight into ongoing disputes, disputes that often divide a field, with little chance of resolution. Influenced by Thomas Kuhn (1970), some might go so far as to say that scientific disputes will be settled by politics or charisma rather than reason (e.g., Feyerabend, 1975). Although scholars are guided by disciplinary methods and principles, they cannot rest assured of their interpretations. Nor are their inferences sealed off from personal history and local circumstance. Moreover, scholarly interpretations can be tenable while conflicting. In a sense, the better one's education, the greater and more varied are one's uncertainties. Of course, this lack of assurance provides some protection against dogmatism. For better or worse, some uncertainties about subject matter will therefore survive, no matter how well teachers are educated.

Teachers' Uncertain Authority

Uncertainties about assessment, teaching effects, and instructional content merge in an overarching uncertainty about teacher authority in the classroom. Recognizing their uncertain intellectual footing, teachers may feel that they have little reason to contradict pupils who assert their own interpretations. Teachers are unsure about how much students already know, about what will happen if students go along with the planned lesson, and about whether the claims in the text are really the last word on the subject at hand. While having to make decisions, teachers have no unshakable bases for choosing one academic task or form of classroom organization over another.

For beginners, uncertainty about managerial authority is more salient than uncertainty about intellectual authority (Veenman, 1984). Novice teachers want students to like them and may even feel more affinity with students than with colleagues. Yet they have to maintain discipline and assign grades. Often, beginning teachers rightly doubt their capacity to control students. The common advice not to smile until Christmas suggests a solution that reduces uncertainty, but such simple escapes from self-doubts may not be the most appropriate ways of coping.

Questions of authority are complicated by teachers' moral obligation to respect students' personal autonomy (Strike, 1982). People have a right to hold opinions. Indeed, teachers often strive to foster student self-expression and autonomy. Yet teachers have a potentially conflicting obligation to help shape logical and aesthetic standards for judgment (Elbow, 1986). Tensions between preserving student autonomy and exercising intellectual and social leadership in the classroom are perennial.

ON BEING PREPARED FOR UNCERTAINTIES

What should educators do to prepare future teachers for their uncertainties? One deceptively attractive answer is that they should warn teachers of the myriad uncertainties and give them the wherewithal to reduce those uncertainties to a minimum. This "know [and smite] thine enemy" approach has advantages but is incomplete and somewhat misguided. Teachers should know how to reduce some uncertainties by developing routines and their knowledge and skills. But the quest for certainty needs to be tempered, and supplemented with ways to teach responsibly in the presence of uncertainties.

Is More Certainty Always Better?

Certainty has its advantages. If one could predict results of action accurately, one could choose the most efficient strategies for desired outcomes. If teachers could be more certain about the effects of different teaching approaches, they might choose instructional strategies based on probable impact on student learning, rather than on manageability and fit with current practice (Cohen, 1987). If they had a good grasp of how to share authority with students, teachers could avoid disturbing confrontations and heavy-handed actions that suppress students' sense of responsibility.

Seeking more certainty, however, can create attachments to teaching goals, topics, and methods where certainty is easiest to obtain. Since the future is uncertain, striving for certainty pulls attention away from long-term plans and inspiring ideas to what is immediate, specific, and seemingly obvious. A teacher in quest for certainty may favor content that can be tested by traditional objective examinations, rather than making decisions in light of worthwhileness. Rigidity and narrowness in classroom life, rather than flexibility and breadth, may be outcomes of a quest for certainty.

Too much uncertainty may be disabling, but too much certainty can lead to boredom and stagnation or to the mistaken sense that teaching is mechanical. Suppose that instead of "uncertainty," one spoke of "openness," "awareness of possibilities," "fluidity," or "freedom from rigidity." Uncertainty may be vital to practice in all professions (Schön, 1983). Benefits of greater certainty must also be weighed against disadvantages arising from ways an increase may be obtained. Teachers can, for example, reduce uncertainty about student understanding by asking more questions. Yet benefits of questioning "must be weighed not only against its potential discomfort to individual students but also against the strain it puts on the social relationships within the classroom as a whole" (Jackson, 1986, p. 69). As an essential, driving force in teaching, uncertainty is a tension that cannot and should not be removed (McDonald, 1986).

The virtues of uncertainty are obscured by its negative connotations. In part, teaching is an art whose impact comes through interweaving the expected and the surprising. An artistic work of depth continues to reveal new facets. A lesson or assignment likewise has depth if, while conforming on the whole to a pattern, it provides unexpected opportunities for teaching and learning. Teachers should entertain these tempering thoughts about certainty's virtues, so that they can take a moderate stance, rather than rooting out uncertainty wherever they find it. Balancing openness and predictability is difficult and dependent on context, while crucial to teaching and the learning of students and teachers alike. Understanding the various aspects of uncertainty should help in continuing to strive for a productive balance, as well as in reducing uncertainties where appropriate.

Learning About Uncertainties

Teachers will become aware of many uncertainties on their own, especially uncertainties about teaching, learning, and classroom authority. Other aspects of uncertainty are less visible. Consider that constructivist views of student and expert knowledge are at odds with the commonly held assumptions that children will understand things properly if they are clearly explained and that the received truths of the curriculum can be taken for granted. Also, some awareness of uncertainty seems to diminish over time. Thus, teachers often become used to their modes of assessment and forget that inferences about student learning may be partial or mistaken.

Being prepared for uncertainties includes understanding them. Apart from its intrinsic value, understanding is important for developing an appropriate stance toward uncertainty, maintaining openness and flexibility, and deciding when uncertainties might be reduced through study and effort. But how much should beginning teachers understand about the uncertainties they face? Should educators feel satisfied that teachers are likely to recognize some uncertainties, or should they try to bring their full range to teachers' attention? Should teacher educators keep awareness of uncertainty from slipping away?

As adult learners, teachers have a large say in their curriculum— probably larger than they realize. In college courses, they can choose where to put their energies, where to go beyond requirements, and where to seek help from faculty and peers. In their first years, teachers can decide what to continue studying, and how and when to seek assistance or advice. In either case, teachers play a primary role in assessing their progress: What are they learning? What good will it do them as teachers or as people? How much more can they expect to learn? Their relative autonomy means that teachers also face perplexing choices about what to study, whom to consult, whether to admit their uncertainties, or what to do about them.

Appreciating the extent and varieties of uncertainty can, after all, be unsettling. Dangers of confusion, loss of confidence, or anarchy complicate teacher preparation. Teacher educators must prepare their students for uncertainties without suggesting that there are no bases for authority, order, and instructional choices. Compared with most of their students, teachers know more about instructional content, including criteria of worth. Teachers may not be dead certain about what and how to teach or why, but they have better grounds for assessing most choices than their students. Witless relativism or the cynical positions that "anything goes as long as you can come up with a reason" or "nothing works, so why bother" confuse uncertainty with anarchy. Just as teachers should be judicious in their pursuit of certainty, teacher educators should be prudent in their efforts to raise teachers' awareness of uncertainty. Uncertainty militates against dogmatism, but it is no excuse for anarchy.

One possible compromise would be to limit attention in preservice programs to uncertainties most salient to beginners, who are otherwise in danger of being overwhelmed. Further uncertainties could then be introduced in inservice education. This staged approach has two drawbacks. First, since the content of inservice education is often largely at their discretion, many teachers might not choose to learn more about uncertainty. Growing understanding of uncertainties in teaching would then be avoided rather than postponed. Second, teachers may establish convictions of certainty that will be difficult to shake. The belief that instructional content is unproblematic, for example, is often supported by teachers' own school experiences. If the seeds of some uncertainties are not planted in preservice programs, they may never be able to take root.

It is, therefore, desirable to help teachers see a greater range of uncertainties than most will discover on their own, even though this may entail raising their levels of anxiety and concern. Everyday classroom experience is unlikely to surface some uncertainties (e.g. about social organization or instructional content) because they do not interfere with running a well-functioning classroom. Raising awareness of hidden uncertainties can draw teachers' attention to more distant, yet inspiring, aims, such as long-term learning that is faithful to evolving disciplinary knowledge and ideals of autonomy and responsibility for teachers and students.

It is instructive to compare teaching with public management. Public managers also have greater uncertainties than they typically recognize. From their own perspective, these managers have few incentives to increase their awareness of uncertainty. They can function well with a false sense of certainty, because their success is judged by whether they can make a decision that others accept, not by whether their decisions are most likely to increase the general good. From the public's point of view, however, it would be better for these managers to recognize how their policies might go awry.

Uses and Limits of Routines

Understanding could lead to despair if teachers had no hope of re-ducing their uncertainties to manageable and productive levels. This is not the case. Increasing pedagogical knowledge and skills helps teachers to make reasonable, rapid choices, anticipate events, assess understand-ings, and find acceptable postures of authority. Habits of thought and action reduce perceived complexity and increase predictability. If stu-dents regularly exchange critiques of each other's work, both teachers and students know what to do. If a teacher always constructs social stud-ies quizzes by writing one item for each textbook section, testing uncer-tainties diminish. Mastering routines and learning how to generate them prepares teachers to structure classroom events and also frees their atten-tion for dealing with the unexpected (Clark & Peterson, 1986).

Routines are a specific response to the general problems of uncer-tainty; hence considerations raised earlier apply here also. While routines can reduce uncertainties, having more routines does not entail better teaching. Some routines have questionable instructional results. Imagine, for example, mathematics instruction entirely composed of routines for handing out and correcting ditto sheets, or a classroom in which discus-sion and student ideas were paramount at all times. Or consider instruc-tional planning reduced to turning textbook pages. In some cases, in-creasing uncertainty is preferable to relying on routines.

Routines can become so entrenched that teachers continue using them even when their results are not satisfactory (Clark & Peterson, 1986). Conversely, "teachers are often temporarily confused by unexpected suc-cess (simply because it is unexpected) . . . [or find] that unexpected events are somehow troubling even when desirable (because we tend to become well adjusted to and eventually to prefer what we have come to expect)" (Brophy, 1983b, p. 651). Unexpected opportunities and difficulties may be good reasons for interrupting standard procedures. Lacking capacities for ready adaptation may lead to foregone teachable moments (Shroyer, 1981/1982). Being prepared for uncertainty includes being flexible enough to break out of a routine when appropriate *and* being able to do something sensible after abandoning the shelter of established patterns (Bromme & Brophy, 1986).

Increasing Certainty Where Appropriate

Teachers can reduce some uncertainties by deepening and strength-ening their pedagogical knowledge and skills during initial preparation or later in their careers. At times, though, getting insights from colleagues, books, or college faculty may be impossible or too time-consuming. Preparing for uncertainties includes knowing both how and when to attempt their reduction. A great support for continuing learning is being generally alert to what (inconveniently) contradicts one's assumptions. While one may feel, for example, that eager discussions are to be prized, it is helpful to be on the lookout for contributions that suggest wild misunderstandings, or to call on quiet students when that can be done in a tactful way.

A more specific goal is developing a sense of when it is worth the costs to work for greater mastery of teaching subjects. Teachers cannot study everything intensively, and the best rule for learning need not be to study whatever makes one feel least sure of oneself. Being prepared here means pursuing routes to subject knowledge that are propitious and practicable.

RESPONSIBLY COPING WITH RESIDUAL UNCERTAINTIES

Even given routines and continuing learning, teaching remains uncertain. While a reasonable measure of uncertainty adds interest and challenge, stress is a side effect. Worrying about one's knowledge and effectiveness can add to the mental and emotional costs of an already demanding job. Students may also suffer if they sense a teacher's lack of confidence. Part of being prepared for uncertainty is knowing how to cope with residual uncertainties—by talking, for instance, with other teachers and combining brisk assurance with second thoughts.

Communicating Teachers' Sense of Uncertainty

Talking to other teachers can ease the strain of residual uncertainties in three ways. First, being able to talk about one's doubts and fears with one's comrades is a relief. Recognizing that uncertainties are endemic can relieve unjustified feelings of personal failure. Second, their conversations can remind teachers that uncertainty is an essential driving force in teaching, not merely a deficiency and worry. Third, if teachers can articulate uncertainties among themselves, they may become able to communicate them to others, which might reduce inappropriate pressure for certainty. The organization of U.S. schools, their norms, and facts of classroom life, however, inhibit teacher talk and admissions of uncertainties. In addition, theories of teaching and educational policy often suppose that "teaching is at best simply the rational application of means to given ends. In this light, all the ambiguity, irrationality, and conflict which teachers are used to feeling in their bones, if not used to talking about, are simply evidence of teaching failure" (McDonald, 1986, p. 377).

Yet McDonald (1986) also describes how barriers have been surmounted. In monthly meetings over beer and pizza, he and other teachers discussed incidents in their work lives. Their conversations deepened appreciation of certainty's limits and resulted in essays about educational scholarship and policy through which the group broadened public awareness.

> What if teachers, recognizing the uncertainty in their work, raised their voices instead of growing silent? And what if theorists recognized that intimate knowledge of this uncertainty was exactly what was missing from both their theories and the policies these theories provoke? (McDonald, 1986, p. 362)

Combining Brisk Confidence with Second Thoughts

Nevertheless, teaching and learning require decision, not helpless hesitation. Decisive action, however, may give the appearance of certitude. Indeed, it is this appearance that deceives novice teachers into thinking that their experienced colleagues are sure of their subjects, students, and efficacy. Brisk confidence can still be helpful. Time spent agonizing about each action or interpretation could put a stop to classroom life. Learners can throw themselves into their studies if they believe in their teachers' confidence; parents, likewise, can then trust in the direction of their children's learning. Both parties are—and should be—relieved by teachers' acceptance of responsibility.

Brisk confidence does not mean that teachers should behave as though their actions could never be questioned. Projections of absolute certainty would be dishonest, as would constant professions of doubt. Both would interfere with teaching and learning to teach. Hence, teachers must combine reliance on themselves and their students with a habit of reconsidering the sources and consequences of their actions. Their confidence must be based on openness to changes suggested by second thoughts (Buchmann, 1984b), not on the false assumption that teachers always know best. Like policy makers and researchers, teachers must maintain a "double consciousness" (Scheffler, 1984, p. 163), committed to taking action and to probing and revising their practice in the light of empirical and normative consequences.

CHAPTER 11

Coherence, The Rebel Angel

Margret Buchmann and Robert E. Floden

In calling for coherence in U.S. teacher education, people express abiding concerns about the effects of education. Scholars maintain that teachers go through their preparation relatively untouched, relying instead on common sense and their experience of schooling (Buchmann, 1987; Lortie, 1975). Pitted against these prior learnings, a fragmented curriculum is likely to have little or no effect (Barnes, 1987). Seeking to strengthen teacher education by making its elements more consistent, reformers often cite "increasing program coherence" as a central principle and even as the primary indicator of curricular worth (see, e.g., Howey & Zimpher, 1989). The highly publicized Holmes Group Report implicitly supports these views: "Basically a 'nonprogram' at present, professional studies are rarely interrelated or coherent. . . . Students . . . wander about rather than progressing systematically . . . through their programs" (Sedlak, 1987, p. 321).

People thus turn to a family of concepts that seem guardian angels of reform: program, system, direction, coherence, and consistency. Our argument is that—within this company—coherence is a rebel angel, advancing human learning but escaping control. We contrast coherence with consistency, two concepts with several resemblances: First, both satisfy the sensible criterion of nonfragmentation in the curriculum or the requirement that it should not be a collection of small bits and pieces. Denoting connectedness, coherence and consistency share, second, a status of relative terms, for understanding each depends on some clarity about what is supposed to "hang together" with what else, how, in what aspects, and to what ends. Connoting order, unity, and intelligibility, the concepts of coherence and consistency carry, finally similar positive implications of value. Despite their resemblances, however, these two concepts are not interchangeable. Thus, while *consistency* implies logical relations and the absence of contradictions, *coherence* allows for many kinds of connectedness, encompassing logic but also associations of ideas and feelings, intimations of resemblance, conflicts and tensions, previsagements and imaginative leaps.

Plain thinking, theories of choice, philosophy, the arts, and literature can alert one to the differences between coherence and consistency as forms of connectedness. Yet when educators invoke coherence—especially "program coherence"—they veer toward consistency as a proxy of worth and effectiveness. An incident at a meeting about research on teacher education highlights some of the meanings and values associated with coherence and related concepts. Speaking as if he expected immediate understanding and agreement, a well-known scholar recommended that the assembled investigators abandon their studies of teacher education, "because you already know that there aren't any programs." The blithe recommendation was rooted in assimilating the idea of a tightly structured curriculum to the concept of program, perhaps even of education. The denial of apparent facts (i.e., researchers thought they had already spent hundreds of hours studying a set of programs) provoked puzzlement and counter-denial.

START MAKING SENSE!

Let us build on this incident by imagining that a member of the audience jumped up—quite irate—to attack the notion that only tightly structured programs are good for teachers. "What's all this talk about programs got to do with *education?*" our voluble critic begins. "Of course we want coherence in education and professional preparation, if you mean eschewing meaningless babble. People have to be able to make sense, in some fashion, of what they hear, read, and do. But implicit adherence to consistency brings in a lot more regimentation than we need to rise above randomness. A program that is too consistent fits students with blinders, deceives them, and encourages complacency. Remember that being focused is good only if people are heading in a good direction and are not blind as bats.

"I fear that the call for program coherence comes out of the same longing for certainty, order, and control that lies behind movements for all sorts of social engineering. It may be appealing to think one could design programs to turn out model teachers or learners, with the same reliability and precision that we can fabricate cars or refrigerators, being able to calculate the percentage of 'lemons' with some accuracy. But teaching people to depend on others in making sense is not serving them well in the long run. Processing people through 'pre-fab' experiences can't guarantee worthwhile learning.

"I am also bothered by hints that everything people are learning should be repeatedly reinforced. We know that significant change often comes through adventure—through running up against the unexpected, chancing upon things that are conflicting or that are memorable but mysterious. I don't think learners are well served by having all paths laid down for them. That might be all right for *some* technical training, but if people are to engage with the everyday problems of teaching and learning, they need practice in *figuring out* how different elements—even those that seem incongruous—can be connected and made to work together in acting and thinking.

"Please understand that, in teacher preparation and elsewhere, I'm not arguing for a shopping-mall education. I'm keen, instead, on an approach to curriculum and learning that fosters the weaving and reweaving of beliefs. That approach depends on loose ends, animating ideas, and patterns. There are, of course, connections, but there are also fuzzy bits and new threads of experience and meaning, with outworn or odd patches being worked over, stashed away for future use, or discarded. If the phrase 'lifelong learning' means anything at all, this is it! Contrary to my emphasis on ruminative, productive thinking, I fear that some people trusting in program coherence could come to treat learners, inadvertently, as objects gradually shaped to one mold. To produce their outputs, programs may relentlessly chip away at students, just as Tyler (1949) likened education to drops of water slowly eroding a stone.

"Let's pause to think about the assumptions underlying this disturbing image: assumptions about learners and the rightful use of power in unilateral human change. Can we tolerate the mechanistic views that surround complacent, hazy talk about *'cumulative* learning experiences' and 'maximizing educational *impact'* on ethical and epistemological grounds—I mean, as appropriate for our moral relations with students and appropriate considering the limited depth and certitude of our knowledge about the world, people, education, and teacher learning? While things need to change, we have to sort out what we mean when talking about program coherence."

OVERLAPPING VOICES OF EXPLICATION AND DISSENT

Let us get even more fanciful and imagine a symposium at which Israel Scheffler, Charles Lindblom, Leszek Kolakowski, Northrop Frye,

Richard Wollheim, Richard Rodriguez, Stuart Hampshire, Elias Canetti, and George Lakoff and Mark Johnson speak to issues of consistency and coherence, from contexts including philosophy, political science, literature and the arts, educational autobiography, and personal diaries. With multiple differences and points of contact, these overlapping voices stress people's evolving constructions of coherence, rather than presuming that the world could or should be portrayed as neatly consistent. Moreover, if learners are repeatedly presented with objects of thought that others have trimmed to fit patterns, they lack opportunities for responsibly making sense. Less agitated than the critic, the diverse speakers distinguish consistency from coherence, seeing the latter form of connectedness as more hospitable to change and growing imagination, while true to the many sides of concepts and experiences.

The Benefits of Disintegration

Itself of different kinds, experience is open to legitimately different and changing interpretations. Ordered by their orientations to their subjects, the disciplines of knowledge reflect, elaborate, and codify these variations and disagreements, thus making them available to study and discussion. Because of its adequacy of knowing and learning, Israel Scheffler (1973) stresses, some "disintegration" actually has educational benefits.

> It is a fact of life that the modes of experiences are various and that they generate differing perspectives, norms, and sensibilities. It is, it seems to me, an educational experience of the highest value to be confronted with these differences at an appropriate age, and to learn at first hand the disjointednesses and incongruities which no administrative integration can forever hide. . . . It is highly desirable, I think, for the student to learn that the opinions and approaches of experts differ violently, that the community of truth-seekers is not just one happy family. . . . A student who gets all his education screened through some neat integrative framework imposed in advance by others, without being forced to make his own sense of the discordances and discrepancies patent in experience, has been effectively protected from thinking altogether. (p. 106)

While learning should not be made unnecessarily difficult, educational experiences must not sell students short. The differences and *incongruities* that characterize the disciplines of knowledge, moreover, likewise characterize life and action; they challenge students' capacity to form intentions and make connections whose reach, complexity, and flexibility indicate their learning's worth. Though learning depends on structures, it is also fostered by enticing uncertainties, eye-opening experiences, and honest difficulties. Hence denying or eliminating conflicts within and among the disciplines is foolish.

Scheffler sees, however, that helping students orient themselves in a world of multiplying and disjointed ideas and experiences is a serious problem. While he finds no solution in increasing consistency by imposing "an overarching framework or shell to contain or encase variation within fixed limits" (p. 107), mere faculty intuition or inertia is not an answer either. Scheffler puts forward the balancing idea "of unity through internal structure, a unity that would not set fixed limits to variation but would infuse it as it varied" (p. 107).

Inconsistency and Unifying Intentions

Calls for systematic progress in teacher learning lean toward the notion that teaching knowledge can be dovetailed in a neat system, displaying relations among ideas, facts, and principles—all smoothly joined in theory and practice. A similar faith in consistency and conflict elimination has undergirded models of choice based on goal hierarchies. Echoing Scheffler, Charles Lindblom reflects that life is not so simple. People may wish to order the multiplicity of human goods by finding principles of super- and subordination that eliminate doubts and bring an end to searching. Yet their open-ended tasks of thinking and willing are at once more demanding and more meaningful. As Lindblom (1990) explains, the difference between discovering value hierarchies and creating networks of volition implicates a distinction between consistency and coherence.

> One examines many interrelationships among volitions in all directions and achieves at best a greatly flawed consistency that might be called coherence. . . . Coherence is admittedly a loose concept, but its obvious alternative, "consistency," is too rigid. . . . What ordinary people do to achieve coherence does not greatly differ in main outline from what scientists do in their scientific work. . . . The structure of one's volitions, then, takes the form of a web rather than a hierarchy, a web "stretched across the ground of experience, serving as one of the structures that unifies it." . . . For any one person, the search for coherence becomes an extension of the task not of finding but of forming, creating, or willing. (pp. 39–41)

Thus Lindblom views coherence in thought and action as an affirmation of people's capacity to weave structures responsive to the world as it is and could be. Fashioning relationships that stretch across the ground of experience in teaching will likewise result in a flawed consistency—temporarily redeemed by unifying intentions.

Teaching requires an inconsistency that is no mere inconsequence—want of logical sequence, connection, or relevance—but, instead, consequential upon, and adequate to, its tension-ridden moral structure. Teachers must attend to many human goods whose diversity cannot be translated into set hierarchies without educational and moral losses. It would, actually, be illogical to conclude that their conflicting nature alone disposes of the claims that values make upon us. Evoking previous speakers at this fictive symposium, Leszek Kolakowski (1968) points out that people's inconsistency "is simply a secret awareness of the contradictions of this world" (p. 214).

People respond to their dilemmas by temporarily suspending attention to some goods without, however, denying or abandoning them. If this is inconsistency, Kolakowski concludes, then inconsistency is reasonableness and strict consistency an evasive ideological fiction. In stressing life's implacable contradictions, he runs through a list of compelling fidelities that hold also true for teaching.

> Our lives are bound up in conflicting loyalties that we must choose between in concrete situations. We must break one bond in favor of another, while still not questioning the first. Loyalty to the individual, to one's own outlook on the world, to human communities in which we find ourselves either accidentally or of free choice, loyalty to nations, parties, government, friends, to ourselves and those close to us, to our own nature and our convictions, to the present and the future, to concrete things and universalities. (pp. 218–219)

Reasonable inconsistency lays the ground for modesty and perceptive tolerance. If one admits that human goods and loyalties that bear on one's decisions always exceed present capacities for attention, one concedes not only abiding imperfections but possibilities for error and needs for enlarging one's heart and vision.

Coherent Narratives Without Linear Logic

Like the disciplines of knowledge, literature can be seen in Lindblom's terms: as a web, indeed manifold webs, engaging with experience in responsive impulses of imagination. For fiction, Northrop Frye (1976) argues that two types of narrative differ revealingly in their principles of connection. The "hence" narrative makes events seem to grow naturally, almost inevitably, out of preceding events and character traits. The "and then" narrative, by contrast, contains incidents that happen to protagonists, yet these events bear no necessary relations to one another. While testifying to their spellbinding nature, the recollection of "and then" nar-ratives allows people to make connections that deepen and spread. Their pattern and openings draw readers in, impelling them to form ideas and perspectives.

Differences in authorial roles, perhaps intentions, are associated with these types of narrative connection. If the overflowing details and name-less fascination of "what happened *then* . . . and then . . . and then" keep people bound up in the story while calling on—and extending—their imaginative resources, the "hence" narrative enjoins readers to "follow the leader" who, in claiming to display causal chains, does not seem to lead—choosing, directing, persuading—but to obey, instead, necessity or logic.

Although it is not clear to what extent "hence" narratives do capture causalities or laws of logic, their pretense of mirroring the given in its inevitable movements ironically converts art and authorship into forms of objective authority. Insofar as "freedom in perception and understand-ing . . . is one of the recognized values art possesses," Richard Wollheim (1968, p. 155) comments, overly determinate narratives dispossess their readers; this is a point of educational, indeed, social significance beyond the arts. Comparing (prestigious) literary "realism" with romantic tradi-tions, Frye (1976) further explicates forms and processes of narrative con-nection by juxtaposing images of movement in space that imply con-trasting reader roles and outcomes in reading: The realist, with his sense of logical and horizontal continuity, leads us to the end of his story; the romancer, scrambling over a series of disconnected episodes, seems to be trying to get us to the top of it" (p. 50).

John Keats contends: "We hate poetry that has a palpable design upon us—and if we do not agree, seems to put its hand in its breeches pocket" (Forman, 1952, p. 95). Artists are characteristically many-minded and their intentions need not be homogeneous; neither a work nor an interpretation can therefore be correlated, unambiguously, with a "mean-ing" or "message." (See Wollheim, 1968, pp. 154–156.) While coherence is valued in art, its case for coherence is hence not one of overdetermination. Yet art's indeterminacy is no bland vagueness either: Competing interpre-tations are constrained by demands that art and literature make of people and that art itself makes of its practitioners. Wollheim (1968) therefore sees coherence as a construction midway between artist and audience, both of whom must create unity—in composing and interpreting; creat-ing and re-creating—but neither of whom should impose a unifying structure upon the other. The dangers of overly determinate constructions apply regardless of who frames them: authors, curriculum designers, or learners themselves.

Missing the Point of Education?

A curriculum needs a consistent message no more than a work of literature needs a story line in which each event has a linear (causal or logical) connection to the ones before it. Education can be coherent without being always consistent; and coherence is not just a feature of design—curriculum structures—or unifying intentions, but a characteristic of learners' formative responses. Transgressing impositions must likewise be avoided: *neither* side must take liberties with the other. Students can draw on a variety of understandings in reading narratives that can be interpreted at many levels (e.g., as descriptions, archetypes, or metaphors). Some educational practices, however, reduce literature's meanings to a list or set of main points and themes, encapsulated in textbooks and study guides. Held by many students who do well in school, related views of literature ignore education's main value and misrepresent its contents and processes.

In an educational autobiography, *Hunger of Memory*, Richard Rodriguez (1982) makes sense of his school experiences. As a Mexican-American, he benefited from learning English and being in public school. Still Rodriguez (1982) judges that he never recognized what there was to be learned:

> In the sixth grade I simply concluded that what gave a book its value was some major idea or theme it contained. If that core essence could be mined and memorized, I would become learned like my teachers. . . . After reading *Robinson Crusoe*, I wrote that its theme was 'the value of learning to live by oneself.' (p. 62)

Rodriguez distinguishes learning that yields perspectives from his own bookishness, associated with piecemeal accumulation and a bucket theory of learning. "Merely bookish, I lacked a point of view when I read. . . . I vacuumed books for epigrams, scraps of information, ideas, themes—anything to fill the hollow within me and make me feel educated" (Rodriguez, 1982, p. 64). What helped him understand his experiences was Hoggart's (1957) analysis of the "scholarship boy," a composite picture of a British working class student who likewise succeeds at schooling without growing in imagination and learning. Rodriguez devotes an entire chapter in *Hunger of Memory* to looking back at himself as a "scholarship boy," who

> tends to over-stress . . . the piling-up of knowledge and of received opinions. He discovers a technique of apparent learning, of the acquiring of facts

> rather than of the handling and use of facts. . . . He rarely feels the reality of
> knowledge, of other men's thoughts and imaginings, on his own pulses. . . .
> He has something of the blinkered pony about him. (p. 243)

Even higher education left Rodriguez initially dispossessed. His retrospective analysis fits with Dewey's (1916/1966) general conclusion that
"because of our education we use words, thinking they are ideas, to dispose of questions, the disposal being in reality simply such an obscuring
of perception as prevents us from seeing any longer the difficulty" (p.
144). Accumulating them as external givens, a learner does not feel, as
Hoggart (1957) stresses, "other men's thoughts and imaginings on his
own pulses"; this leaves him at the mercy of seeming facts. For all its
suggestion of upward mobility, success in moving through a formal curriculum may be meaningless, even disabling. Rodriguez, again, might
concur with Dewey's (1916/1966) assessment that—where education is
taken as ready-made studies set from above—their stratification over experience may be oppressive:

> Ordinary experience is not even left as it was, narrow but vital. Rather, it
> loses something of its mobility. . . . It is weighed down and pushed into a
> corner by a load of unassimilated information. It parts with its flexible re-
> sponsiveness and alert eagerness for additional meaning. (p. 209)

Learning from the Disparate and Unexpected—in Time

Elias Canetti (1973/1978) wrote in his diaries: "Learning has to be
an adventure, otherwise it's stillborn" (p. 75). Most people remember experiences with sudden, but lasting effects: images, chance encounters, a
phrase or conversation that makes one see things "in a different light"
(see also Bandura, 1982). Because such experiences are personal and may
have few qualities that presage their power, they cannot be purposely
built into a program—except indirectly, that is, by including content and
activities that reward recollection and are open to manifold responsive
engagements. To take advantage of such potentials, education must deliberately leave room for the unexpected while preparing students to make
the most of their adventures. Because chance and unpredictability—the
unplanned and the unexplained—play such key roles in human learning,
the arts, and sciences, Stuart Hampshire (1989) emphasizes that *careful*
deliberation must figure in the unexpected. Hence, an acting, thinking
person ought always

> to be open to surprises, discoveries, and uncertainties. Through an accident
> of experience he may discover in himself a disposition that he had never

believed that he could have, or he may find a deep significance, and a source of enlightenment, in an activity which he had thought was trivial and worthless. We cannot know *a priori* what is superficial and what is profound from the standpoint of the developed and free imagination. (p. 133)

Learning often unfolds in slow motion, relieved by visitations of the past and leaps of the imagination. This is another argument against educators working too hard at connecting things for learners in one programmatic whole and systematic progression. Elias Canetti's (1973/1978) reflections on his urgent, monumental, self-imposed task of pulling together everything that might conceivably clarify phenomena of "crowds and power" illuminates the perplexing relations of time, unification, and earnest efforts in learning.

> Perhaps it was lucky for me that I never let myself be overwhelmed by my material in earlier years, that I always kept it detached from me. Thus every single part had its own, lasting effect. I could think about things which would otherwise have suffocated one another. Many things had time to meet and link up in memory, whereas otherwise they would have had a short and turbulent existence on the surface. Thus I can understand why the enormous material I have looked at during the past few months has not inspired any truly new ideas in me—it has only confirmed older ideas and given me new—I would say—*scientific* courage. (p. 136)

In the end, the author worked for 30 years on *Crowds and Power* (1960/ 1962).

It strengthens our argument that Canetti's (1973/1978) reflections leave doubts and difficulties. Consider that, in the attempt to fit his thoughts into our section, we might have been tempted to stop the quotation above with "confirmed older ideas." Trying to be true to his thinking, we are left wondering what the author meant by saying that he gained "scientific" courage. Looking at science in terms of *results*—collective knowledge sedimented in methods, formulas, and propositions—it appears that science is one thing, and courage another. But personal bravery—being steadfast and willing to take risks—does enter into scientific work or into its *processes*. The concept of courage focuses attention, in detail, on the latter aspects, themselves part of the multidimensional structure of our concept of science.

Metaphorical Coherence

In asking what it may mean for multiple metaphors, each of which partially structures a concept, jointly to provide conceptual understanding, George Lakoff and Mark Johnson (1980) contrast coherence and consistency. When metaphors *overlap*—that is, describe some characteristics in similar terms—they are *coherent*. For example, since "journey" and "container" metaphors for argument both use increasing amount to represent progress, people can readily mix them: "We got a long way toward the conclusion by filling logical gaps." No single image fits the two metaphors (journey, container); hence, they are not consistent. Yet we need both (and more) to clarify features of "argument" as well as of education. For the journey, or process, metaphor includes the important aspect of direction (e.g., implying that one can go astray) absent from the container, or content, metaphor.

> The difference between coherence and consistency is crucial. Each metaphor focuses on one aspect of the concept ARGUMENT: in this, each serves a single purpose. Moreover, each metaphor allows us to understand one aspect of the concept in terms of a more clearly delineated concept. (pp. 94–95)

By extension, a larger set of metaphors is coherent when every metaphor has *some* overlap with some other members of the set. Thus, although "journey," "growth," and "adventure" metaphors for education all connote change, journeys have destinations, growth indicates given potentials, and adventure—entailing chance and daring—adds a touch of the unknown. Still, people going on a journey also show initiative. And so on. Rather than advancing conceptual understanding, metaphorical consistency is a restriction that can stand in the way of learning.

Consider cutting diamonds or weaving cloth as further metaphors for education. Though not coincident, each suggests a structure for education and coherence that highlights different aspects of both concepts. Lustrous diamonds are cut skillfully, prefiguring a pattern and changing effects. Cutting involves many planes that are angled *against* each other; moreover, it brings out and enhances a diamond's *inherent* powers to shine (i.e., refractive power). Lively sparks depend also on how one holds this durable jewel in contemplation, life, and enjoyment. Does the owner let it get dulled with grime or leave it in its box, thus never allowing the diamond to emit bright, fitful flashes of light or glow with a steady fire?

Diamonds do not sparkle in the rough. What one can make of precious stones—in fashioning and responding to them—depends on knowledge, skills, and developing sensibilities. Still, boundary conditions are set by the inflexible object at hand: This is an important entailment of the diamond metaphor. Once cut, a stone can be recut, though its parts cannot be rejoined. As the irate critic suggested, education can, on the other hand, be likened to an unfinished woven cloth: an artifact less given but more pliable, drawing on materials that can be found *and* that are made by people. While this textured metaphor encompasses the pleasures of feeling and seeing, of making patterns and devising ornaments, it has aspects of everyday need, of wear and tear, that are missing from the diamond metaphor. Yet the image of weaving and reweaving also gives more scope to spirited variation, participation, and remediable errors.

FRAMING OCCASIONS FOR EDUCATIONAL AND VOCATIONAL COHERENCE

The voices heard at the fictive symposium overlap in encouraging educators to do what people already seem to be doing in choosing a place to live, composing a painting or poem, interpreting data, and recalling fairy tales. Distinguishing coherence from consistency as forms of connectedness, our speakers posit manifold webs of concepts, metaphors, and volitions that stretch across the ground of experience, occasionally getting on top of it. Making sense does not require either singleness of conception, equable harmony, or uniform progression. In brief, the advice to educators is: "Frame occasions for constructing coherence: Do not fabricate consistency!" Where the curriculum veers toward consistency, it verges toward narrowness, rigidity, and a dispossession of learners. What unites the voices we assembled is a quality of mature reflection that transcends schools of thought and disciplines in resonating to the infinite contradictions of the world.

Educational Coherence

The metaphor of an evolving web or woven cloth clarifies which points on the continuum of consistency and disjointedness are educative. Educational coherence depends on patterns *and* loose ends; on workable materials, animating ideas, and formative activities. Threads interlace, but there are fuzzy bits and dangling strands of experience and meaning, with outworn or thin patches being worked over or unraveled over time. Resulting from the way it is woven, a fabric may be strong and matted or filmy and insubstantial.

Briefly exposing students to numbers of disparate ideas and practices may hardly touch them; it may lead to a web with so few connections that learners cannot orient themselves and that many parts of the web will escape their attention or recollection. A course of studies aiming to tie up all loose ends, on the other hand, will be tightly structured; it may lead to a sturdy web that is densely entwined, yet with such a smooth boundary and filled-in texture that it admits few opportunities for making connections to new ideas or readily meeting the unexpected. Educational coherence is found where students can discover *and* establish relations among various areas of sensibility, knowledge, and skill, yet where loose ends remain, anticipating a reweaving of beliefs and ties to the unknown.

In the university, faculty autonomy pulls the curriculum toward incongruities and fragmentation, as professors teach with regard to what they know best but with less regard to students' ease or difficulty in putting things together. But imposing consistency risks depriving students of specific and general educational benefits: being taught in areas of special faculty competence and being challenged to make sense of their disparate studies. Learners' chances for unifying their experiences with flexible responsiveness increase, furthermore, as teaching stays close to professors' live scholarship, the essence of which is creating coherence. In part, a move toward consistency may stem from the difficulties faculty have framing curricular occasions for constructing coherence. It is easier to repair fragmentation by using simplified frameworks than by crafting educational experiences in which most students understand both grounded structures and legitimate discrepancies in, for example, mathematics or teacher education.

Program Coherence in Teacher Education

While a fragmented curriculum may hardly touch ideas derived from their own schooling, curricular consistency sells teachers short. Concepts central to their education—such as teaching and learning—have multiple aspects no single perspective can contain. Attention to pupil learning, for instance, can encompass practicing a tennis serve, paying attention to the ideas of others, memorizing the spelling of "mosquito," and conceiving relations between geometry and algebra.

Though not coincident, different learning theories do have points of contact. In principle, all such theories must consider the roles of background knowledge, practice, and motivation, for instance. More specifically, a behaviorist theory of motor learning and an associationist theory of concept formation both feature repetition, albeit in different ways. (For an extension of this argument, see also Campbell's [1988, pp. 437–439] "fish-scale model of collective omniscience.") Even where faculty make no attempts to create overlaps, a curriculum including both theories could, in effect, be coherent—if teachers had developed the capacity and inclination to figure out ways in which these two accounts of learning do or do not fit together in thought and in practice.

As Romano Guardini (1954) avers, university learning prepares students for their vocations. Because education must rest on a sense of intellectual responsibility and vigorous questioning, it cannot be ill-defined or boundless. Form and flexibility are interdependent.

> There must be a whole: something that lends itself to a mental survey and in terms of which one can work practically. It must take a shape capable of incorporating new materials and problems without disintegrating: forever unfinished yet never unformed. And this whole takes its shape not only from subject matters, but from a form of prospective practice—embodying, accordingly, a living image of what it means to be a teacher, a man of law, or an engineer. (p. 8, *author's translation*)

Methods of inquiry and stirring ideas offer students bridges to learning. Teachers and other professionals can also look to their future practice: Images of teaching can serve as living links that offer connections forward and backward in time, as well as infusing understanding with personal meaning. Learning means hazarding structures and intentions amid the variations of life.

Separating the Dark from the Dark

Steven Weiland

More than most critics and theorists, Margret Buchmann and Robert Floden welcome philosophical and literary discourse into today's complex conversation about teaching and teacher education. Their work, as I see it, is part of the rethinking in higher education generally of how teaching and learning work across the curriculum, how scholarship in the academic disciplines might represent pedagogical themes, and how teacher education is affiliated with the other domains of academic life. They specialize in the education of teachers, but they everywhere recognize how working with ideas can be specialized only as ideas themselves allow or prompt it.

Philosophy and literature inspire and instruct us in the uses of uncertainty and the variability of coherence. These are Deweyan principles, mainstays of liberal pedagogy. Buchmann and Floden bring them up-to-date as part of their intention to bring teacher education into the history of ideas, including those that have contributed to current conflicts over the liberal arts curriculum. Questions remain, however, about the consequences of developments in intellectual life and higher education where the epistemological transformations of the academic disciplines and the pressures they have put on the curriculum have had the effect of presenting a new round of problems to a professional field—teacher education—with enough of its own. Buchmann and Floden make of this circumstance a promising domain of educational inquiry. In what follows I often address what is implicit or even incomplete in their arguments, but why do otherwise with writers who urge us to live and work more deeply in our uncertainties?.

REDESCRIBING PEDAGOGIC LIBERALISM

Buchmann and Floden are important voices in teacher education for a point of view in intellectual life that claims, among other things, that

236

we do not have the terms we need to do the work we want to do. Or at least we need to rethink the uses of some of our favorite words. As Richard Rorty (1989), the most Deweyan of influential philosophers, has put it, "We need a redescription of liberalism as the hope that culture as a whole can be 'poeticized' rather than as the Enlightenment hope that it can be 'rationalized' or 'scienticized'" (p. 53).

Rorty reads philosophers as poets and novelists and turns to novels for the lessons we have often found in philosophy. Buchmann and Floden favor literature too (or the thinking of poets and other writers), because it teaches "uncertainty" and the difference between "consistency" and "coherence" by actually representing them, though Rorty would favor "contingency" to supplement their choices. But Rorty's stance is an especially useful one from which to appreciate their distinctive contribution and the questions it raises. For as teacher education searches for its place within today's tangle of cultural, intellectual, and policy disagreements, it is difficult to think that we will have much to gain by making a case for "uncertainty" and against "consistency." These are proposals, I think, for the kind of "redescription" Rorty sees at the center of the post-modern revolution in scientific and intellectual life.

What kind of intellectual lives do Buchmann and Floden wish for teachers and teacher educators? And what kinds of classrooms can be imagined for them to work in? For Rorty, "the citizens of my liberal utopia would be people who had a sense of the contingency of their language of moral deliberation, and thus of their consciences, and thus of their community" (p. 61). Are Buchmann and Floden philosophers of the liberal utopia of teacher education? Or are they curriculum reformers in higher and professional education who can guide practice? If they are both, how can these critical identities be integrated?

TEACHERS AS ADULT LEARNERS

Few people are convinced that there is any continuity among the levels of formal education (or among the ideas and texts they may be made to share), much less that lifelong education is a theme worth the attention of scholars otherwise interested in, say, the poet Keats and the political philosopher Kolakowski (as Buchmann and Floden are). Preparing today's teachers to welcome uncertainty and any other strategies of pedagogic and intellectual disruption require the long view in which formal teacher education is part of a teaching career, a point in learning where many of the benefits of uncertainty and of resistance to consistency can only be anticipated.

In "Between Routines and Anarchy," Floden and Buchmann begin with a dictionary definition as if to assert, with suitable irony, that defining "certain" reifies the problem in teaching and learning that interests them. But preparing for uncertainty is not quite like preparing to teach a subject, which is, of course, never only that. What is required is a "stance" or a "posture," a point of view in the classroom that is chastening first with regard to knowing what exactly it is that students learn. Floden and Buchmann have what social and behavioral scientists call the life-span perspective, a useful one in light of the fact that the results of teaching often do not show themselves within the chronological constraints of a class or a course. As they say in a pointed understatement, "the long-term effects of teaching are variable and surprising."

The problem is not just time, it is also particularity. The influential anthropologist Clifford Geertz (1983) has made the case for the priority of "local knowledge" not just as a rationale for far-flung ethnographic inquiry but for the peculiarities of disciplinary ideas and methods and the settings in which they are taught and learned. Writing of the "local knowledge" of teaching and its resistance often to the uses of research in illuminating why some kinds of teaching work and others don't, Buchmann and Floden say, "It does not, and will probably never, permit accurate predictions of what *this* child will learn from *this* lesson taught in *this* way by *this* teacher in *this* school." I take that as an assertion of the valuable constraints of thinking locally at a time when many critics of the schools (and of higher education) are eager for assurances that the next national reform will guarantee successful teaching.

Buchmann and Floden are not against assessment (nor am I). But neither are they indifferent to how it is that teaching and learning derive from discrete ideas and experiences that gain their value precisely from what is difficult to measure. True enough, as I will explore below, they are vulnerable to the case being made against epistemological, cognitive, and curricular relativism. But in their argument for "uncertainty" in judging what is learned, they are asking for "local knowledge" as a form of counterpoint to generalizing inquiry, a source of "second thoughts" that make for better learning and living.

"Second thoughts" is, in my view, one of the most appealing of Buchmann and Floden's critical and practical formulations for teaching and learning at any level, and in formal or informal settings. When they consider the problem of locating accurately the results of teaching, Buchmann and Floden are speaking of "teacher effects," but one might add that what they say of change among students is true as well for the lives of their teachers. We cannot generalize very well about teachers as adult learners, but we can, as they sensibly urge us to do, still think about the structure of adult development and cognition as a guide to thinking about the whole of a teaching career. For as Buchmann and Floden know, teachers develop just as students do, though the adult development of teachers has not had nearly the attention that the development of their students has had, and certainly not according to emerging themes and dilemmas in life-span developmental research (exceptions are Sprinthall and Thies-Sprinthall, 1983 and Huberman, 1989b). To be sure, there is an adult developmental dimension in educational tradition. Dewey (1938), for example, made his polemical text *Experience and Education* the occasion for thinking about how the durability of subject matter is sustained across the life-span of the learner.

> Keeping track is a matter of reflective review and summarizing, in which there is both discrimination and record of the significant features of a developing experience. To reflect is to look back over what has been done so as to extract the net meanings which are the capital stock for intelligent dealing with further experiences. It is the heart of intellectual organization and of the disciplined mind. (p. 87)

In this intimation of our current preoccupation with narrative in the humanities and now, too, in the social and behavioral sciences, Dewey advanced a developmental principle that gave cognitive depth and plasticity to maturity.

Buchmann and Floden have a similar confidence in teachers to move beyond the problems they may sense in a curriculum that fosters uncertainty and appears "incoherent." For teachers are only beginning their professional and intellectual careers as college students. What may be presented to them as fixed forms of inquiry and classroom practice needlessly ignores the opportunities to "keep track"; or as they put it, "Teachers must combine reliance on themselves and their students with a habit of reconsidering the sources and consequences of their actions." From "second thoughts" come greater depth in intellectual life and the motive for practical change in the classroom. While these seem to be familiar enough ideas within the orbit of "reflective practice" as it has been advocated by Donald Schön (1987) and others, there is a timely implication in Buchmann and Floden's work that such "reflection" must be both directed at the subject matter of teaching and carried out within the life-span framework of a teaching career. They are "briskly confident" (to use one of their own exhortations) about the uses of uncertainty because they see its possibilities and its problems in the many opportunities that present themselves to teachers, especially those enabled by what they do not know or cannot be sure of.

Though the title Floden and Buchmann chose for their chapter stresses the *preparation* of teachers for uncertainty, they also recognize the problems of sustaining or deepening uncertainty even as teaching experience helps to mitigate the effects of intellectual confusion. They see inservice learning as (ironically enough) too unplanned to guarantee the necessary orientation to uncertainty as a teaching ideal, so they make the case for the preparatory approach in the curriculum. The problem, of course, is that contact with competing intellectual ideas and ideals is uncertain in the workaday world of the school. That is a good reason to stress the preparatory years, obligating teacher education colleagues to join them in a demanding intellectual task. Still, they cannot resist looking ahead: "Raising awareness of hidden uncertainties can draw teachers' attention to more distant, yet inspiring, aims, such as long-term learning that is faithful to evolving disciplinary knowledge and ideals of autonomy and responsibility for teachers and students."

Teachers deserve attention as adult learners, though in terms reflecting something more than the often sloganized and self-congratulatory domain of "adult ed" or even the orientation to problem solving found in standard professional development programs. Both are lagging behind the most important developments in theorizing adult personality and cognitive development (Baltes, 1987; Dannefer & Perlmutter, 1990; Featherman & Lerner, 1985). At the border of psychological and sociological approaches, a "family of perspectives" is now available from which to inquire into newly conceptualized relations between growth and decline, personality and cognition, the meanings of "context" for development, and the role of "wisdom" and other traditional constructs in relation to information-processing models of the brain and mind (Baltes, 1987).

There is a thriving tradition of neo-Piagetian positions that may be especially illuminating for the careers of teachers and for the unusual professional norms at the center of Buchmann and Floden's ideas for educating teachers as they prepare for and grow in their profession. For just as they urge a commitment to uncertainty, developmental psychologists have found the potential for dialectics to be a defining feature of adulthood. In one important formulation, adult dialectics is offered as a middle ground between "universalist formal thinking," having the structure of a fixed order of things, and "relativistic thinking" that sees only plural and incompatible worlds (Basseches, 1984). Dialectics is the cognitive activity of searching for what unity is possible without sacrificing doubt and difference.

Buchmann and Floden are (as noted above) interested too in how autonomy might be translated into professional ideals of responsibility. The problem of "autonomy" is one that has attracted attention in recent work in adult development. In an inventive proposal for the relations between the forms of mature structures of logic, Gisela Labouvie-Vief (1982) asserts her intention to extend work by others in the "progressive inclusion of uncertainty into one's logical program [as] the very mechanism by which development proceeds.... [The] ability to endure and even embrace uncertainty as a mechanism by which the self creates an impetus for change" (p. 168). As individuals move into (and out of) different institutional settings that provide formats of inquiry and values, they both adapt and resist. While other theorists (e.g., Perry, 1970) have charted for the undergraduate years the gradual evolution of intellectual independence, or the habits of relativism and acceptance of uncertainty, Labouvie-Vief shows how in mid- and late-life development autonomy is deepened as people evolve their own self-regulating systems of cognition and affect. "This reconstructive process permits a newly differentiated concept of personalized truth to arise: Truth no longer propagates itself, as it were, but it is created and propagated by individuals. Questions of truth thus acquire dimensions that are unabashedly pragmatic, social, ethical, moral, and personal" (p. 183). Uncertainty is functional in prompting greater self-consciousness of the relations between ideas, actions, and institutional life.

For Buchmann and Floden, "mature reflection" grasps what is distinctive about disciplinary knowledge even as it "transcends schools of thought." Is "maturity" of this kind within the reach of the beginning teacher? Some of the most influential life-span theorists have cautioned against age-linked models of development (especially those that are stage-structured). Teaching and learning toward such maturity, however, is better fitted to the life-span perspective, as it is generally implicit in *Detachment and Concern*. Where it is explicit, it is in the strong voice that opens Buchmann and Floden's imaginary conversation in their chapter on coherence. The speaker finds the essence of "lifelong learning" in the imagery of "weaving and reweaving" of patterns out of "loose ends" and "new threads of experience." In their own voice, Buchmann and Floden reassert the principle of "second thoughts," this time in a form that reaches across disciplines and forms of practice, and with a moral as well as cognitive imperative for human and professional development across the life-span:

Reasonable inconsistency lays the ground for modesty and perceptive tolerance. If one admits that goods and loyalties that bear on one's decisions always exceed present capacities for attention, one concedes not only abiding imperfections but possibilities for error and needs for enlarging one's heart and vision.

Cognitive dialectics can seem a remote exercise if we forget how it is that teachers and other professionals must make their way in organizational life while they grapple with the place of their subjects in their evolving life course. Still, the gifts of "maturity" appear to be very uneasily related to the domains of teacher education without the integration (as uneasy as this term will make Buchmann and Floden if it is applied too formally) of a life-span perspective into the curriculum. Where do short-term (*getting* ready to teach) and long-term (*being* ready to have "second thoughts" or to concede error) perspectives meet?

KNOWLEDGE OF SUBJECTS AND ADULT DEVELOPMENT

The great advantage of a more developmental idea of lifelong teacher learning is the framework it provides for assimilating the demands of greater subject-matter knowledge into a satisfying career. With their program for "second thoughts," the core of Floden and Buchmann's essay (Chapter 10), I think, is its effort to find the relations between the managerial and intellectual aspects of teacher uncertainty. While they are not inattentive to the former, it is the latter that count the most for them. There is the appearance of inconsistency, but only that, when they look for the space between true intellectual development and how learning fortifies the teacher's role (and legitimate authority) even as it continuously destabilizes one's personal epistemology or sense of intellectual coherence. Hence, at one point they say that "further studying . . . will not bring certainty. The deeper one goes into a subject, the more one gets insight into ongoing disputes, disputes that often divide a field, with little chance of resolution." Later they acknowledge the functional role of professional intellectual development: "Increasing pedagogical knowledge and skills helps teachers to make reasonable, rapid choices, anticipate events, assess understandings, and find acceptable postures of authority. Habits of thought and action reduce perceived complexity and increase predictability."

In the end, they say that "teachers can reduce some uncertainties by deepening and strengthening their pedagogical knowledge and skills during initial preparation or later in their careers." The key, again, is mobilizing the potential for dialectics. "A great support for continuing learning is being generally alert to what (inconveniently) contradicts one's assumptions." As the class hour unfolds, look for "wild misunderstandings" as a way to advance learning, the student's and the teacher's. But Floden and Buchmann know when to adapt their views to developmental choices. In a statement of generosity and wisdom, they recognize the dialectics of individual human development (the trajectory of a teach-er's life and career) by proposing that what is practical and still intellectu-ally compelling may lie beyond knowing how to lead a classroom discus-sion. "A more specific goal [than searching out all curricular uncertainties] is developing a sense of when it is worth the costs to work for greater mastery of teaching subjects. Teachers cannot study every-thing intensively, and the best rule for learning need not be to study what-ever makes one feel least sure of oneself. Being prepared here means pursuing routes to subject knowledge that are propitious and practical."

By rejecting absolutism for subject-matter knowledge, Buchmann and Floden do not question its priority. And by encouraging teachers to choose how far to carry it into their vocations, they pose compelling prob-lems of lifelong learning. But the "propitious" and the "practical" are localized, too, and how can we know when they simply cancel out—in the name of individual differences in adult development—the gains be-ing made by teacher education programs to bring subject matter to the forefront?

TEACHER EDUCATION AND INTELLECTUAL LIFE

In his 1991 AERA Presidential Address, Larry Cuban (1992) identified what he understood to be an unexplored relation between the problems of precollegiate and undergraduate teaching.

> The glaring neglect of analysis of undergraduate and graduate teaching and its linkages with pre-collegiate classrooms is seen in the scarcity of explicit intellectual discourse and conversations among scholars and practitioners about these teaching commonalities. The argument I make, then, is that seri-ous scholarly examination of the uncertainties, ambiguities, and moral di-lemmas of teaching students at different levels of formal schooling is pre-cisely one basis for assembling intellectual communities among educators. Such collaborative inquiry into core teaching activities common to all levels of schooling invigorated by respect of professors for wise practitioners and of practitioners for thoughtful professors could forge coherent communities of researchers, professional educators, and practitioners. (p. 9)

His statement suggests some degree of consensus about the uses of un-certainty, or at least the priority that it should have in the study of teacher learning and development.

Cuban speaks, I think, as an organizer, as his invocation of "coher-ence" suggests. But a "coherent" community derives its power from the same "rebel angel" (in Buchmann and Floden's terms) that makes ordering the curriculum so problematic. Where would the coherence come from? The different roles that Cuban names show how particular priorities are institutionalized and how those in these roles resist coherence as much as they appear to crave it. What constitutes the "wisdom" of practice or the "thoughtfulness" of professors is far from settled, even if there were agreement that both groups could be described in such terms. Indeed, if they were "redescribed," as Rorty would have it, then the polarized categories of practice and thinking would give way to a more supple idea of professional work (including teaching) that identified elements of each in the other and inquired into how the ratio of each to the other shapes particular practices, at particular times, in particular places, and in the case of education, in the teaching of particular subjects. These accumulated particularities ("local knowledge" again) are what make teaching so "uncertain" or "contingent" and what chasten our plans for a consistent curriculum. Buchmann and Floden welcome rebelliousness and look for the patterning that may emerge from the interminable action of "second thoughts" and correcting errors. They would be the ironists (Rorty's preferred stance) on Cuban's committee. Still, Buchmann and Floden also believe in the scarcity of conversations, or perhaps that the conversation currently underway is not suitable to its themes and purposes.

I understand the structure of Buchmann and Floden's essay on coherence and consistency (Chapter 11) to mean that the committee Cuban wishes for is also too small. The intellectual luminaries they invoke provide models of discourse even while they underline how far the conversation about teacher education is from other kinds of intellectual discourse. Indeed, many campus observers (and invariably critics, too) of teacher education teaching in departments of the liberal arts and sciences lament the isolation of colleges of education from other parts of the university curriculum. The Holmes Group (Sedlak 1987) and Project 30 Alliance (1991), recognizing this as more than a matter of university organization but as a sign of the incompleteness of traditional teacher education, are seeking to remedy the problem with inventive projects and revised programs. Such efforts may come to have the flaws of inconsistency that bedevil some curriculum theorists and (privately, perhaps) delight others. Buchmann and Floden believe that reasserting connections should not depend on curricular projects and programs (they will, among other things, have the flaw of deceptive coherence) but on reasserting the place of scholarly and disciplinary traditions at all levels of learning, and for learning at all ages once formal schooling is complete.

One name that has been given to such potential continuity, or at least to how it is that the disciplines of the arts and sciences (and other domains) are represented in pedagogy, is "pedagogical content knowledge."

This is an appealing program, and Lee Shulman (1987) is an articulate spokesman for the intellectual demands of teaching that derive from disciplinary particulars. Professors in English or history departments, and teacher educators, have taken much (false) pride in asserting the differences in their premises and practices. Cuban is right in asserting that the stratification of university departments has delayed the integration of teaching and learning according to this model. But Shulman's proposals could not have come at a more difficult time for an idea like "content knowledge." I mean, of course, not only the shifting borders among disciplines and the proliferation of new fields of inquiry but also that within old and new fields alike disciplinary epistemologies are threatened and knowing of many kinds has been made "uncertain." The problem is acute because it is general *and* discipline-specific. That is, as the historian Peter Novick (1988) has demonstrated in a masterful overview of the intellectual environment and its consequences for his field, "pedagogical content knowledge" (a designation Novick would not recognize but which is part of his argument) is more like a web of the classic texts and methods and the fresh theories and problems that have infiltrated all disciplines even as each has deepened its specialized concerns.

Can teacher educators (even those well focused on disciplinary concerns) and their students keep up if scholars in the disciplines can't? By highlighting "uncertainty," Buchmann and Floden affiliate teacher education with the largest problems of the disciplines of the arts and sciences. But these have entered the liberal arts curriculum only unevenly. Can these two overlapping curricular projects be undertaken in ways that help to close the gaps between intellectual, educational, and professional interests?

The role for teacher education, implicit everywhere in Buchmann and Floden's work, is the redirection of intellectual dilemmas toward the classroom. Despite their uneasiness about the problem of resolving intellectual disputes, in their search for an intellectually responsible pedagogy they are joined by an influential literary theorist. In an inventive and practical response to the problem of uncertainty in the liberal arts curriculum, Gerald Graff (1988) has proposed in many recent essays that we actually "teach the conflicts" that divide faculty members across the disciplines. He recognizes the dangers but agrees with Buchmann and Floden about the pointlessness of staging intellectual development:

> We need to ask whether confusion has really been held at bay by the practice of protecting students from premature exposure to intellectual dissonance. There is something curious about the standard academic assumption that only in the advanced stages of disciplinary inquiry do students qualify to

be let in on the news that the experts frequently disagree. The deeper sources of student confusion may lie not in the conflicts in and between the disciplines, but in the failure of the university to negotiate these conflicts out in the open where students would have a chance to grasp what is at stake. (pp. 106–107)

Adapting this approach to teacher education, as Buchmann and Floden imply, would make students their colleagues in discovering how it is that ideas are never certain because conflicting ideas prompt constant "second thoughts." But does teaching the conflicts simply institutionalize in the classroom the polarization of contemporary scholarship around ideological differences and hence deny to students the help they need in seeing beyond them? Students may grasp what is at stake, but for whom? As Buchmann and Floden know, this is a vivid problem for prospective teachers who take very seriously their role in the disciplines they teach. And what is at stake for their students? Should they be let in on the news also? Buchmann and Floden have shown how the discourse of teacher education might be assimilated to multidisciplinary debates. Is "Teach the Conflicts" the strong version of "Preparing Teachers for Uncertainty"? Or is "Preparing Students for Uncertainty" a needlessly modest version of "Teach the Conflicts," a step away from fully problematizing the teacher education curriculum in terms of the major debates in the arts and sciences that are undercurrents in the subject-matter preparation of teachers?

CONCLUSION: HOW MUCH UNCERTAINTY AND INCONSISTENCY ARE ENOUGH?

Philip Levine's *What Work Is* (1991—it won the National Book Award for Poetry) includes, surprisingly, poems about schooling. In one he remembers a teacher from his youth during World War II in Detroit who once drew a diagonal line on the blackboard, seemingly to prompt the junior high school students to reflect about mathematics, space, and art. The teacher asks, "What have I done?" and Levine notes with (retrospective) admiration the response of one precocious student: "You've begun to separate the dark from the dark." A pessimist about today's urban schools, Levine offers this poetic anecdote as an emblem of the kind of teaching and learning—metaphoric or even philosophic—most likely to last.

Metaphors can instruct even as they tempt us to overstate their uses. Floden and Buchmann temper their case with suitable caution. "Teacher

educators must prepare their students for uncertainties without suggesting that there are no bases for authority, order, and instructional
choices." The same spirit inhabits their call for resisting consistency by
embracing coherence in what may be called its aesthetic mode, with regard to overall patterning rather than strict internal consistency. A "moderate stance," they say, is the best one

> Balancing openness and predictability is difficult and dependent on
> context, while crucial to teaching and the learning of students and
> teachers alike. Understanding the various aspects of uncertainty
> should help in continuing to strive for a productive balance, as well
> as in reducing uncertainties where appropriate.

Still, in their closing paragraph they cite Israel Scheffler on the need for
teachers to maintain a "double consciousness," meaning active and reflective at once.

I find in "double consciousness" a strong hint of Rortyan irony, a
skeptical and even subversive stance based on the power of redescription
in a field so committed to practice. After all, Buchmann and Floden do
their work mainly in words, the audience for their essays being not
teacher education students, but colleagues in education and, in the best
of worlds, across the disciplines of arts and sciences. The philosopher
Richard Bernstein (a different kind of Deweyan) has said that "we may
feel increasingly uneasy with Rorty's master strategy—to separate private irony and public hope" (1990, p. 51). I have found irony in Buchmann
and Floden's stance, but it is fair also to say that they demonstrate how it
is possible in teacher education not to sacrifice public ideals to intellectual ones.

Moving About in Worlds Not Realized

Margret Buchmann and Robert E. Floden

> I can redescribe
> Not only where some segment silver-true
> Stays clear, but where the breaks of black commence.
> —Robert Browning, 1871/1981, "Prince Hohenstiel-
> Schwangau"

Steven Weiland chose his response's heading from Levine's (1991) marvelous poem about teaching arts and sciences in a Detroit middle school in 1942. For the rejoinder's title, we drew on Wordsworth's ode of recollection, which celebrates the vivid, dream-like splendor of vision and the "obstinate questionings" of childhood. Weiland extends and probes our analyses by making connections to life-span development and to the current soul searching among academics in the liberal arts; he draws attention, furthermore, to the stance we take toward our work and readers.

Our respondent sees redescription as central to our essays, but "redescription" has more than one sense and irony, too, can mean different things. Our work and vision are closer to practice and improvement than Weiland appears to think. Citing Rorty, he brings up conflicts of philosophical irony and public hope; in response, we return to the *Oxford English Dictionary*.

Unlike other dictionaries, the *OED* is no register of lexical properties. Instead, it richly documents life histories of words, their origins and changes of form and meaning (see Murray, 1977). Its first editor, James Murray, sought contributions from anyone and anywhere in efforts to include not only "common"—literary and colloquial—English, but foreign words, terms and expressions that were scientific and technical, and those belonging to dialects and slangs. Slang terms can also be technical; dialects may pass into foreign languages, or foreign words move into scientific terminology. James Murray saw the English language accordingly as

> one of those nebulous masses familiar to the astronomer, in which a clear and unmistakable nucleus shades off on all sides, through zones of decreasing brightness, to a dim marginal film that seems to end nowhere, but to lose itself imperceptibly in the surrounding darkness. (cited in Murray, 1977, p. 193)

Take, for instance, redescription. When looking up "redescribe" and the source quotation from Browning (see the epigraph above), one is reminded that contemporary meaning knits together redescription and change, whereas earlier usages associated redescription with repetition and reiteration. Recalling the life histories of words is a form of widening and branching, of creating dissonances and resonances where univocality may be assumed. Considering irony, one needs to distinguish where what is "ironical" is meant to characterize features of the world or of a peculiar stance toward other people or their behavior or beliefs. As sarcasm or ridicule, irony can become a privileged rhetorical control, veering toward hierarchy and alienation. By contrast, the *OED* cites Thomas Hardy's book title, *Life's Little Ironies,* to exemplify irony as a sense of things turning out, upon reflection, in unexpected or contradictory ways. This generalizing observation comes with the supposition that many perplexing experiences are shared and equalizing in effect.

Thus Boring (1929/1963) points out that scientists are limited by certain human paradoxes; what drives people toward "laborious research and to the braving of public criticism with their conclusions, is the drive which perseveres and makes them persist against criticism" (p. 78). The more you fight for truth, in short, the less you see it. Looking inward, people's lives seem haunted by an apparition that is both familiar and unidentifiable—a presence known, forgotten, half-recalled. Numerous other such examples and observations are woven throughout this book.

We can, therefore, accept irony in what may be termed the *noticing* sense (designating a condition of affairs or events) as a redescription of tensions thematic to this book. Our cautious dealings with common sense, emphasis on guided adventures in learning, and cleaving to conversation as a tender romance of reason, however, show that we back off from the *distancing* sense of irony as possibly treacherous, for both sides. Departing far from Dewey, Rorty's (1989) dichotomy of private, philosophical irony and public, liberal hope casts relations of detachment and concern in terms of a contraction and withdrawal with which we feel no affinity or reason to agree.

When one does not realize that words have different meanings, such as distinct senses of irony, or changing senses of redescription, one fails to grasp with clearness and detail aspects of language and human reality that are available and fluid. This is one interpretation of Wordsworth's line, "Moving about in worlds not realized." Another interpretation invokes the sense of "realize" as "to make real," or to give reality to something imagined or planned. Moving forward and backward in time, both senses of realization are connected in life and thought: coherent but not consistent.

Although time is implicit in all conversations about education, Steven Weiland illustrates how making temporality explicit intensifies second thoughts in their importance. Preparation implies learning for future situations. Appropriate responses to uncertainty will change as teachers solidify aspects of their craft, developing enabling and constraining habits of mind and action. A developmental view implies differentiating the learning of beginners from that of experienced teachers and considering how what may be learned today could bear fruits tomorrow, next month, and in years to come.

Considering learning in time strengthens the case for coherence, while revealing depths and directions of curriculum thinking. Consistency backfires where it inhibits students' growing abilities to make connections. Curricular coherence sacrifices some degree of neat and present integration (and, perhaps, of student comfort) in view of future capacities for making meaning in situations that instructors cannot foresee. Differences in students' knowledge and maturity will shape their perceptions of a curriculum as full of possibilities or as a jumble. We also embrace a life-span perspective in the chapters on teacher thinking (Part III), yet we are unsure about how much it should be made salient in teachers' curricula. Teacher education students might be best served by allowing them to figure out how their stance toward uncertainties should change over time. In any case, the life-span perspective may be most valuable to the teacher *educator.*

Our essays and surrounding interchanges about teaching, learning, research, and teacher education are redescriptive in anticipating new openings while reminding authors and audience of connections and commitments with which texts and concepts resonate. If we endorse local knowledge, we stress its textured varieties and degrees of distance to contingent selves—neither with a sense of "homey cheerfulness" nor "metaphysical malaise," as Geertz (1983, p. 163) put it. Yet in the end we need more than an efflorescence of local knowledge: "We need a way of turning its varieties into commentaries upon one another, the one lightening what the other darkens" (Geertz, 1983, p. 233). We close with Dewey's (1934) words from *Art as Experience:*

> Important as are the distinctions and relations thus made possible, the story does not end here. There are more opportunities for resistance and tension, more drafts upon experimentation and invention, and therefore more novelty in action, greater range and depth of insight and increase of poignancy in feeling. (p. 23)

Conclusion

Lee S. Shulman

> If it be true that good wine needs no bush, 'tis true that a good play needs no epilogue. Yet to good wine they do use good bushes; and good plays prove the better by the help of good epilogues.
>
> —Shakespeare, *As You Like It*, Rosalind's Epilogue

A good play needs no epilogue, and by implication, neither does a fine book. Nonetheless, having been invited to essay this final chapter, I shall proceed, hoping that my observations will prove neither redundant nor misguided. I prefer to consider this contribution an epilogue, or even less pretentiously, an afterword. I dare not attempt to draw a simple conclusion, to provide closure or summation to this group of essays. Buchmann and Floden persuasively attack the quest for certainty and consistency in discussions of teaching and teacher education. As a teacher educator, all I can claim with confidence is the last word. It is a position of advantage in both courts of law and books of essays. I accept it gratefully.

What is the role of the last word in this provocative volume of essays, critiques, and responses? My colleague-at-a-distance Maxine Greene has already done all the heavy lifting. In her introduction (which I prefer to view as a prologue or foreword) she has summarized the arguments of all the essays and of the critiques, as well as adding a few well-crafted glosses and elaborations of her own. With all the serious work having been completed, I am left with the envious opportunity to suspend the rules, to reminisce and recount, to explicate and pontificate, as befits the last player to leave the stage. I will indeed offer my observations as if I had been sitting silently at Margret's table during this marvelous set of conversations. Now that the last of the guests has left, and I am helping Margret and Bob clean up, I can offer gratuitous comments on the contributions of their guests, and sage advice to the hosts themselves.

As befits the late hour, my remarks will wander over several topics. I will first offer slight emendation to Maxine Greene's suggestion that

Professor Buchmann is reminiscent of Virginia Woolf's Mrs. Ramsay, orchestrating conversations at her dinner table. I will then offer a personal reminiscence of the early years of the Buchmann/Floden careers, proffering an explanation for the unusual focus of their work on teacher education and the particularly Deweyan and Schwabian character of their perspectives.

What is the context in which Buchmann and Floden offer their analyses? Although philosophers may lay claim to timelessness, their work commands even more interest if it is timely. They philosophize in an era where the functions of teaching and teacher education are beset by a particularly excruciating ambiguity. The juxtaposition of national standards and national examinations on the one hand, and the growth of site-based management and local school control on the other, establishes a tricky tension within which teachers must work through their roles and responsibilities. In this setting, philosophers offer their critiques and analyses to lend sober reflection to the enthusiasms of their peers.

Out of this analysis, I will suggest that the policy environment introduces a tension between teacher as policy implementor and teacher as local problem solver. I will suggest an image of teacher as curriculum broker and transformer, using a conception of pedagogical reasoning and action as my model. How does one prepare teachers for such a demanding role? I will suggest the need to develop a dramatically new approach to the pedagogy of teacher education, with the use of cases and case methods at its heart.

Finally, lest we forget that teaching is more than an exquisitely complex form of reasoning and judgment, I will follow Buchmann and Floden's lead and draw from the literary wisdom of several writers for a countervailing image of teaching, one that emphasizes the necessary hope and trust that must undergird the teacher's intellectual capacities. Now, if you will assist me in clearing the cups and saucers, we can proceed from the dining room, where norms of gentility may reign, into the kitchen, where we can speak less formally and more frankly about the evening's conversations.

AT MRS. RAMSAY'S DINNER TABLE

What are the contributions of philosophers to the educational conversation? Maxine Greene, in her role as my partner bookend, compares Margret Buchmann with Virginia Woolf's Mrs. Ramsay at her dinner table. "She is the Mrs. Ramsay who strives to create a space of calm consideration in the noisy, banal domains of teaching and teacher education: a space where probing questions can be posed; where the tensions can be lived out between what is and what ought to be." The image of a calming and coherent space among the noisy and banal cacophony of voices in teaching and teacher education is soothing. Many philosophers of education attempt to accomplish as much, to make education's rough places smooth. Nevertheless, in this set of essays, I don't find the team of Buchmann and Floden offering calm and coherence to their brothers and sisters in teacher education. They provoke and challenge received wisdom, providing breeze to the becalmed but blowing them in directions for which they are ill-prepared. They are less like Mrs. Ramsay, I would suggest, than they are like the "tummlers" at a Catskills resort.

In their heyday, I am told, every resort in the "Jewish Alps" of the Catskill Mountains north of New York City had a valued employee known as the "tummler." The etymology of this Yiddish word may derive equally from "tumult" and "tumbler," but his function (and I suspect he was usually a "he") was utterly indispensable. His job was to keep things stirred up. Remarkably like Mrs. Ramsay, he was listed on the books as the "social director." And his responsibility was to create "trouble," but of a socially productive sort. He rousted guests out of their comfortable deck chairs beside the pool and induced them into hotly contested games of shuffleboard. He taught the rhumba and the cha-cha-cha. Amateur night was his responsibility, and he probably did stand-up comedy in the lounge before the handsome young singer (named either Fisher or Damone) sang popular love songs by Irving Berlin or Rodgers and Hammerstein. The tummler's role was to replace calm with cacophony; where quiet reigned, there would tumult be.

Why are Buchmann and Floden more like a Catskills tummler than like Mrs. Ramsay? Or, more likely, why would Virginia Woolf's protagonist have been considered a tummler had she presided over her dining room at Grossinger's rather than Ramsay's? I find the world of teacher education all too comfortable and consensual in its attitudes. Whether advocating the magic of reflective practice, the routine of Madeline Hunter, or the organizational rhetoric of professional development schools, this beleaguered field has circled its wagons and developed the appearance of consensus far too readily. Our philosophers have detected this quiet self-satisfaction and, like good tummlers, have set out to create a disturbed space amid the dull consistencies. They argue that the needed coherence will result only from a struggle with the disarray they must create.

The worlds of teaching and teacher education are not places where most philosophers dwell. While Maxine Greene, Thomas Green, and Gary Fenstermacher have addressed problems in that domain, it remains relatively free of philosophers. Why do we find Buchmann and Floden in the heat of the teacher education kitchen instead of in the safer and more benign places where most philosophers do their work?

WHAT'S A NICE PHILOSOPHER LIKE YOU DOING IN A PLACE LIKE THAT?

Most philosophers shy away from the analysis of teaching. Even among philosophers of education, questions of truth, beauty, morality, and virtue are far more attractive topics than that prosaic commonplace, teaching. And if teaching is unpopular, teacher education is toxic. How does it happen, then, that two gifted philosophers devote their attention almost exclusively to the educationally rich but philosophically prosaic problems of teachers and their preparation? In her introductory remarks, Maxine Greene urges our philosophers to devote more attention "to situation, to location . . ." in the analysis of education. I shall address the question of philosophical choices by reference to situation and location, employing biography more than philosophy to suggest an answer. In the spirit of the kitchen counter kibbitzer rather than the dining table sage, I shall reminisce in quite personal terms.

Bob Floden and Margret Buchmann arrived at Michigan State University from Stanford's gentle climate on a Christmas eve when the temperature was barely at zero Fahrenheit and the wind-chill was well below that mark. They came to work in an organization that was a department neither of philosophy nor of educational foundations. Instead, they would begin to teach and to conduct research in a department of teacher education and a newly founded Institute for Research on Teaching. The institute, whose direction I shared with Professor Judith Lanier, was founded on a number of premises. We believed that problems of education were far too complex to be addressed by members of any one discipline or educational specialty. Inspired in part by Joseph Schwab's image of practical deliberation informed by a disciplined eclectic, we had begun to organize an institutional cloak of many disciplines, a place where psychologists, teacher educators, economists, anthropologists, linguists, policy analysts, curriculum specialists, philosophers and practicing school teachers could work together in the study of teaching. Yes, even philosophers. Hence, Margret and Bob. We also believed that the study of teaching had to be tempered by a continuing taste of reality. We therefore continued strong connections between the institute's work and the continuously reforming teacher education programs at Michigan State. We ensured that each research program included a practicing classroom teacher as a full participant, typically purchasing half the teacher's contract so he or she could spend substantial time with other members of the research teams.

While both were completing Ph.D.s in philosophy of education at Stanford, their backgrounds and orientations were quite different. Margret's dissertation was on Dewey and Hegel, with substantially more of the latter than the former. She brought a background in political and social theory. She came to these philosophical studies from a strong foundation in the classical curriculum of the German *gymnasium*. Bob's earlier studies had been in philosophy and mathematics. At Stanford his work in philosophy sometimes was subordinated to his activity with the Evaluation Consortium directed by Professor Lee J. Cronbach, itself a remarkable interdisciplinary research and deliberation group. Indeed, his dissertation topic reflected this hybrid vigor, as he studied the uses of analysis of covariance in evaluation research from the perspective of philosophical investigations of the logic of reasoning from counterfactuals.

Among the most memorable occasions in the early history of the institute were the transdisciplinary staff seminars taught by visiting University of Chicago philosopher Joseph Schwab. In those seminars he modeled the power of deliberations across disciplines in the examination of educational questions. He certainly influenced the intellectual climate of the institute. I believe he also continued to inspire our growing image of the centrality of philosophical criticism and analysis to the study of educational theory and practice. He also had a profound effect on the thinking of both Buchmann and Floden.

The traditional role of the philosopher vis-à-vis empirical research is of the outsider, the critic, speaker of the last word. We held the view that even philosophers should be insiders, participating actively in all phases of research, thereby lending a critical and normative cast to aspects of a project's activity. Similarly, we appointed practicing teachers as members of each research team, not as "research translators" but as full collaborators. Thus, shortly after their arrival in Michigan, Margret began working on a project studying how teachers integrate across subject matters in teaching the language arts; Bob worked on a long-term study of the impacts of state testing and curriculum policies on teachers' decisions about what topics to teach in elementary school mathematics. Shortly afterward, both added teaching in the teacher education program to their roster of responsibilities.

Why do I bother with such an extended account of the context in which Buchmann and Floden assumed their first (and continuing) academic appointments? With Greene, I believe that situation and location are essential to understanding any enterprise. I also believe in the importance of the kind of philosophical work contained in this book, in which philosophers who are deeply involved in the activities of teacher education and research on teaching write as philosophical insiders about the complexities of those worlds. Therefore, I must try to explain what kinds of locations and situations make such scholarship flourish. Organizations like the Institute for Research on Teaching and its progeny at Michigan State and elsewhere, where philosophers work actively with colleagues from other fields of study on problems of practice and policy, become the locations and settings for this kind of work. The vitality and value of the essays in this book serve as elegant argument against the continued separation of the educational foundations—philosophy, psychology, history—from the practice of teacher education and the empirical study of teaching.

WHAT'S A NICE PHILOSOPHER LIKE YOU DOING IN AN EDUCATIONAL POLICY ENVIRONMENT LIKE THIS?

Another aspect of "situation and location" is the policy environment in which considerations of teaching and teacher education occur. Buchmann and Floden's analysis of the teacher's needed capacities and dispositions is particularly relevant to the demands that the current directions of educational reform are likely to place on teachers. Through the multitude of educational reform proposals, a few common themes are emerging. They outline a new countenance for education and significantly more demanding conditions for America's teachers. Commitment to these commonplaces, for example, was one of the few areas of agreement between the contending 1992 presidential campaigns of Clinton and Bush.

Higher national standards in the core subject areas and national examinations for all students are the twin foundation stones atop which a national policy for educational reform is being erected. The most enlightened reform proposals reject the curricular impulse derived from those who believe that a fairly fixed body of cultural literacy must be conveyed to all students. They disclaim the view that our students simply do not know enough history, science, mathematics, literature, or geography. They argue with those advocates who propose a coordinated system of national curriculum and standard examinations that will hold educators and students responsible for knowing what they must know. In the more enlightened view, the national goals would not take the form of prescribed syllabi, however, but of detailed curriculum frameworks tied to quite different systems of student assessment. Teachers would be free to select from the options offered by the curriculum frameworks and to fashion programs of study that would prepare their students for the new genres of national examinations.

Alongside this apparent nationalization of educational renewal, however, was a countervailing move. Schools and teachers would become more autonomous and responsible at the local level to fashion programs that would gain student interest and be responsive to local needs, interests, culture, and values. Teachers would still be expected to help students reach the national standards and do well on the national examinations. But the belief was that a lockstep national curriculum tethered to narrowly defined traditional examinations would be harmful for American education. There should be a way to share common goals and standards while permitting, even encouraging, locally responsive variations in methods, emphases, and values. Thus national definitions of educational goals and national examinations could be paired with greater site-based management and local control.

What kinds of national curriculum frameworks and examinations permit the coexistence of such contradictory directions? The proposals are somewhat utopian, perhaps almost quixotic. Here we see curriculum frameworks rather than mandated curricula, eschewing the stereotype of French or German education in which an entire nation of fourth graders is on the same page of every text on the second Tuesday in May. Examinations would be conducted in the spirit of Lauren Resnick and Marc Tucker's *New Standards Project* or of Ted Sizer's *Coalition of Essential Schools*, in which performance assessments, projects, and portfolios worthy of exhibition and display replace the machine-scored answer sheet.

The new view of assessment carries with it striking new images of teaching. The teacher is a coach, much more in the spirit of advanced placement (AP) tests than of standardized tests. In standardized tests the teacher is unprofessional if she teaches to the test; in APs the teacher is unworthy if she doesn't. Indeed, she knows what should be on the test and actively coaches the students to perform well on it. Unlike advanced placement tests, however, the forms of assessment are vigorously local even as the tests are scored in light of national standards, no small challenge for the psychometricians but no small revolution in educational thinking.

"Less is more" and the rediscovery of Zipf's Law. A key element in the image of new standards, whether following the model of the mathematics standards of the National Council for Mathematics Education (NCTM) or the science, mathematics, and technology standards of Project 2061 of the prestigious American Association for the Advancement of Science, is Sizer's motto, "Less is more!" (borrowed wisely from the architect Ludwig

Mies Van der Rohe, who probably borrowed it in turn from someone else in the spirit of Robert Merton's [or was it Whitehead's] line, "Everything of importance has been said before by someone who did not invent it").

The countervailing impulse of reform through national goals also reflects the belief that national standards may be needed to guide the reform of American education. However, advocates of "less is more" begin by challenging the assumption that our conceptions of needed knowledge are adequate. They deny that we need only develop a "delivery system" to ensure that the intellectual goods get from suppliers to clients. This perspective argues that we must radically reconstruct our conception of what knowledge is of most worth. We must replace the emphasis on coverage and the audit of results with the need for selectivity, depth, and the demonstration and display of accomplishments. The "less is more" principle calls for the curriculum to eschew coverage and to replace that seductively simple virtue with the exploration in depth, variation, and richness of the essential questions and central ideas of the disciplines and interdisciplines. The principle is hardly new, and no less valuable for its age or lineage. In our century, Dewey, Whitehead, Bruner, and Schwab are among the thinkers who argued for the idea. The principle is revolutionary, however, especially as it relates to significant consequences for the work of students and teachers in schools.

When we emphasize the core essential ideas of disciplines or interdisciplines, we do not merely reduce the amount of material to be covered nor do we take a shorter list of ideas and merely address them more deeply. The ideas themselves change character. Indeed, I would argue, the more central and hence essential are ideas to any field, the more likely they are to be ambiguous, elusive, and multidimensional in their complexity. Thus, not only is less more valuable than more, less is more complex and difficult to learn than more.

Which finally brings us back to Zipf's Law. Who, you may ask, is Zipf, and what is he suddenly doing in our kitchen? George Kingsley Zipf was a Harvard instructor whose passion was comparative philology. Zipf (1935, 1949) verified that, in nearly all languages, word frequency is correlated with word shortness. The more frequently words are used, the shorter and less phonemically complex they are or they become. The process of abbreviation and curtailment that apparently produces this effect, however, also leads to one of the great agonies of second-language learning.

We all remember the ease with which we negotiated the first few months of high school Spanish or French. The regular conjugations were straightforward, and so—regular. Then we discovered that these languages engage in the ultimate *bait-and-switch* operation with respect to the regularities of grammar and syntax. The verbs we really needed to use, the verbs "to go" and "to be" and others like them, turned out to be regularly irregular in their conjugations! That's a manifestation of Zipf's Law, a pattern he attempted to apply to many features of human individual and collective behavior as a manifestation of the "principle of least effort."

Shulman's corollary to Zipf's Law is quite simple. The more central a concept, principle, or skill to any discipline or interdiscipline, the more likely it is to be irregular, ambiguous, elusive, puzzling, and resistant to simple propositional exposition or explanation. Thus, if we are to make less into more, we had better recognize that less is harder than more, less is more complex than more, less is more enigmatic or cryptic than more. It is far easier to remember how a bill becomes a law than to understand *democracy* as a concept.

What will be the role of the teacher in this form of education? Teachers will serve as honest brokers between the ideas, skills, and dispositions contained in national and state curriculum frameworks, and the specific conditions, understandings, and interests of students, schools, and communities. Bruner has used the term "intellectual honesty" to characterize the teacher's pedagogical imperative. Teachers must discern the most significant ideas contained in the curriculum frameworks and examine them critically from their own perspectives, which combine the wisdom of subject-matter experts and pedagogues. They must simultaneously examine the minds and motives of their students, sensing the knowledge and experience they bring to the table, and the kinds of thinking that will help the students make the most sense out of the curriculum's ideas. To teach in an intellectually honest way is to create instructional representations that are faithful simultaneously to the structure of the subject matter, on the one hand, and to the constructive understandings of students, on the other.

The great challenge of teaching these less-is-more essential ideas is that they do not permit clear, clean, direct propositional expositions. You can't just learn the definitions. They require instead a "criss-crossing of the landscape," the active application of multiple representations through metaphors, analogies, narratives, and inventive examples. They require student constructions, iterations, and, most important, dialogues and debates. Policy makers will need to abandon their illusions about the remote control of teaching. Teachers will need to depend even more on their own deep subject-matter understanding and their abilities to transform that knowledge into powerfully adaptive representations that connect with the experiences and preconceptions of students. They must learn to employ groupwork, for example, not as a fashion, but as an indispensable crucible in which ideas are tempered and internalized through collaboration, competition, and exchange. Teachers must then be in a position to monitor and respond to the active, multiple constructions of meaning by their students.

The essential feature of teaching is its uncertainty and unpredictability. Teaching cannot be directed by formal theory, lockstep national syllabi, or centralized procedural policies, yet remain responsive to both student insights and misconceptions. Moreover, as our educational goals increasingly emphasize higher-order thinking and reasoning and student collaborations around real problems, the education of teachers must emphasize their development of flexibly powerful pedagogical understanding and judgment. Therefore, discourse on teaching must go beyond broad principles and propositions as its objects. This set of conditions not only defines the difficult conditions for teaching; it also identifies the reasons why the education of teachers represents a challenge of the first magnitude.

When confronted with so much uncertainty and unpredictability, teachers will find only temporary value in simple admonitions and checklists. Recipes for teaching and prefabricated lesson plans will work only as long as conditions remain within the predicted range. This is the reason I advocate the development of new approaches to the education of teachers, a long-overdue reinvention of the pedagogy of teacher education. Consistent with Buchmann and Floden's critiques, we cannot improve teacher education merely by increasing the amount of firsthand experience. Nor will more theory or more practical maxims suffice. A case-based curriculum strikes the ideal middle ground between the high impact of direct experience and the thoughtful reflection engendered by fine literature, insightful theory, and engaging discussions (Shulman, 1992).

Knowledge of teaching comprises combinations of cases and principles. Future teachers can be guided to develop a repertoire of cases that can help to guide their thinking and reflections on their own teaching. They can then use their experience with cases, their own and those of others, as lenses for thinking about their work in the future. Their development as teachers can be guided through their study of prototype cases written by others, as well as through reflecting on their own teaching and crafting cases of their own.

By reading and discussing such cases, we begin to detoxify the recounting of failures and make the possibilities for learning from such experiences more real. We try to help our students celebrate their failures if they can learn from them, rather than denying them to avoid embarrassment. Bosk (1979) has written about learning in the surgical residency, in a book that carries the wonderful title *Forgive and Remember*. The title communicates the message that internships are occasions in which errors must be made. They will be forgiven only if they can be remembered and reflected upon and become a source of learning. "Forgive and forget" is a motto for good relationships without growth. "Forgive and remember" is a slogan for all practical internships and an inspiration for those who would learn from cases.

Thus far I have been in fundamental agreement with Buchmann and Floden, supporting their more complex and uncertain view of teaching and their eschewal of highly rationalized approaches to teacher preparation. However, there are limits to the degree to which human agents can be asked to tolerate ambiguity and unpredictability. To the outsider, coping with the demands of an inconsistent curriculum may seem like a great humanistic adventure. To the insider who is undergoing the experience, the price may be far too high.

MANAGING COMPLEXITY

For our philosophers, coherence is a rebel angel and the quest for consistency and simplicity is foolish and misguided. They argue that teachers and teacher educators must learn to live with the necessary ambiguities and complexities that are inherent in education. Yet, they ask of educators what may well be unreasonable to ask of anyone—to seek to complicate rather than simplify their lives. The issue may not be a matter of choice or preference. The need to reduce complexity or ambiguity to optimal or tolerable levels may well be wired into our nervous systems.

An example from medicine may illustrate my point. When Arthur Elstein and I were studying how gifted internists arrived at difficult diagnoses (Elstein, Shulman, & Sprafka, 1978), we first read the standard textbooks of medicine. They instructed physicians to gather the patient information they needed from medical histories, physical examinations, and routine laboratory procedures, all the while *maintaining an open mind*. We therefore approached our first direct observations of diagnostic work in internal medicine fully expecting to document inductive search procedures. To our amazement, when we worked with our first physician, he proceeded to generate several diagnostic hypotheses within the first minutes of the patient encounter, long before he had collected much information at all. What, we wondered, had happened to the open mind? He devoted much of the ensuing investigation to pitting his working hypotheses against one another as he continued to collect new information.

As our studies continued, we came to understand that the first physician was not an anomaly or exception. Indeed, all the experienced physicians we studied employed essentially the same heuristic. They sized up the presenting complaint and rapidly moved toward generating one or more diagnostic hypotheses. This early closure did not doom them to frequent error. The method of multiple hypotheses, as we came to call the strategy, was remarkably robust. Yet it appeared to violate both the tenets of the medical textbooks and the principles of open-minded inductive reasoning!

We came to understand our findings in terms of the management of complexity. Examined closely, the admonition to gather all the information needed while maintaining an open mind was a recipe for madness. The modest capacities of human memory were quickly overwhelmed by the burdens of unscaffolded information-gathering. Even though the search could be divided into history, physical, and laboratory phases, and some of those processes could be further organized by anatomical location (proceeding cephalocaudally, from head to toes), the sheer volume of information accumulates much too rapidly to be held in mind efficiently. Simply put, the textbook admonitions were impossible to follow. Inductive, open-minded diagnostic work was an illusion. Physicians regularly generated multiple working hypotheses because without them they couldn't find their place. The intellectual world of medical diagnosis would be unmanageably complex if the inductive imperative were followed.

Why then generate *multiple* working hypotheses if the primary motivation is simplification? A single hypothesis would be quite enough. But the motivation is not solely to avoid complexity. The diagnostician seeks to control complexity within the bounds of real problems that demand solution. The great danger of early hypothesis generation is, indeed, premature closure around a favored hypothesis that has not been adequately challenged. The method of multiple competing hypotheses serves the dual purpose of memory management and safeguarding the reasoning process from inappropriately early narrowing of the field. And in this example, I believe, we find an important moral for our analysis of teaching and teacher education.

The physician addresses diagnostic problems of great complexity against a background of stability and routine. The order and contents of the medical history, the physical examination, and the ordering of laboratory tests is stable and routine. The physician engages with a single patient at a time, both in the examining room and in the operating room. When the task becomes more complex, as in a surgical procedure, the physician works as part of a team, including nurses and other physicians.

When a diagnostic problem exceeds her range, the physician readily so-licits the consultation of peers. Both the internal structure of medical work and the organizational structure of medical practice combine to control the complexity and unpredictability of the physician's work. This is not so in teaching.

Except for a busy emergency room (always staffed by a team), no medical context approximates the flux of an elementary school classroom. The teacher faces the uncertainties of teaching as a solo practitioner, and with responsibility for two or three dozen lives and minds at any one time. Critics of teaching and teacher education who wish to celebrate complexity and the importance of seeking coherence must be mindful of the potentially overwhelming demands of life in classrooms. The proper education of teachers as well as the needed restructuring of schools must take account of the need to provide a stable and supportive set of condi-tions within which teachers might then be expected to cope with ambigu-ity and uncertainty.

Coherence and Experience: Twin Rebel Angels?

As befits the vocation of tummlers, this collection of essays begins and ends with challenges to a conventional wisdom that celebrates two of the pillars of contemporary teacher education programs: firsthand ex-perience and program consistency. Belief in the importance of these two principles has supported attempts to reform the preparation of teachers for nearly a century. How can these be questioned?

We are first urged to be suspicious of the great value ascribed to experience, hands-on direct involvement with life in classrooms through observation, participation, and internship. In the spirit of those who have admonished that we learn not from experience, but from thinking about our experience, our authors warn that too much experience will likely fail to yield the advertised skill and wisdom. Instead, it might well bring about unwarranted confidence, uncritical habits of practice, and limita-tions to pedagogical imagination and inventiveness.

The book's final chapter praises "coherence, the rebel angel." Need-lessly confused with the "guardian angels" of systemic educational re-form such as consistency, direction, and program, coherence is of a differ-ent species, valuable in quite different ways. Coherence actually presupposes inconsistency, complexity, a modicum of disorder and con-tradiction that can be negotiated by future teachers only if they actively transform the inconsistencies into coherence. Consistency can be a char-acteristic of programs or curricula; coherence must be constructed by the learners themselves.

The image of the rebel angel is telling. Rebel angels are said to have resisted the control and discipline of God and defied his commands. They descended from heaven, mated and matriculated with human beings, taught them the secrets of divine wisdom, and thus robbed humankind of its innocence. Buchmann and Floden argue that program consistency, by oversimplifying the world of classrooms and schools, breeds a form of pedagogical innocence. This innocence must be challenged by the cacophonies of mismatched theories and incompatible principles that make up the useful teacher education program. The rebel angel of coherence teaches mortal pedagogues to cope with the complexities of their responsibilities and to construct the meaning and order needed to guide their work.

This provocative claim by our two tummlers stimulates me to express both assent and dissent. The magical properties of student teaching guided by the invisible hand of systematic teaching models certainly make teaching appear far more orderly and regular than is warranted. Nevertheless, there are lessons to be learned from experience, both one's own and that of others. Coherence is a worthy goal, but one unlikely to be accomplished by students working alone. They will need considerable support from thoughtful and sensitive faculty members who are prepared to create the conditions that make for coherence without falling prey to the temptation to do the work on behalf of the students. (Deborah Ball's conception of mathematics teaching in the elementary grades is a good model for this delicate balance.)

Here again, I see particular value in the potential of case methods in teacher education. Cases are powerful representations of experience, secondhand experience if you will. While "secondhand" is generally a term of derision in the world of clothing or automobiles, secondhand experience may actually have advantages over its firsthand counterpart for some aspects of teacher development. As I discussed earlier, I see value in both the study of cases and the crafting of one's own. When a student studies, discusses, analyzes, and wrestles with the facts, feelings, and issues in a well-crafted case, she re-frames the experiences of the case to make them her own. Thus, learning with cases entails two complementary processes—one studies the secondhand accounts of others' firsthand experiences, transforming them vicariously into one's own. One also writes cases based on firsthand experiences, and this process of case-making renders the merely firsthand experiences into a form of reflective practice. The teacher not only has immediate experience, he constructs it. Constructing one's own teaching, like composing one's life, confronts and captures it in new ways.

The ease with which we attack experience, however, leaves me uneasy. I grant that mere experience is an overrated condition for developing expert pedagogical judgment. Nevertheless, it seems so typical for academics to demean that which *hoi polloi* have in far greater abundance than do professors. Varieties of firsthand experience are the prerequisite for secondhand experience. One cannot think about experiences one has never had, and even cases gain their educative power through their interchange with direct experience.

In yet another sense, experience's value may lie less in how it guides our actions, and more in how it permits us wisely to refrain from action. In her novel *The Cannibal Galaxy* Cynthia Ozick portrays a philosopher named Hester Lilt, who delivers a lecture on the nature of pedagogy. She reads to her audience the following *midrash*, a tale from the Jewish sources.

> There ran the little fox . . . on the Temple Mount, in the place where the Holy of Holies used to be, barren and desolate, returned to the wild, in the generation of the Destruction. And Rabbi Akiva was walking with three colleagues, Rabbi Gamliel, Rabbi Elazar, and Rabbi Joshua, and all four saw the little fox dash out. Three of the four wept, but Akiva laughed. Akiva asked, "Why do you weep?" The three said, "Because the fox goes in and out, and the place of the Temple is now the fox's place." Then the three asked Akiva, "Why do you laugh?" Akiva said, "Because of the prophecy of Uriah and because of the prophecy of Zechariah. Uriah said, 'Zion shall be ploughed as a field, and Jerusalem shall become heaps.' Zechariah said, 'Yet again shall the streets of Jerusalem be filled with boys and girls playing.' So you see," said Rabbi Akiva, "now that Uriah's prophecy has been fulfilled, it is certain that Zechariah's prophecy will also be fulfilled." And *that*, said Heather Lilt, "is pedagogy. To predict not from the first text, but from the second. Not from the earliest evidence, but from the latest. To laugh out loud in that very interval which to every reasonable judgment looks to be the most inappropriate—when the first is accomplished and future repair is most chimerical. To expect, to welcome, exactly that which appears most unpredictable. To await the surprise which, when it comes, turns out to be not a surprise after all, but a natural path." Again she lifted her head. "The hoax is when the pedagogue stops too soon. To stop at Uriah without the expectation of Zechariah is to stop too soon. And when the pedagogue stops too soon, he misreads every sign." (Ozick, 1983, pp. 67–68)

The wisdom of Akiva suggests a caution for Buchmann and Floden's elegant critiques of experience. The value of experience may lie less in providing grounds for action than in offering sound reasons for inaction. Strategic action may depend far less on the contributions of experience than most professional educators are wont to believe. But the wisdom of practice is often the wisdom to forbear, to withhold, "to predict not from the first text, but from the second." It is no accident that young parents are always seeking ways to act when confronted with a problem, while more mature parents recognize the prudence of patience and the wisdom of forbearance.

In a novel by Canadian author Robertson Davies, ironically titled *The Rebel Angels*, a character observes that fine teaching often takes on a surprising character.

> Only those who have never tried it for a week or two can suppose that the pursuit of knowledge does not demand a strength and determination, a resolve not to be beaten, that is a special kind of energy, and those who lack it or have it only in small store will never be scholars or teachers, because real teaching demands energy as well. To instruct calls for energy, and to remain almost silent, but watchful and helpful, while students instruct themselves, calls for even greater energy. To see someone fall (which will teach him not to fall again) when a word from you would keep him on his feet but ignorant of important danger, is one of the tasks of the teacher that calls for special energy, because holding in is more demanding than crying out. (Davies, 1981, p. 87)

Thus, teachers need to give heed to that voice of wisdom that courageously yells, "Wait!" when the crowds clamor for the attack, or softly whispers "Listen," when the teacher's every instinct is to tell. Experience, whose teachings can be so misleading and dangerous, may also be a second rebel angel, whose gift is the wisdom to withhold, to permit learning to replace teaching as the essential feature of classroom life. Perhaps the lesson of experience is that two significant nouns are missing in the glib phrase "less is more." Less *teaching* is more *learning*. If we wish students to learn more, teachers may have to teach less. And both groups will discover that they can use the time profitably.

Epilogue. "It is not the fashion to see the lady epilogue; but it is no more unhandsome than to see the lord the prologue." So Rosalind comments on both her person and her position as she concludes Shakespeare's great comedy. It is certainly not the fashion to see the teacher educator the epilogue in a book of philosophical analysis, but perhaps no less worthy than to have given a distinguished philosopher the prologue. It is only civil for the tummlers to give their clients the last word. We are the ones whose serenity is so rudely, albeit fruitfully, disturbed by their analyses.

Since good plays need no epilogue, Shakespeare used this device only once more among his prodigious creations. In his very last play, *The Tempest*, he provides a closing valedictory for his alter ego, Prospero. This wise philosopher-duke recognizes that neither the storm with which the play opens nor its absence, perfect calm, is a suitable setting for human progress. He sagely blesses his children, therefore, with the promise of "calm seas, auspicious gales." Without the combination of both, we can enjoy neither the serenity of peace nor the adventures of progress and growth. The safe setting of a calm ocean can permit sailors to risk raising all their largest sails and thus take advantage of strong winds. In a similar fashion, the field of teacher education will flourish if we can find the proper balance of consistency and coherence, a judicious blend of calm seas and auspicious gales to permit our fields to accomplish their needed reforms. The competing images of a calming Mrs. Ramsay and an abrasive tummler suggest that our philosophers may play both roles in turn as they help guide the educational conversation.

References

Anderson, C. W., & Roth, K. J. (1989). Teaching for meaningful and self-regulated learning of science. In J. Brophy (Ed.), *Advances in research on teaching* (Vol. 1, pp. 265–309). Greenwich, CT: JAI Press.

Anscombe, G. E. M. (1957). *Intention*. Ithaca, NY: Cornell University Press.

Arendt, H. (1978a). *The life of the mind: Vol. 1. Thinking*. New York: Harcourt Brace Jovanovich. (Original work published 1977).

Arendt, H. (1978b). *The life of the mind: Vol. 2. Willing*. New York: Harcourt Brace Jovanovich.

Au, K. H.-P., & Jordan, C. (1981). Teaching reading to Hawaiian children: Finding a culturally appropriate solution. In H. T. Trueba, G. P. Guthrie, & K. H.-P. Au (Eds.), *Culture and the bilingual classroom: Studies in classroom ethnography* (pp. 139–152). Rowley, MA: Newbury House.

Auerbach, E. (1953). *Mimesis: The representation of reality in Western literature* (W. R. Trask, Trans.). Princeton, NJ: Princeton University Press. (Original work published 1946)

Ausubel, D. P. (1968). *Educational psychology: A cognitive view*. New York: Holt, Rinehart & Winston.

Ball, D. L. (1993a). Halves, pieces and twoths: Constructing representational contexts in teaching fractions. In T. Carpenter, E. Fennema, & T. Romberg (Eds.), *Rational numbers: An integration of research* (pp. 157–196). Hillsdale, NJ: Erlbaum.

Ball, D. L. (1993b). With an eye on the mathematical horizon: Dilemmas of teaching elementary school mathematics. *Elementary School Journal, 93*(4), 373–397.

Ball, D. L. (1991). Beginning a conversation about the NCTM Professional standards for teaching mathematics: Improving teaching, not standardizing it. *Arithmetic Teacher, 39*, 18–22.

Baltes, P. (1987). Theoretical propositions of life-span developmental psychology: On the dynamics between growth and decline. *Developmental Psychology, 5*, 611–626.

Bambrough, R. (1986). Question time. In S. G. Shanker (Ed.), *Philosophy in Britain today* (pp. 58–71). London: Croom Helm.

Bandura, A. (1982). The psychology of chance encounters and life paths. *American Psychologist, 37*, 747–755.

Bardach, E. (1984). The dissemination of policy research to policymakers. *Knowledge, 6*, 125–144.

Barnes, H. L. (1987). The conceptual basis for thematic teacher education programs. *Journal of Teacher Education, 38*(4), 13–18.

Barth, K. (1961). *Church dogmatics: Vol. III. The doctrine of creation: Part 4* (G. W. Bromiley & T. F. Torrance, Eds.). Edinburgh: T & T Clark.

Basseches, M. (1984). *Dialectical thinking and adult development.* Norwood, NJ: Ablex.

Belenky, M. F., Clinchy, B. M., Goldberger, N. R., & Tarule, J. M. (1986). *Women's ways of knowing: The development of self, voice, and mind.* New York: Basic Books.

Bell, D. (1980). The social framework of the information society. In T. Forester (Ed.), *The microelectronics revolution: The complete guide to the new technology and its impact on society* (pp. 500–549). Oxford: Basil Blackwell. (Original work published 1979)

Bell, M. (1991). *Meaning in Henry James.* Cambridge, MA: Harvard University Press.

Berger, P. L. (1967). *The sacred canopy: Elements of a sociological theory of religion.* New York: Doubleday.

Berliner, D. C. (1986). In pursuit of the expert pedagogue. *Educational Researcher, 15*(7), 5–13.

Bernstein, R. (1990). Rorty's liberal utopia. *Social Research, 57,* 31–72.

Black, M. (1968). *The labyrinth of language.* New York: Frederick A. Praeger.

Black, M. (1972). Reasonableness. In R. F. Dearden, P. H. Hirst, & R. S. Peters (Eds.), *Education and the development of reason* (pp. 194–207). London: Routledge & Kegan Paul.

Blake, W. (1963). *The marriage of heaven and hell.* Coral Gables, FL: University of Miami Press. (Original work published c. 1790)

Blonsky, M. (1992). *American mythologies.* New York: Oxford University Press.

Bodenheimer, E. (1962). *Jurisprudence: The philosophy and method of the law.* Cambridge, MA: Harvard University Press.

Boring, E. G. (1963). The psychology of controversy. In R. I. Watson & D. T. Campbell (Eds.), *History, psychology, and science: Selected papers* (pp. 67–84). New York: John Wiley. (Original work published 1929)

Bosk, C. L. (1979). *Forgive and remember: Managing medical failure.* Chicago: University of Chicago Press.

Boswell, J. (1953). *Life of Johnson.* London: Oxford University Press. (Original work published 1799)

Bourdieu, P. (1971). Systems of education and systems of thought. In M. F. D. Young (Ed.), *Knowledge and control: New directions for the sociology of education* (pp. 189–207). London: Collier-Macmillan. (Original work published 1967)

Bradley, F. H. (1927). *Ethical studies.* Oxford: Clarendon Press. (Original work published 1876)

Brann, E. T. H. (1979). *Paradoxes of education in a republic.* Chicago: University of Chicago Press.

Britton, J. (1982). Spectator role and the beginnings of writing. In M. Nystrand (Ed.), *What writers know: The language, process, and structure of written discourse* (pp. 149–169). New York: Academic Press.

Bromme, R., & Brophy, J. (1986). Teachers' cognitive activities. In B. Christiansen, A. G. Howson, & M. Otte (Eds.), *Perspectives on mathematics education: Papers submitted by members of the Bacomet group* (pp. 99–139). Dordrecht, The Netherlands: Reidel.

Brophy, J. E. (1982). *Fostering student learning and motivation in the elementary school classroom* (Occasional Paper No. 51). East Lansing: Michigan State University, Institute for Research on Teaching.

Brophy, J. E. (1983a). Conceptualizing student motivation. *Educational Psychologist, 18*, 200–215.

Brophy, J. E. (1983b). Research on the self-fulfilling prophecy and teacher expectations. *Journal of Educational Psychology, 75*, 631–661.

Brophy, J. E. (1990). Teaching social studies for understanding and higher-order applications. *Elementary School Journal, 90*, 351–417.

Browning, R. (1895). Two in the Campagna. In H. E. Scudder (Ed.), *The complete poetic and dramatic works of Robert Browning* (p. 189). Boston: Houghton Mifflin. (Original work published 1855)

Browning, R. (1981). Prince Hohenstiel-Schwangau, Saviour of Society. In J. Pettigrew (Ed.), *Robert Browning: The poems* (Vol. 1, p. 952). Harmondsworth: Penguin Books. (Original work published 1871)

Bruner, J. S. (1972). Nature and uses of immaturity. *American Psychologist, 27*, 687–708.

Bruner, J. S., & Olson, D. R. (1977–78). Symbols and texts as tools of intellect. *Interchange, 8*(4), 1–15.

Buber, M. (1947a). Dialogue. In *Between man and man* (pp. 1–39; R. G. Smith, Trans.). London: Routledge & Kegan Paul. (Original work published 1929)

Buber, M. (1947b). Education. In *Between man and man* (pp. 83–103; R. G. Smith, Trans.). London: Routledge & Kegan Paul. (Original work published 1926)

Buchmann, M. (1983). *Role over person: Justifying teacher action and decisions* (Research Series No. 135). East Lansing: Michigan State University, Institute for Research on Teaching.

Buchmann, M. (1984a). The priority of knowledge and understanding in teaching. In L. G. Katz & J. D. Raths (Eds.), *Advances in teacher education* (Vol. 1, pp. 29–50). Norwood, NJ: Ablex.

Buchmann, M. (1984b). The use of research knowledge in teacher education and teaching. *American Journal of Education, 92*, 421–439.

Buchmann, M. (1987). Teaching knowledge: The lights that teachers live by. *Oxford Review of Education, 13*, 151–164.

Buchmann, M. (1988). Argument and contemplation in teaching. *Oxford Review of Education, 14*, 201–214.

Buchmann, M. (1990). Beyond the lonely, choosing will: Professional development in teacher thinking. *Teachers College Record, 91*, 481–508.

Campbell, D. T. (1975). On the conflicts between biological and social evolution and between psychology and moral tradition. *American Psychologist, 30*, 1103–1126.

Campbell, D. T. (1988). *Methodology and epistemology for social science: Selected papers* (E. S. Overman, Ed.). Chicago: University of Chicago Press.

Camus, A. (1955). *The myth of Sisyphus.* New York: Knopf.

Canetti, E. (1962). *Crowds and power* (C. Stewart, Trans.). New York: Viking. (Original work published 1960)

Canetti, E. (1978). *The human province* (J. Neugroschel, Trans.). New York: Seabury. (Original work published 1973)

Carew, J. V., & Lightfoot, S. L. (1979). *Beyond bias: Perspectives on classrooms.* Cambridge, MA: Harvard University Press.

Carter, K., Sabers, D., Cushing, K., Pinnegar, S., & Berliner, D. C. (1987). Processing and using information about students: A study of expert, novice, and postulant teachers. *Teaching and Teacher Education, 3,* 147–157.

Clark, C. M., & Peterson, P. L. (1986). Teachers' thought processes. In M. C. Wittrock (Ed.), *Handbook of research on teaching* (pp. 255–296). New York: Macmillan.

Clement, J. (1982). Students' preconceptions in introductory mechanics. *American Journal of Physics, 50,* 66–71.

Clifford, G. J. (1975). *The shape of American education.* Englewood Cliffs, NJ: Prentice-Hall.

Cohen, D. K. (1987). Educational technology, policy, and practice. *Educational Evaluation and Policy Analysis, 9,* 153–170.

Cohen, D. K. (1989). Teaching practice: Plus que ça change . . . In P. W. Jackson (Ed.), *Contributing to educational change: Perspectives on research and practice* (pp. 27–84). Berkeley, CA: McCutchan.

Cohen, D. K., & Garet, M. S. (1975). Reforming educational policy with applied social research. *Harvard Educational Review, 45,* 17–43.

Coleridge, S. T. (1951). To William Wordsworth. In D. A. Stauffer (Ed.), *Selected poetry and prose of Coleridge* (pp. 74–77). New York: Modern Library. (Original work published 1817)

Coles, R. (1989). *The call of stories: Teaching and the moral imagination.* Boston: Houghton Mifflin.

Commission on National Aid to Vocational Education. (1974). Report. In M. Lazerson & W. N. Grubb (Eds.), *American education and vocationalism: A documentary history 1870–1970* (p. 116–132). New York: Teachers College Press. (Original work published 1914)

Connelly, F. M., & Clandinin, D. J. (1985). Personal practical knowledge and the modes of knowing: Relevance for teaching and learning. In E. Eisner (Ed.), *Learning and teaching the ways of knowing* (84th yearbook of the National Society for the Study of Education, pp. 174–198). Chicago: National Society for the Study of Education.

Connelly, F. M., & Clandinin, D. J. (1987). On narrative method, biography and narrative unities in the study of teaching. *Journal of Educational Thought, 21,* 130–139.

Cronbach, L. J., Ambron, S. R., Dornbusch, S. M., Hess, R. D., Hornik, R. C., Phillips, D. C., Walker, D. F., & Weiner, S. S. (1980). *Toward reform of program evaluation.* San Francisco: Jossey-Bass.

Cuban, L. (1992). Managing dilemmas while building professional communities. *Educational Researcher, 21,* 4–11.

Cusick, P. A. (1983). *The egalitarian ideal and the American high school: Studies of three schools.* New York: Longman.

Dannefer, D., & Perlmutter, M. (1990). Development as a multi-dimensional process: Individual and social constituents. *Human Development, 33,* 108–137.

Davies, R. (1981). *The rebel angels.* New York: Viking.

Delpit, L. (1988). The silenced dialogue: Power and pedagogy in educating other people's children. *Harvard Educational Review, 58,* 280–298.

Dewey, J. (1902). *The child and the curriculum.* Chicago: University of Chicago Press.

Dewey, J. (1915). Education vs. trade-training—Dr. Dewey's reply. *New Republic, 3,* 42–43.

Dewey, J. (1933). *How we think: A restatement of the relation of reflective thinking to the educative process.* Boston: D. C. Heath.

Dewey, J. (1934). *Art as experience.* New York: Capricorn Books.

Dewey, J. (1938). *Experience and education.* New York: Macmillan.

Dewey, J. (1956). *The child and the curriculum.* Chicago: University of Chicago Press. (Original work published 1902)

Dewey, J. (1958). *Experience and nature.* New York: Dover Publications. (Original work published 1925)

Dewey, J. (1959). The child and the curriculum. In M. S. Dworkin (Ed.), *Dewey on education* (pp. 91–111). New York: Teachers College Press. (Original work published 1902)

Dewey, J. (1959). My pedagogic creed. In M. S. Dworkin (Ed.), *Dewey on education* (pp. 19–32). New York: Teachers College Press. (Original work published 1897)

Dewey, J. (1959). The school and society. In M. S. Dworkin (Ed.), *Dewey on education* (pp. 33–90). New York: Teachers College Press. (Original work published 1900)

Dewey, J. (1960). Context and thought. In R. J. Bernstein (Ed.), *On experience, nature, and freedom: Representative selections* (pp. 88–110). New York: Liberal Arts Press. (Original work published 1931)

Dewey, J. (1966). *Democracy and education: An introduction to the philosophy of education.* New York: Free Press. (Original work published 1916)

Deyle, D., Hess, G., & Lecompte, M. (1991). Approaching ethical issues for qualitative researchers in education. In M. Lecompte, J. Preissle, & M. Millroy (Eds.), *Handbook of qualitative research in education* (pp. 597–641). New York: Academic Press.

Drabble, M. (1980). *The middle ground.* New York: Knopf.

Drabble, M. (1987). *The Radiant Way.* New York: Ivy Books.

Dunn, W. N. (1982). Reforms as arguments. *Knowledge: Creation, Diffusion, Utilization, 3,* 293–326.

Eaton, J. F., Anderson, C. W., & Smith, E. L. (1984). Students' misconceptions interfere with science learning: Case studies of fifth-grade students. *Elementary School Journal, 84,* 365–379.

Edelman, M. (1975). *The language of inquiry and the language of authority* (Discussion Paper No. 257–75). Madison: University of Wisconsin, Institute for Research on Poverty.

Eisele, J. C. (1980). Defining education: A problem for educational history. *Educational Theory, 30,* 25–33.

Elbaz, F. (1983). *Teacher thinking: A study of practical knowledge.* London: Croom Helm.

Elbaz, F. (1990). Knowledge and discourse: The evolution of research on teacher thinking. In C. Day, M. Pope, & P. Denicolo (Eds.), *Insight into teachers' thinking and practice* (pp. 15–42). London: Falmer.

Elbow, P. (1986). *Embracing contraries: Explorations in learning and teaching.* New York: Oxford University Press.

Eliot, C. W. (1974). Equality of educational opportunity. In M. Lazerson & W. N. Grubb (Eds.), *American education and vocationalism: A documentary history 1870–1970* (pp. 136–138). New York: Teachers College Press. (Original work published 1908)

Eliot, T. S. (1964a). The perfect critic. In *The sacred wood: Essays on poetry and criticism* (pp. 1–16). London: Methuen. (Original work published 1920)

Eliot, T. S. (1964b). Tradition and the individual talent. In *The sacred wood: Essays on poetry and criticism* (pp. 47–59). London: Methuen. (Original work published 1920)

Eliot, T. S. (1971). Little gidding. In *Four quartets* (pp. 49–59). New York: Harcourt Brace Jovanovich. (Original work published 1943)

Elstein, A. S., Shulman, L. S., & Sprafka, S. (1978). *Medical problem solving: An analysis of clinical reasoning.* Cambridge, MA: Harvard University Press.

Emerson, R. W. (1966). Self-reliance. In H. M. Jones (Ed.), *Emerson on education: Selections* (pp. 102–132). New York: Teachers College Press. (Original work published 1841)

Erlwanger, S. H. (1973). Benny's conception of rules and answers in IPI mathematics. *Journal of Children's Mathematical Behavior, 1*(2), 7–26.

Featherman, D., & Lerner, R. (1985). Ontogenesis and sociogenesis: Problematics for theory and research about development and socialization across the lifespan. *American Sociological Review, 50,* 659–676.

Feiman, S., & Floden, R. E. (1980). A consumers guide to teacher development. *Journal of Staff Development, 1*(2), 126–147.

Feyerabend, P. K. (1975). *Against method: Outline of an anarchistic theory of knowledge.* Atlantic Highlands, NJ: Humanities Press.

Fisher, C. W., Filby, N. N., Marliave, R., Cahen, L. S., Dishaw, M. M., Moore, J. E., & Berliner, D. C. (1978). *Teaching behaviors, academic learning time and student achievement: Final report of Phase III-B, Beginning Teacher Evaluation Study* (Technical Report No. V-1). Washington, DC: U.S. Department of Health, Education and Welfare; National Institute of Education.

Fiumara, G. C. (1990). *The other side of language: A philosophy of listening* (C. Lambert, Trans.). London: Routledge.

Floden, R. E. (1985). The role of rhetoric in changing teachers' beliefs. *Teaching and Teacher Education, 1,* 19–32.

Floden, R. E., & Klinzing, H. G. (1990). What can research on teacher thinking contribute to teacher preparation? A second opinion. *Educational Researcher, 19*(5), 15–20.

Forman, M. B. (1952). *The letters of John Keats.* London: Oxford University Press.

Fox, R. C. (1957). Training for uncertainty. In R. K. Merton, G. G. Reader, & P. L.

Kendall (Eds.), *The student-physician: Introductory studies in the sociology of medical education* (pp. 207–241). Cambridge, MA: Harvard University Press.

Frankel, C. (1973). The nature and sources of irrationalism. *Science, 180,* 927–931.

Frederiksen, N. (1984). The real test bias: Influences of testing on teaching and learning. *American Psychologist, 39,* 193–202.

Fried, C. (1978). *Right and wrong.* Cambridge, MA: Harvard University Press.

Frye, N. (1967). The knowledge of good and evil. In M. Black (Ed.), *The morality of scholarship* (pp. 1–28). Ithaca, NY: Cornell University Press.

Frye, N. (1976). *The secular scripture: A study of the structure of romance.* Cambridge, MA: Harvard University Press.

Frye, N. (1990). *Words with power: Being a second study of "The Bible and Literature".* San Diego, CA: Harcourt Brace Jovanovich.

Fuller, F. F. (1969). Concerns of teachers: A developmental conceptualization. *American Educational Research Journal, 6,* 207–226.

Gadamer, H.-G. (1975). *Truth and method* (G. Barden & E. Cumming, Eds. and Trans.). New York: Seabury. (Original work published 1965)

Garrison, J. W. (1988). Democracy, scientific knowledge, and teacher empowerment. *Teachers College Record, 89,* 487–504.

Geertz, C. (1975). Common sense as a cultural system. *Antioch Review, 33*(1), 5–26.

Geertz, C. (1980). Blurred genres: The refiguration of social thought. *American Scholar, 49,* 165–179.

Geertz, C. (1983). *Local knowledge: Further essays in interpretive anthropology.* New York: Basic Books.

Geertz, C. (1986). The uses of diversity. *Michigan Quarterly Review, 25,* 105–123.

Gergen, K. (1978). Toward generative theory. *Journal of Personality and Social Psychology, 36,* 1344–1360.

Gladwin, T. (1970). *East is a big bird: Navigation and logic on Puluwat Atoll.* Cambridge, MA: Harvard University Press.

Glass, G. (1979). Policy for the unpredictable. *Educational Researcher, 8,* 12–15.

Goodlad, J. (1984). *A place called school: Prospects for the future.* New York: McGraw-Hill.

Goodman, N., & Elgin, C. (1988). *Reconceptions in philosophy and other arts and sciences.* Indianapolis, IN: Hackett.

Goody, J., & Watt, I. (1968). The consequences of literacy. In J. Goody (Ed.), *Literacy in traditional societies* (pp. 27–68). Cambridge: Cambridge University Press. (Original work published 1963)

Gouldner, A. W. (1968). The sociologist as partisan: Sociology and the welfare state. *American Sociologist, 3,* 103–116.

Graff, G. (1988). Teach the conflicts: An alternative to educational fundamentalism. In B. J. Craig (Ed.), *Literature, language and politics* (pp. 99–109). Athens: University of Georgia Press.

Green, T. F. (1971). *The activities of teaching.* New York: McGraw-Hill.

Grice, H. P. (1975). Logic and conversation. In P. Cole & J. L. Morgan (Eds.), *Syntax and semantics: Vol. 3. Speech acts* (pp. 41–58). Orlando, FL: Academic Press.

Grubb, W. N., & Lazerson, M. (1975). Rally 'round the workplace: Continuities and fallacies in career education. *Harvard Educational Review, 45,* 451–474.

Guardini, R. (1954). Die Verantwortung des Studenten für die Kultur. In R. Guardini, W. Dirks, & M. Horkheimer, *Die Verantwortung der Universität: Drei Vorträge* (pp. 5–35). Würzburg: Werkbund-Verlag.

Guardini, R. (1965). *The world and the person* (S. Lange, Trans.). Chicago: Henry Regnery.

Gusfield, J. (1976). The literary rhetoric of science: Comedy and pathos in drinking driver research. *American Sociological Review, 41*, 16–34.

Gusfield, J. R. (1981). *The culture of public problems: Drinking-driving and the symbolic order.* Chicago: University of Chicago Press.

Habermas, J. (1973). Wahrheitstheorien. In H. Fahrenbach (Ed.), *Wirklichkeit und Reflexion: Walter Schulz zum 60. Geburtstag* (pp. 211–265). Pfullingen, Germany: Neske.

Habermas, J., & Luhmann, N. (1971). *Theorie der Gesellschaft oder Sozialtechnologie— Was leistet die Systemforschung?* Frankfurt am Main: Suhrkamp.

Haezrahi, P. (1956). *The contemplative activity: A study in aesthetics.* New York: Abelard-Schuman.

Hallpike, C. R. (1979). *The foundations of primitive thought.* Oxford: Clarendon Press.

Hampshire, S. (1967). Commitment and imagination. In M. Black (Ed.), *The morality of scholarship* (pp. 29–55). Ithaca, NY: Cornell University Press.

Hampshire, S. (1989). *Innocence and experience.* Cambridge, MA: Harvard University Press.

Hare, W. (1985). *In defence of open-mindedness.* Kingston, Ontario: McGill-Queen's University Press.

Hawkins, D. (1974). I, thou, and it. In *The informed vision: Essays on learning and human nature* (pp. 48–62). New York: Agathon Press. (Original work published 1967)

Heath, S. B. (1982). Questioning at home and at school: A comparative study. In G. Spindler (Ed.), *Doing the ethnography of schooling: Educational anthropology in action* (pp. 102–131). New York: Holt, Rinehart & Winston.

Hegel, G. W. F. (1931). *The phenomenology of mind* (J. B. Baillie, Trans.). London: George Allen & Unwin. (Original work published 1807)

Hegel, G. W. F. (1952). *Hegel's philosophy of right* (T. M. Knox, Trans.). London: Oxford University Press. (Original work published 1821)

Heidegger, M. (1968). *What is called thinking?* (F. D. Wieck & J. G. Gray, Trans.). New York: Harper & Row. (Original work published 1954)

Heller, E. (1988). Rilke and Nietzsche with a discourse on thought, belief and poetry. In *The importance of Nietzsche: Ten essays* (pp. 87–126). Chicago: University of Chicago Press.

Hexter, J. H. (1971). *Doing history.* Bloomington: Indiana University Press.

Highet, G. (1950). *The art of teaching.* New York: Knopf.

Hoggart, R. (1957). *The uses of literacy: Aspects of working-class life, with special reference to publications and entertainments.* London: Chatto & Windus.

Hölderlin, F. (1972). Remembrance. In F. Hölderlin & E. Mörike, *Selected poems* (pp. 90–93; C. Middleton, Trans.). Chicago: University of Chicago Press. (Original work published 1807)

Howey, K. R., & Zimpher, N. L. (1989). *Profiles of preservice teacher education: Inquiry into the nature of programs.* Albany: State University of New York Press.

Huberman, M. (1983). Recipes for busy kitchens: A situational analysis of everyday knowledge use in schools. *Knowledge, 4,* 478–510.

Huberman, M. (1987). Steps towards an integrated model of research utilization. *Knowledge, 8,* 586–611.

Huberman, M. (1989a). Predictors of conceptual effects in research utilization: Looking with both eyes. *Knowledge in Society, 2,* 6–24.

Huberman, M. (1989b). The professional life cycle of teachers. *Teachers College Record, 91,* 31–57.

Huberman, M. (1990). Linkage between researchers and practitioners: A qualitative study. *American Educational Research Journal, 27,* 363–391.

Huberman, M., & Gather-Thurler, M. (1991). *De la recherche à la pratique: Eléments de base et mode d'emploi* [*Putting research into practice—with a user's manual*]. Berne, Switzerland: P. Lang.

Husserl, E. (1931). *Ideas: General introduction to pure phenomenology.* (W. R. B. Gibson, Trans.). London: George Allen & Unwin.

Jackson, P. W. (1986). *The practice of teaching.* New York: Teachers College Press.

James, H. (1896). The figure in the carpet. In H. James, *Embarrassments: The figure in the carpet, glasses, the next time, the way it came* (pp. 1–66). London: Heinemann.

James, W. (1969). The moral philosopher and the moral life. In J. K. Roth (Ed.), *The moral philosophy of William James* (pp. 169–191). New York: Thomas Y. Crowell. (Original work published 1891)

James, W. (1981). *The principles of psychology* (Vol. I). Cambridge, MA: Harvard University Press. (Original work published 1890)

Jonson, B. (1953). *Timber or discoveries* (R. S. Walker, Ed.). Syracuse, NY: Syracuse University Press. (Original work published 1641)

Karlinsky, S. (Ed.). (1973). *Letters of Anton Chekhov* (M. H. Heim, Trans.). New York: Harper & Row.

Keel, A. (1991). Nachwort. In H. Ibsen, *Die wildente* (pp. 119–136). Stuttgart: Philipp Reclam.

Kennedy, M. (1967). *Together and apart.* London: Virago. (Original work published 1936)

Kolakowski, L. (1968). In praise of inconsistency. In *Toward a Marxist humanism: Essays on the left today* (pp. 211–220; J. Z. Peel, Trans.). New York: Grove Press.

Kolakowski, L. (1989). *The presence of myth* (A Czerniawski, Trans.). Chicago: University of Chicago Press. (Original work published 1972)

Kolakowski, L. (1990). *Modernity on endless trial.* Chicago: University of Chicago Press.

Kuhn, T. S. (1970). *The structure of scientific revolutions.* Chicago: University of Chicago Press.

Kundera, M. (1991). *Immortality* (P. Kussi, Trans.). New York: Grove Weidenfeld.

Labouvie-Vief, G. (1982). Dynamic development and mature autonomy: A theoretical prologue. *Human Development, 25,* 161–191.

Labov, W. (1982). Competing value systems in the inner-city schools. In P. Gilmore & A. A. Glatthorn (Eds.), *Children in and out of school* (pp. 148–171). Washington, DC: Center for Applied Linguistics.

Lakoff, G., & Johnson, M. (1980). *Metaphors we live by.* Chicago: University of Chicago Press.

Lampert, M. (1985). How do teachers manage to teach? Perspectives on problems in practice. *Harvard Educational Review, 55,* 178–194.

Laudan, L. (1977). *Progress and its problems: Towards a theory of scientific growth.* Berkeley: University of California Press.

Laudan, L. (1990). Demystifying underdetermination. In C. Wade Savage (Ed.), *Scientific theories* (Vol. XIV of Minnesota Studies in the Philosophy of Science, pp. 267–297). Minneapolis: University of Minnesota Press.

Lave, J., Murtaugh, M., & de la Rocha, O. (1984). The dialectic of arithmetic in grocery shopping. In B. Rogoff & J. Lave (Eds.), *Everyday cognition: Its development in social context* (pp. 67–94). Cambridge, MA: Harvard University Press.

Leavis, F. R. (1962). *Two cultures? The significance of C. P. Snow.* London: Chatto & Windus.

Leinhardt, G. (1988). Situated knowledge and expertise in teaching. In J. Calderhead (Ed.), *Teachers' professional learning* (pp. 146–168). London: Falmer.

Leites, N. (1969). *The rules of the game in Paris* (D. Coltman, Trans.). Chicago: University of Chicago Press. (Original work published 1966)

Levi, I. (1980). *The enterprise of knowledge: An essay on knowledge, credal probability, and chance.* Cambridge, MA: MIT Press.

Levi, P. (1984). *The periodic table* (R. Rosenthal, Trans.). New York: Schocken Books. (Original work published 1975)

Levine, P. (1991). *What work is.* New York: Knopf.

Lindblom, C. E. (1990). *Inquiry and change: The troubled attempt to understand and shape society.* New Haven, CT: Yale University Press.

Lindblom, C. E., & Cohen, D. K. (1979). *Usable knowledge: Social science and social problem solving.* New Haven, CT: Yale University Press.

Lipsky, M. (1980). *Street-level bureaucracy: Dilemmas of the individual in public services.* New York: Russell Sage Foundation.

Little, J. W. (1981). *School success and staff development: The role of staff development in urban desegregated schools.* Executive summary (NIE No. 400-79-0049). Boulder: University of Colorado, Center for Action Research.

Locke, J. (1959). *An essay concerning human understanding* (Vol. II). New York: Dover. (Original work published 1690)

Lortie, D. C. (1975). *Schoolteacher: A sociological study.* Chicago: University of Chicago Press.

Lowell, R. (1977). *Day by day.* New York: Farrar, Straus & Giroux.

MacIntyre, A. (1981). *After virtue: A study in moral theory.* Notre Dame, IN: University of Notre Dame Press.

MacLean, N. (1976). *A river runs through it.* Chicago: University of Chicago Press.

Mann, T. (1982). *Lotte in Weimar.* Frankfurt am Main: S. Fischer. (Original work published 1939)

Marsh, D., & Glassick, J. (1988). Knowledge utilization in evaluation efforts. *Knowledge, 9,* 223–241.

Marx, K. (1963). *Early writings* (T. B. Bottomore, Ed. & Trans.). London: C. A. Watts. (Original work published 1844)

Marx, K. (1963). *The eighteenth Brumaire of Louis Bonaparte.* New York: International Publishers. (Original work published 1852)

Maxwell, J. (1992). *Types of validity in qualitative research.* Cambridge, MA: Harvard Graduate School of Education.

Mayer, R. E. (1979). Twenty years of research on advance organizers: Assimilation theory is still the best predictor of results. *Instructional Science, 8,* 133–167.

McDonald, J. P. (1986). Raising the teacher's voice and the ironic role of theory. *Harvard Educational Review, 56,* 355–378.

McDowell, J. (1978). Are moral requirements hypothetical imperatives? *Proceedings of the Aristotelian Society* (Supplementary Volume), *52,* 13–29.

McLaughlin, M. W., & Marsh, D. D. (1978). Staff development and school change. *Teachers College Record, 80,* 69–94.

Meehl, P. E. (1971). Law and the fireside inductions: Some reflections of a clinical psychologist. *Journal of Social Issues, 27*(4), 65–100.

Meredith, G. (1947). *The egoist: A comedy in narrative.* London: Oxford University Press. (Original work published 1879)

Merleau-Ponty, M. (1964). *The primacy of perception: And other essays on phenomenological psychology, the philosophy of art, history and politics.* (J. M. Edie, Ed.). Evanston: Northwestern University Press.

Merton, R. K. (1957). The role-set: Problems in sociology theory. *British Journal of Sociology, 8,* 106–120.

Merton, R. K. (1973). The normative structure of science. In N. W. Storer (Ed.), *The sociology of science: Theoretical and empirical investigations* (pp. 267–278). Chicago: University of Chicago Press. (Original work published 1942)

Meyers, W. (1986). When research does not help teachers. *American Educator, 10,* 18–23.

Mill, J. S. (1900). *A system of logic.* London: Longmans, Green. (Original work published 1843)

Mill, J. S. (1962). Bentham. In G. Himmelfarb (Ed.), *Essays on politics and culture* (pp. 77–120). Garden City, NY: Anchor Books. (Original work published 1838)

Mill, J. S. (1962). Coleridge. In G. Himmelfarb (Ed.), *Essays on politics and culture* (pp. 121–172). Garden City, NY: Anchor Books. (Original work published 1840)

Mill, J. S. (1971). *John Stuart Mill on education* F. W. Garforth, Ed.). New York: Teachers College Press. (Original work published 1873)

Minkus, P. A. (1980). Arguments that aren't arguments. In J. A. Blair & R. H. Johnson (Eds.), *Informal logic: The first international symposium* (pp. 69–76). Inverness, CA: Edgepress.

Montefiore, A. (1975). Objectivity, impartiality, and open-mindedness. In A. Montefiore (Ed.), *Neutrality and impartiality: The university and political commitment* (pp. 17–30). London: Cambridge University Press.

Murdoch, I. (1970). *The sovereignty of good.* London: Routledge & Kegan Paul.

Murray, K. M. E. (1977). *Caught in the web of words: James A. H. Murray and the Oxford English Dictionary.* New Haven, CT: Yale University Press.

Musil, R. (1990). Helpless Europe: A digressive journey. In B. Pike & D. S. Luft (Eds.), *Precision and soul: Essays and addresses* (pp. 116–133). Chicago: University of Chicago Press. (Original work published 1922)

Nagel, T. (1979). *Mortal questions.* New York: Cambridge University Press.

National Council of Teachers of Mathematics. (1989). *Curriculum and evaluation standards for school mathematics.* Reston, VA: Author.

National Council of Teachers of Mathematics. (1991). *Professional standards for teaching mathematics.* Reston, VA: Author.

Nemerov, H. (1978). *Figures of thought: Speculations on the meaning of poetry and other essays.* Boston: David R. Godine. (Original work published 1975)

Nisbett, R., & Ross, L. (1980). *Human inference: Strategies and shortcomings of social judgment.* Englewood Cliffs, NJ: Prentice-Hall.

Noddings, N. (1984). *Caring: A feminine approach to ethics and moral education.* Berkeley: University of California Press.

Noddings, N. (1986). Fidelity in teaching, teacher education, and research for teaching. *Harvard Educational Review, 56,* 496–510.

Novick, P. (1988). *That noble dream: The 'objectivity question" and the American historical profession.* New York: Cambridge University Press.

Nussbaum, J., & Novak, J. D. (1976). An assessment of children's concepts of the earth utilizing structured interviews. *Science Education, 60,* 535–550.

Nussbaum, M. C. (1986). *The fragility of goodness: Luck and ethics in Greek tragedy and philosophy.* Cambridge: Cambridge University Press.

Nussbaum, M. C. (1990). *Love's knowledge: Essays on philosophy and literature.* New York: Oxford University Press.

Oakeshott, M. (1962). The voice of poetry in the conversation of mankind. In *Rationalism in politics and other essays* (pp. 197–247). New York: Basic Books. (Original work published 1959)

Oakeshott, M. (1989a). A place of learning. In T. Fuller (Ed.), *The voice of liberal learning: Michael Oakeshott on education* (pp. 17–42). New Haven, CT: Yale University Press. (Original work published 1975)

Oakeshott, M. (1989b). Political education. In T. Fuller (Ed.), *The voice of liberal learning: Michael Oakeshott on education* (pp. 136–158). New Haven, CT: Yale University Press. (Original work published 1951)

Olson, D. R. (1977). The languages of instruction: The literate bias of schooling. In R. C. Anderson, R. J. Spiro, & W. E. Montague (Eds.), *Schooling and the acquisition of knowledge* (pp. 65–89). Hillsdale, NJ: Erlbaum.

The Oxford English Dictionary (2nd ed.). (1989). Oxford: Clarendon Press.

Ozick, C. (1983). *The cannibal galaxy.* New York: Knopf.

Ozick, C. (1989). *Metaphor and memory.* New York: Knopf.

Pascal, B. (1910). Thoughts. (W. F. Trotter, Trans.). In C. W. Elliot (Ed.), *Blaise Pascal: Thoughts, letters, minor works* (pp. 7–322). New York: P. F. Collier & Son.

Passmore, J. (1970). *The perfectibility of man.* London: Duckworth.

Peirce, C. S. (1955). The fixation of belief. In J. Buchler (Ed.), *Philosophical writings of Peirce* (pp. 5–22). New York: Dover. (Original work published 1877)

Perelman, C., & Olbrechts-Tyteca, L. (1969). *The new rhetoric: A treatise on argumentation* (J. Wilkinson & P. Weaver, Trans.). Notre Dame, IN: University of Notre Dame Press. (Original work published 1958)

Perry, W. (1970). *Forms of intellectual and ethical development in the college years.* New York: Holt, Rinehart & Winston.

Peters, R. S. (1966). *Ethics and education.* London: George Allen & Unwin.

Peters, R. S. (1977). The place of philosophy in the training of teachers. In *Education and the education of teachers* (pp. 135–150). London: Routledge & Kegan Paul. (Original work published 1964)

Philips, S. U. (1983). *The invisible culture: Communication in classroom and community on the Warm Springs Indian Reservation.* New York: Longman.

Phillips, D. C. (1988). On teacher knowledge: A skeptical dialogue. *Educational Theory, 38,* 457–466.

Platt, J. (1973). Social traps. *American Psychologist, 28,* 641–651.

Polanyi, M. (1959). *The study of man.* Chicago: University of Chicago Press.

Polanyi, M. (1962). *Personal knowledge: Towards a post-critical philosophy.* Chicago: University of Chicago Press. (Original work published 1958)

Polanyi, M. (1967). The growth of science in society. *Miverva, 5,* 533–545.

Popper, K. R. (1962). On the sources of knowledge and of ignorance. *Encounter, 19*(3), 42–57.

Popper, K. R. (1972). *Objective knowledge: An evolutionary approach.* Oxford: Clarendon Press.

Posner, G. J., Strike, K. A., Hewson, P. W., & Gertzog, W. A. (1982). Accommodation of a scientific conception: Toward a theory of conceptual change. *Science Education, 66,* 211–227.

Powell, A. (1955). The acceptance world. In *A dance to the music of time/1: Spring.* New York: Popular Library.

Powell, A. G., Farrar, E., & Cohen, D. K. (1985). *The shopping mall high school: Winners and losers in the educational marketplace.* Boston: Houghton Mifflin.

Project 30 Alliance. (1991). Two year report: Institutional accomplishments. Newark: University of Delaware, College of Education.

Prosser, C. A., & Allen, C. R. (1925). *Vocational education in a democracy.* New York: Century.

Proust, M. (1956). *Swann's way* (C. K. S. Moncrieff, Trans.). New York: Modern Library. (Original work published 1913)

Quine, W., & Ullian, J. (1978). *The web of belief.* New York: Random House.

Raspa, A. (1975). Introduction. In J. Donne, *Devotions upon emergent occasions* (pp. xiii–lvi). Montreal: McGill-Queen's University Press.

Resnick, L. B. (1987). *Education and learning to think.* Washington, DC: National Academy Press.

Rich, R. F. (1981). Knowledge in society. In R. F. Rich (Ed.), *The knowledge cycle* (pp. 11–39). Beverly Hills, CA: Sage.

Rodgers, D. T. (1978). *The work ethic in industrial America 1850–1920.* Chicago: University of Chicago Press.

Rodriguez, R. (1982). *Hunger of memory: The education of Richard Rodriguez.* Boston: David R. Godine.

Rogoff, B., & Lave, J. (Eds.). (1984). *Everyday cognition: Its development in social context.* Cambridge, MA: Harvard University Press.

Rorty, R. (1982). *Consequences of pragmatism (Essays: 1972–1980).* Minneapolis: University of Minnesota Press.

Rorty, R. (1989). *Contingency, irony, and solidarity*. Cambridge: Cambridge University Press.

Royce, J. (1969). The philosophy of loyalty. In J. J. McDermott (Ed.), *The basic writings of Josiah Royce* (Vol. 2, pp. 855–1013). Chicago: University of Chicago Press. (Original work published 1908)

Sacks, O. (1984). *A leg to stand on*. New York: Summit.

Sartre, J.-P. (1988). *"What is literature?" and other essays*. Cambridge, MA: Harvard University Press. (Original work published 1948)

Scheffler, I. (1960). *The language of education*. Springfield, IL: Charles C. Thomas.

Scheffler, I. (1965). *Conditions of knowledge: An introduction to epistemology and education*. Chicago: Scott, Foresman.

Scheffler, I. (1973). Science, morals, and educational policy. In *Reason and teaching* (pp. 97–115). London: Routledge & Kegan Paul. (Original work published 1956)

Scheffler, I. (1977a). In praise of the cognitive emotions. *Teachers College Record, 79*, 171–186.

Scheffler, I. (1977b). Justifying curriculum decisions. In A. A. Bellack & H. M. Kliebard (Eds.), *Curriculum and evaluation* (pp. 497–505). Berkeley, CA: McCutchan. (Original work published 1958)

Scheffler, I. (1979). *Beyond the letter: A philosophical inquiry into ambiguity, vagueness and metaphor in language*. London: Routledge & Kegan Paul.

Scheffler, I. (1984). On the education of policymakers. *Harvard Educational Review, 54*, 152–165.

Scheffler, I. (1985). *Of human potential: An essay in the philosophy of education*. Boston: Routledge & Kegan Paul.

Schmidt, W. H., & Buchmann, M. (1983). Six teachers' beliefs and attitudes and their curricular time allocations. *Elementary School Journal, 84*, 162–171.

Schön, D. A. (1983). *The reflective practitioner: How professionals think in action*. New York: Basic Books.

Schön, D. A. (1987). *Educating the reflective practitioner*. San Francisco: Jossey-Bass.

Schopenhauer, A. (1956). Third book: The world as idea: Second aspect. In I. Edman (Ed.), *The philosophy of Schopenhauer* (pp. 135–214). New York: Modern Library. (Original work published 1844)

Schrag, F. (1981). Knowing and doing. *American Journal of Education, 89*, 253–282.

Schrag, F. (1983). Social science and social practice. *Inquiry, 26*, 107–124.

Schutz, A. (1962). On multiple realities. In M. Natanson (Ed.), *Collected papers: Vol. I. The problem of social reality* (pp. 207–259). The Hague: Martinus Nijhoff. (Original work published 1945)

Schwab, J. J. (1978a). Education and the structure of the disciplines. In I. Westbury & N. J. Wilkof (Eds.), *Science, curriculum, and liberal education: Selected essays* (pp. 229–272). Chicago: University of Chicago Press.

Schwab, J. J. (1978b). The "impossible" role of the teacher in progressive education. In I. Westbury & N. J. Wilkof (Eds.), *Science, curriculum, and liberal education: Selected essays* (pp. 167–183). Chicago: University of Chicago Press. (Original work published 1959)

Schwandt, T. (1990). Paths to inquiry in the social disciplines: Scientific, constructivist and critical theory methodologies. In E. Guba (Ed.), *The paradigm dialogue* (pp. 258–276). Newbury Park, CA: Sage.

Schwartz, A. (1979). Aristotle on education and choice. *Educational Theory, 29*, 97–107.

Schwille, J., Porter, A., Belli, G., Floden, R., Freeman, D., Knappen, L., Kuhs, T., & Schmidt, W. (1983). Teachers as policy brokers in the content of elementary school mathematics. In L. S. Shulman & G. Sykes (Eds.) *Handbook of teaching and policy* (pp. 370–391). New York: Longman.

Scribner, S., & Cole, M. (1973). Cognitive consequences of formal and informal education. *Science, 182*, 553–559.

Scribner, S., & Cole, M. (1981). *The psychology of literacy.* Cambridge, MA: Harvard University Press.

Sedlak, M. W. (1987). Tomorrow's teachers: The essential arguments of the Holmes Group Report. *Teachers College Record, 88*, 314–325.

Shaw, B. (1903). *Man and superman: A comedy and a philosophy.* New York: Brentano's.

Shiff, R. (1979). Art and life: A metaphoric relationship. In S. Sacks (Ed.), *On metaphor* (pp. 105–120). Chicago: University of Chicago Press. (Original work published 1978)

Shklar, J. N. (1984). *Ordinary vices.* Cambridge, MA: Belknap.

Shroyer, J. C. (1982). Critical moments in the teaching of mathematics: What makes teaching difficult? (Doctoral dissertation, Michigan State University, 1981). *Dissertation Abstracts International, 42*, 3485-A.

Shulman, J. H. (Ed.). (1992). *Case methods in teacher education.* New York: Teachers College Press.

Shulman, L. S. (1987). Knowledge and teaching: Foundations of the new reform. *Harvard Educational Review, 57*, 1–22.

Simmel, G. (1950). The secret and the secret society. In K. H. Wolff (Ed.), *The sociology of Georg Simmel* (pp. 305–376). Glencoe, IL: Free Press. (Original work published 1906)

Simmel, G. (1959). The adventure. In K. H. Wolff (Ed.), *Georg Simmel, 1858–1918* (pp. 243–258). Columbus: Ohio State University Press. (Original work published 1911)

Sizer, T. R. (1984). *Horace's compromise: The dilemma of the American high school.* Boston: Houghton Mifflin.

Skvorecky, J. (1984). *The engineer of human souls.* (P. Wilson, Trans.). New York: Knopf.

Smith, E. L., & Anderson, C. W. (1984). *The planning and teaching intermediate science study: Final report* (Research Series No. 147). East Lansing: Michigan State University, Institute for Research on Teaching.

Smith, F. (1975). *Comprehension and learning: A conceptual framework for teachers.* New York: Holt, Rinehart & Winston.

Snedden, D. (1924). Education for a world of team-players and team-workers. *School and Society, 20*, 552–557.

Snow, C. P. (1963). *The two cultures and the scientific revolution.* New York: Cambridge University Press. (Original work published 1959)

Soltis, J. F. (1981). Education and the concept of knowledge. In J. F. Soltis (Ed.), *Philosophy and education* (80th yearbook of the National Society for the Study of Education, Part I, pp. 95–113). Chicago: National Society for the Study of Education.

Soltis, J. F. (Ed.). (1987). Reforming teacher education: A symposium on the Holmes Group Report [Special issue]. *Teachers College Record, 88*(3).

Sprinthall, N., & Thies-Sprinthall, L. (1983). The teacher as an adult learner: A cognitive-developmental view. In G. A. Griffen (Ed.), *Staff development*. Chicago: National Society for the Study of Education.

Stephens, J. M. (1967). *The process of schooling: A psychological examination*. New York: Holt, Rinehart & Winston.

Strawson, P. F. (1974a). *Freedom and resentment and other essays*. London: Methuen.

Strawson, P. F. (1974b). Freedom and resentment. In *Freedom and resentment and other essays* (pp. 1–25). London: Methuen. (Original work published 1962)

Strike, K. A. (1982). *Liberty and learning*. Oxford: Martin Robertson.

Struther, J. (1940). *Mrs. Miniver*. New York: Harcourt, Brace.

Taylor, C. (1989). *Sources of the self: The making of the modern identity*. Cambridge, MA: Harvard University Press.

Taylor, R. (1970). *Good and evil: A new direction*. London: Macmillan.

Thelen, H. A. (1973). Profession anyone? In D. J. McCarty and Associates (Eds.), *New perspectives on teacher education* (pp. 194–213). San Francisco: Jossey-Bass.

Thomas Aquinas, Saint. (1966). *Summa theologiæ: Vol. 46. Action and contemplation (2a2æ. 179–182)* (J. Aumann, Ed.). New York: Blackfriars.

Thomas Aquinas, Saint. (1973). *Summa theologiæ: Vol. 47. The pastoral and religious lives (2a2æ. 183–189)* (J. Aumann, Ed.). New York: Blackfriars.

Toulmin, S. (1982). The construal of reality: Criticism in modern and postmodern science. *Critical Inquiry, 9*, 93–111.

Traherne, T. (1966). *Poems, centuries and three thanksgivings* (A. Ridler, Ed.). London: Oxford University Press. (Original work published 1675)

Tribe, L. H. (1971). Trial by mathematics: Precision and ritual in the legal process. *Harvard Law Review, 84*, 1329–1393.

Tversky, A., & Kahneman, D. (1973). Availability: A heuristic for judging frequency and probability. *Cognitive Psychology, 5*, 207–232.

Tyler, A. (1991). *Saint maybe*. New York: Knopf.

Tyler, R. W. (1949). *Basic principles of curriculum and instruction*. Chicago: University of Chicago Press.

Van Manen, M. (1991). *The tact of teaching: The meaning of pedagogical thoughtfulness*. Albany: State University of New York Press.

Veenman, S. (1984). Perceived problems of beginning teachers. *Review of Educational Research, 54*, 143–178.

Viennot, L. (1979). Spontaneous reasoning in elementary dynamics. *European Journal of Science Education, 1*, 205–221.

Vygotsky, L. S. (1962). *Thought and language* (E. Hanfmann & G. Vakar, Eds. and Trans.). Cambridge, MA: MIT Press. (Original work published 1934)

Vygotsky, L. S. (1978). *Mind in society: The development of higher psychological pro-*

cesses (M. Cole, V. John-Steiner, S. Scribner, & E. Souberman, Eds.). Cambridge, MA: Harvard University Press. (Original work published 1930–1966)

Wagner, K. (1980). Ideology and career education. *Educational Theory, 30,* 105–113.

Waller, W. (1961). *The sociology of teaching.* New York: Russell & Russell. (Original work published 1932)

Weaver, R. M. (1953). *The ethics of rhetoric.* Chicago: Henry Regnery.

Weber, M. (1963). "Objectivity" in social science and social policy. In M. Natanson (Ed.), *Philosophy of the social sciences: A reader* (pp. 355–418). New York: Random House. (Original work published 1904)

Weil, S. (1951). Reflections on the right use of school studies with a view to the love of God. In *Waiting for God* (pp. 105–116; E. Crauford, Trans.). New York: G. P. Putnam's Sons. (Original work published 1950)

Weiss, C. (1978). *The many meanings of knowledge utilization.* New York: Columbia University, Bureau of Social Research.

Weizenbaum, J. (1980). Once more, the computer revolution. In T. Forester (Ed.), *The microelectronics revolution: The complete guide to the new technology and its impact on society* (pp. 550–570). Oxford: Basil Blackwell. (Original work published 1979)

Wertsch, J. V. (1979). From social interaction to higher psychological processes: A clarification and application of Vygotsky's theory. *Human Development, 22,* 1–22.

West, R. (1966). *The birds fall down.* New York: Viking.

West, R. (1984). *This real night.* London: Macmillan.

White, J. B. (1985). Doctrine in a vacuum: Reflections on what a law school ought (and ought not) to be. *University of Michigan Journal of Law Reform, 18,* 251–266.

Whitehead, A. N. (1933). *Adventures of ideas.* New York: Macmillan.

Wiggins, D. (1978). Deliberation and practical reason. In J. Raz (Ed.), *Practical reasoning* (pp. 144–152). Oxford: Oxford University Press. (Original work published 1975)

Willis, P. E. (1977). *Learning to labour: How working class kids get working class jobs.* Aldershot, UK: Gower.

Wilson, J. (1963). *Thinking with concepts.* Cambridge: Cambridge University Press.

Wise, A. E. (1979). *Legislated learning: The bureaucratization of the American classroom.* Berkeley: University of California Press.

Wittgenstein, L. (1953). *Philosophical investigations.* Oxford: Basil Blackwell.

Wittgenstein, L. (1980). *Culture and value* (G. H. Von Wright, Ed.; P. Winch, Trans.). Oxford: Basil Blackwell.

Wollheim, R. (1968). *Art and its objects: An introduction to aesthetics.* New York: Harper & Row.

Woolf, V. (1937). *The Years.* New York: Harcourt, Brace.

Woolf, V. (1955). *To the lighthouse.* New York: Harcourt, Brace & World. (Original work published 1927)

Woolf, V. (1956). *Orlando: A biography.* New York: New American Library. (Original work published 1928)

Wordsworth, W. (1904a). On a high part of the coast of Cumberland. In A. J. George (Ed.), *The complete poetical works of William Wordsworth* (p. 705). Boston: Houghton Mifflin. (Original work published 1833)

Wordsworth, W. (1904b). Preface [to *Lyrical ballads*]. In A. J. George (Ed.), *The complete poetical works of William Wordsworth* (pp. 790–799). Boston: Houghton Mifflin. (Original work published 1800)

Wordsworth, W. (1904c). The prelude; or, Growth of a poet's mind: An autobiographical poem. In A. J. George (Ed.), *The complete poetical works of William Wordsworth* (pp. 124–222). Boston: Houghton Mifflin. (Original work published 1850)

Zeichner, K. M., & Teitelbaum, K. (1982). Personalized and inquiry-oriented teacher education: An analysis of two approaches to the development of curriculum for field-based experiences. *Journal of Education for Teaching, 8,* 95–117.

Ziman, J. M. (1968). *Public knowledge: An essay concerning the social dimension of science.* Cambridge: Cambridge University Press.

Ziman, J. M. (1969). Information, communication, knowledge, *Nature, 224,* 318–324.

Zipf, G. K. (1935). *The psycho-biology of language.* New York: Houghton Mifflin.

Zipf, G. K. (1949). *Human behavior and the principle of least effort.* Cambridge, MA: Addison-Wesley.

Zuckerman, H. (1977). *Scientific elite: Nobel laureates in the United States.* New York: Free Press.

Index

About the Authors

Margret Buchmann is Professor and Senior Researcher at the Institute for Research on Teaching, College of Education, Michigan State University. With degrees from Stanford University in philosophy of education, political science, and sociology, she has published widely on the relations of formal knowledge and experience to teaching and education and has presented her work in Europe as well as in the United States. Professor Buchmann has served on the Board of Directors of the Institute for Research on Teaching, Michigan State University, and has recently been elected to the Board of Directors of the national John Dewey Society and the Association for Philosophy of Education (affiliated with the American Philosophical Association). She has been a visiting scholar at the Universities of Oxford and Cambridge in the United Kingdom and at the University of Tübingen in Germany.

Robert E. Floden is Co-Director of the National Center For Research on Teacher Learning and Professor of Teacher Education and Educational Psychology at Michigan State University. He received Ph.D. and M.S. degrees from Stanford University and an A.B. degree from Princeton University. Professor Floden has been Senior Researcher at the Institute for Research on Teaching, an Alexander von Humboldt Fellow at the University of Tübingen in Germany, and an academic visitor at Oxford University's Department of Educational Studies. He is currently Features Editor for *Educational Researcher*. Dr. Floden has written on a wide range of topics, drawing on his expertise in philosophy, statistics, psychology, program evaluation, research on teaching, and research on teacher education.